DATE DUE

BRODART, CO.   Cat. No. 23-221

THE EVOLUTION OF ARMS CONTROL

THE EVOLUTION OF ARMS CONTROL

From Antiquity to the Nuclear Age

RICHARD DEAN BURNS

PRAEGER SECURITY INTERNATIONAL
An Imprint of ABC-CLIO, LLC

Santa Barbara, California • Denver, Colorado • Oxford, England

Library of Congress Cataloging-in-Publication Data

Burns, Richard Dean.
    The evolution of arms control : from antiquity to the nuclear age / Richard Dean Burns.
        p. cm.
    Includes bibliographical references and index.
    ISBN 978-0-313-37574-3 (hard copy : alk. paper) — ISBN 978-0-313-37575-0 (ebook)
    1. Arms control. 2. Arms control—History. I. Title.
JZ5625.B82 2009
327.1'74—dc22   2009006419

13 12 11 10 9   1 2 3 4 5

This book is also available on the World Wide Web as an eBook.
Visit www.abc-clio.com for details.

ABC-CLIO, LLC
130 Cremona Drive, P.O. Box 1911
Santa Barbara, California 93116-1911

This book is printed on acid-free paper ∞

Manufactured in the United States of America

Contents

Preface

The Evolution of Arms Control distills the results of more than four decades of assessing and tracing the lineage of various historical arms control activities which were found scattered in scores of accounts by anthropologists, historians, political scientists, and other writers. Here the focus is on describing arms control's essential techniques and methods, as well as its objectives and processes. As such, it briefly touches on these essentials thus providing an introduction—one reviewer labeled it a virtual "historical dictionary" of arms control and disarmament activities. A fully developed history, of course, would require several volumes.

The brief overview that launches this study is designed to dispel any confusion related to the basic terms "arms control" and "disarmament," and to offer a rationale for examining arms control's historical dimensions. The introduction to Part I presents definitions of six various methods employed to achieve arms control objectives and six arbitrary classifications that demonstrate the evolution of arms control techniques. Subsequent chapters in Part I provide samples of the evolutionary process. It must be recognized that this account, while emphasizing the lineage of arms control techniques, does not claim that all activities are of equal significance. The Treaty of Zama (202 BCE) limiting the number of Carthage's warships, while having considerable importance in its time, obviously is not equal in significance to the SALT and START agreements (1972–1993) that limited and reduced nuclear weaponry.

Part II provides an analytical overview of three essential features of arms control. Chapter 7 employs examples of previously mentioned arms control agreements to examine the implications of domestic and bureaucratic politics, and the conduct of successful/unsuccessful negotiations. Since verification is an essential element of the arms control process, Chapter 8 briefly reviews past examples to illustrate methods that have been employed. Finally, Chapter 9 also uses examples of previous agreements to define and examine the vital issue of compliance and noncompliance.

Not everyone will be satisfied with the broad net—the typography—that that has been used to define arms control in this book. Indeed, others have offered their own versions. It shall be left to the reader to determine whether the one offered here—with the variety of historical examples to control and/or reduce weaponry and military violence—appears adequate to sustain the descriptive structure presented below.

The author's earlier undertakings—a bibliography, *Arms Control and Disarmament* (1977), and the three volumes of *Encyclopedia of Arms Control and Disarmament* (1992)—provide additional information about many of the accords presented here, including bibliography and texts of individual agreements. Not surprisingly, the encyclopedia's essays have been drawn on frequently and their contributions acknowledged in the notes. A list of essential resources appended to this volume also may assist the serious student with directions for further reading and research.

My investigations have left me with far too many debts to librarians and colleagues to attempt acknowledging all individuals. However, I do need to recognize three colleagues who read the recent drafts of the manuscript and whose comments and suggestions significantly improved the text. They were Joseph M. Siracusa, Professor of International Diplomacy and Director of Global Studies at the Royal Melbourne Institute of Technology; Philip E. Coyle, III, Senior Advisor, Center for Defense Information and formerly a U.S. Assistant Secretary of Defense; and Jack Mendelsohn, an adjunct professor at George Washington University and American University, formerly Deputy Director of the Arms Control Association and a member of the U.S. SALT II and START I delegations. Additionally, the manuscript's final revisions took place under the keen editorial eye of Carolyn H. Moriyama.

Having retired a decade and a half ago, I would not have undertaken the preparation of this study except for the encouragement of my wife, Glenda, who has indulged me with more patience than I deserve. Finally, this endeavor has been inspired by the wish that all of our grandkids, Samantha, Christine, Austin, Cassidy, Pierce, Spencer, and Margo, may inherit a much less violent world.

Richard Dean Burns
Claremont, California

Introduction

Various forms of "arms control" and "disarmament"—the products of evolving taboos, imposed terms, and negotiated accords—have been employed among preliterate societies, during ancient and medieval times and between modern nation-states. These techniques took on greater significance when the stability of the modern world was shaken at the dawn of the twentieth century by the introduction of rapid-fire weapons, aircraft, chemical agents, and submarines, and at mid-century by the advent of weapons of mass destruction—nuclear and chemical/bacteriological—and sophisticated delivery systems. The enormous increase in destructive potential brought about by thermo-nuclear weaponry changed the nature of war and, therefore, arms control.

The chapters that follow are designed to provide an introduction to various features of arms control systems and, at the same time, to broaden one's view of their characteristics. To do so, the author has employed historical episodes and contemporary activities. The chapters are divided into two parts. The first part employs the historical and contemporary examples to delineate six arbitrarily defined areas of arms control. The second part uses several of the same examples to focus on the negotiations and politics, various verification arrangements, and issues arising with compliance or noncompliance of arms control activities.

The historical examples cited demonstrate the lineage and evolution of similar arms control methods. Obviously, the author does not mean to infer that the banning of war elephants and nuclear weapons are, for example, of equal strategic or tactical military significance. He does, nevertheless, point out that both Carthage (202 BCE) and Iraq (1991) were defeated states upon which these bans were imposed and that over time both bans posed similar political, verification, and compliance problems to the victors.

DEFINING TERMS

With the advent of modern arsenals came a bewildering array of technical terminology—dealing with weapon systems and strategic scenarios—being expounded by academics, reporters, military officers, and national security analysts. Two of the terms widely used by a variety of people ranging from reporters to policymakers were arms control and disarmament.

Public, and occasionally academic, bewilderment arose from the fact that the terms *arms control* and *disarmament* could be, and indeed often were, used synonymously. Although they often have been employed as umbrella terms to encompass a number of specific techniques to control armaments and reduce martial violence, they also were used independently to suggest two separate systems. Indeed, some people emphasized the distinctions between the two terms and focused on the perceived differences. Many arms controllers have gone on record as favoring measures to ensure international stability and opposing actual arms reductions, whereas some disarmers have dismissed partial or piecemeal arms control measures as meaningless. Often these same disarmers have argued that armaments are the major cause of international instability and that, therefore, only through complete or substantial reduction in the weaponry of all national arsenals can the world achieve lasting peace.[1]

Disarmament. Actually, this term is the older one and was employed for many decades before the introduction of *arms control*. It became fashionable during the nineteenth century, particularly after The Hague peace conference of 1899, to use disarmament to describe all international efforts to limit, reduce, or control the implements of war. While linguistic purists might employ disarmament in the literal sense—that is, the total elimination of armaments and armed forces—most analysts, diplomats and commentators have not. Disarmament "does not mean the disbanding of the whole nor even the greater part of the armed forces of the world," British diplomat and Nobel Prize laureate Philip J. Noel-Baker explained in 1926. "It means, rather, the reduction, the modest but, we may hope, not negligible reduction, of those forces, and their limitation by a general international treaty."[2]

In the post–World War II era, some individuals and institutions have continued to employ the term disarmament as an umbrella term. For example, in his book, *The Strategy of Disarmament,* Henry W. Forbes defined the subject as involving the quantitative and qualitative reduction of armaments, the outlawing of inhumane means of warfare, and the demilitarization of geographic areas. A former director of the United Nations Disarmament Affairs Division, William Epstein, recorded that in the United Nations and its subsidiary agencies, "the term 'disarmament' has in practice been used not as meaning total disarmament but as a generic term covering all measures relating to the field—from small steps to reduce tensions or build confidence, through regulation of armaments or arms control, up to general and complete disarmament."[3]

Arms Control. The desire to control armaments and thereby reduce the likelihood of widespread warfare increased greatly after World War II, stimulated by the development and deployment of nuclear weapons and sophisticated delivery systems with intercontinental reach. As the superpowers' nuclear weapons grew more numerous and powerful during the Cold War, it also became increasingly evident that the chaos and destruction emanating from a nuclear conflict would not only be limited to the principal belligerents, but could also gravely endanger most other nations. Despite the occasional disclaimers from Washington and Moscow that nuclear weapons would never be used, many academics, diplomats, and citizens began to urge the development of measures that might rein in the possible employment of extraordinarily destructive modern military systems.

It was academic specialists in the 1950s, those linking the technology of nuclear weaponry to the strategies of the Cold War, who began substituting the phrase *arms control* for the traditional term—disarmament. As these professionals viewed it, the term disarmament not only lacked semantic precision, it tended to carry a tone of utopianism. "Arms control to be meaningful must be devised in relation to the technological factors which produce the need for it," Professor Henry A. Kissinger wrote in 1960. "It cannot be conceived in a fit of moral indignation. Effective schemes require careful, detailed, dispassionate studies and the willingness to engage in patient, highly technical negotiations. Otherwise arms control may increase rather than diminish insecurity."[4]

Moreover, these new experts believed that arms control better described the Cold War's close military-diplomatic relationship of protracted tension. According to Thomas C. Schelling and Morton H. Halperin, the use of the term arms control rather than disarmament was simply a broadening of the definition to include all forms of military cooperation between potential enemies, in the interest of reducing the likelihood of war, its scope and violence if it did occur, and the political and economic costs of being prepared for it.[5] Allen Ferguson argued in favor of using arms control because it was a more comprehensive term and as such "it embraced all the problems ranging from total disarmament to the selective strengthening of armaments for the purpose of increasing the stability of mutual deterrence."[6]

Consequently, most Cold War strategists who considered the use of arms control concentrated their strategies on tension-reducing mechanisms and, occasionally, on quantitative or qualitative limitations. Their main objective, however, was to improve the stability of the strategic nuclear deterrence system—rather than the elimination of weapons—and, thus, to reduce the prospect of a nuclear war.

Throughout this study, the author has employed the phrase *arms control* as an umbrella term.

HISTORICAL ANALOGIES

While most debates over major foreign and domestic policy issues take place within a historical frame of reference, analysts, policymakers, and citizens dealing with arms control activities far too frequently ignored the history of these activities, considered them dated and, therefore, meaningless, or employed misleading analogies. Diplomat George W. Ball, for example, complained that arms control and disarmament is "more abstruse and arcane" than any other issue in foreign affairs. He also stated that this was "because there is no solid experience to supply a precedent."[7] Meanwhile, Wayland Young explained that "because the field is all hypothesis—nobody has yet *done* any—the very words used to talk about disarmament and arms control are still green."[8] Obviously, the endeavors of both of these observers were focused on efforts to place limits on modern "strategic" weapon systems. Even so, they ignored the experiences of various substantial arms limitation activities that took place between the two world wars, as well as many other, earlier episodes. While historical experiences will not in all likelihood provide answers to contemporary problems, Bernard Brodie pointed out in *War and Peace* that it may, "at its best ... sharpen our receptivity to appropriate insights about those problems."

An enthusiastic supporter of disarmament, Charles A Barker, in yet another example, described the Rush-Bagot pact (1817) as an example of "general and complete disarmament," and chose not to differentiate among the various arms control techniques this agreement used.[9] Contrary to his description, the Rush-Bagot agreement and its subsequent revisions among the United States, Great Britain and, eventually, Canada, did not substantially limit or reduce the main armed forces of any of the signatories. It did, however, essentially "demilitarize" the Great Lakes and, in its initial decades, head off a potentially dangerous local naval race.

The historical record of arms control and disarmament has been either unknown or dismissed because it has been believed, especially in the United States, that historical perspectives could offer little guidance to policymakers. Yet history, if examined, often could have been a refreshing antidote to much of the theoretical nonsense and far-fetched arms, arms control, and disarmament scenarios that were generated during the last half of the twentieth century. As Herman S. Wolk has noted, analysts could have used with profit

> ...historical analogy instead of theory, insight instead of numbers, understanding in place of guesswork, and a facility with language.... Despite the estimable contributions of social science over the ... years, the obsession of many social scientists with methodology, model building, and inexplicable games has produced an astonishing amount of drivel. Part of this massive overdose of gamesmanship proceeded from the kind of macabre incantation leveled by Max Singer of [Herman] Kahn's Hudson Institute: "Experience," he said, "won't serve as a guide any more to practical affairs. The world has become too complicated." When up the creek, throw away the oar.[10]

In many ways, technology has altered the weaponry of the modern era, especially in greatly expanding its destructive capabilities and its range. Unfortunately, the need for political endeavors to induce restraint frequently has gone unrecognized by national leaders in the persistent drive to find security in more and more of these weapons, to the point where the very existence of human civilization was imperiled. Yet several attempts have been made to warn them. "To beget and build in order to kill and demolish is lunacy," General J. F. C. Fuller has written. "And the more powerful becomes the war machine, the more certain is it that war will bring losses far in excess of gains, not only to the vanquished but also to the victors. This is the uncontradictable fact ... the Second World War has revealed to all who still are sane."[11]

Those individuals who reject historical experience as a helpful guide to human undertakings and insist on radical or technical solutions were described by Walter Lippmann as "frightened, irritated, impatient, frustrated and in search of quick and easy solutions."[12] Clearly, many of the basic elements of Cold War arms control activities—negotiating strategies, security considerations, verification techniques, and compliance fears—might have profited with a greater appreciation of historical experiences. While history does not provide us with answers to every question or guarantee us certitude, it does help ensure that we are asking the right questions, and does provide us with a broad perspective in charting a path through the maze of military-political affairs.

The brief descriptions of pacts presented next illustrate different methods and categories of arms control and review various other features of the arms control process.

PART I

Means and Techniques
A Historical Typology

An attempt to establish typologies will almost surely evoke dismay from those individuals who have wrestled with that Aristotelian curse. Yet cannot one discount the argument, posed by James E. Dougherty, that "without definitions, we cannot begin to think or analyze with any ... exactness, much less add anything of value to our knowledge of reality."[1] It is the premise of this study that descriptions grounded in past experiences can sharpen the often abstract definitions of various contemporary approaches to arms control and disarmament, and allow a reasoned assessment of them in a real-world context.

Historical experiences will be employed throughout this section to direct attention to the six means or methods of achieving arms control and disarmament, and to the six additional basic techniques or categories that frequently define the different objectives of these endeavors.

MEANS AND METHODS

The goals of arms control activities have varied widely, but their highest priority has been that of finding a means or method of providing for, or enhancing, the tribe or nation's sense of security. From tribal days to the ancient world to the nation-state, the methods for accomplishing this objective have embraced various choices ranging from extermination to diplomacy.

By examining historical examples, the means or methods through which arms control and disarmament have been accomplished may be classified into three broad categories, each of which, in turn, is subdivided into two additional categories. There are, then, six general means or methods by which the objectives of arms control and disarmament have been achieved.

Retributive Measures

1. *Extermination.* This is a most drastic means of ensuring there will be no future hostile response from one's adversary.

Antiquity provides many examples of the employment of this drastic means of "disarmament" in hopes of guaranteeing that an enemy will never again pose a threat to one's economic and territorial security. The Book of Joshua in the Old Testament tells of the Hebrews' entry into the "promised land." To gain control of the territory, this account records many bloody battles where the victorious Israelites frequently took a city and killed "every living thing" in it, sparing "nothing that drew breath." Various Mongol campaigns, beginning in 1190, would destroy those cities that failed to surrender and then massacre their inhabitants—a technique that made the name of Genghis Khan among the most feared in history. The khan's bloody tactics are estimated to have killed some 18 million people, while his victorious forces devastated the developed Moslem civilization of Central Asia. Timur the Lame followed a century later and was equally as ruthless, as he is remembered for totally destroying resisting cities and stacking the heads of the defeated foes in columns and pyramids in order terrify his next victims into surrendering.

No conqueror outdid Ashurnasirpal II (883–859 BCE) of Assyria, who utilized this means of gaining total control and absolute security in regions where his opponents did not embrace his authority. His account of taking the city of Tela on the slopes of Kashiari that refused to surrender typifies his actions: "Many of their soldiers I took alive; of some I cut off hands and limbs; of others the noses, ears, and arms; of many soldiers I put out the eyes. I reared a column of the living and a column of heads. I hung up on high their heads on trees in the vicinity of the city. Their boys and girls I burned up in the flame. I devastated the city, dug it up, in fire I burned it; I annihilated it."[2] Some 250 years later the Assyrian empire was itself annihilated, accompanied with the utter destruction of its capital Nineveh in 612 BCE, by the Medes, Lydians, Egyptians, and Babylonians.

Another dramatic example of this method was Rome's treatment of Carthage. After the Second Punic War, the victorious Romans imposed extremely restrictive arms control measures upon the Carthaginians. Accusing the Carthaginians of violating these measures some five decades later, the Romans conquered Carthage, sold its 50,000 remaining citizens into slavery, and completely demolished the city. When Carthage ceased to exist, Romans believed that their security was enhanced—and it was, for a time.[3]

In the New World, hostilities among Indian tribes occasionally followed the same pattern. For example, the Iroquois, tired of their protracted conflicts with the Hurons, exterminated their opponent in 1649. The idea, if not the act, continued into the twentieth century. After the Nazis launched World War II, Morley Roberts worried about the outcome. "But if the Germans are again overcome," he wrote, "it must be held that the massacre of a whole population is justified if no other means can secure an inoffensive nation or nationality."[4]

Following World War II, the targeting of nuclear weaponry offered the prospect that its use would create such death and destruction, that it would be difficult to identify who was the victor or the vanquished. We are most fortunate that this did not result in another extreme dimension of "disarmament."

> 2. *Imposition.* This much more limited method seeks to reinforce the security of victorious nations by the prolonged, forced disarmament of their vanquished foes.

Imposed disarmament was employed following some major struggles for empire in ancient times. At the end of Peloponnesian War in 404 BCE, the Spartans contemplated total destruction of Athens but, instead, decided to demand only the destruction of the Long Wall that connected Athens to its port of Piraeus.[5] The Romans reduced the military potential of formally independent states by the terms of its treaties with Carthage at the end of the Second Punic War in 201 BCE, with Macedon after the Second Macedonian War in 196 BCE, and with the Seleucid king Antiochus III in 188 BCE. These treaties imposed significant arms control provisions that restricted their former adversaries freedom to wage war in the future by placing limitations on their military forces, often reinforced by the assessment of severe reparations.

During the English and French wars of the eighteenth century, the victorious British insisted upon the destruction of Dunkirk's fortifications to eliminate a potential base of naval operations. On the other side of Europe, the expansionist Russian and the receding Ottoman Empires were engaged in frequent hostilities. A point of contention, beginning in 1695, was the fortifications at Azov that provided the Russians access to the inland seas; consequently, the Russians built fortifications when victorious, while the Ottoman Turks insisted on razing them when they prevailed.[6]

During the nineteenth and twentieth centuries, the Prussian/German state experienced three episodes of imposed disarmament—following Napoleon's victory in 1806, the Allies' victory in 1919, and the destruction of Hitler's war machine in 1945. The victorious Germans achieved some satisfaction in disarming the French Vichy state in 1940. The most recent example came about when a United Nations coalition, led by the United States, forced restrictions on Iraq's military forces and weaponry after the First Iraqi War in 1992.[7]

Unilateral Measures

> 3. *Unilateral Neglect.* This method (often confused with Unilateral Decision, below) refers to the reduction of a nation's armed forces and/or weaponry via neglect, obsolescence, or postponement.

The distinction between unilateral neglect and unilateral decision is, as Christopher J. Lamb has noted, "an important one, but it is controversial" and, one might add, often not easily defined.[8] A nation's military forces may be allowed to decline without a formally developed arms control policy as a result of a variety of factors, including a false sense of security, public distaste for, or distrust of, the military and, especially, a desire to reduce or reallocate public expenditures. "To my mind," Republican Senator Hugh Scott of Pennsylvania declared, "unilateral obsolescence is even more dangerous than unilateral disarmament, because on unilateral disarmament you can make political adjustments ... , but on unilateral obsolescence you don't know whether your weapons are any good until you suddenly find you need to use [them]. ..."[9]

Some analysts believe that peace and prosperity may bring on a "lulling" effect that may cause the unilateral neglect of a state's military forces. In the case of Rome, J. F. C. Fuller argues, "the dry rot of peace had [by 175 CE] ... eaten into Roman valor." Because they were prosperous, few Romans desired to endure the discomforts of lengthy, distant military service; consequently, the emperor had to hire mercenaries or barbarians to secure the empire's frontiers. Due to a sense of complacency and a "neglect" of duty, the old Roman discipline gradually disappeared and the empire began to crumble.[10]

Sir Charles Oman points to the Wars of the Roses (1455–1487), which saw modern cannon mastering old fortifications, as the beginning of the unilateral decline of England's military. "These wars not only placed Henry Tudor on the throne, but resulted in so deep-seated a dislike for the professional soldier, that for a hundred and fifty years, England was left without an army."[11] Britain's "ten-year rule" during the 1920s and 1930s that delayed expenditures on its military forces was, in large measure, the result of declining treasury receipts due to the Great Depression and the public's reaction to the cost of victory in World War I.

A desire to reduce or reallocate spending motivated the United States' gradual reduction of its Navy after the Civil War. The Northern Navy had built its fleet up to 641 vessels, had made significant technological advances in armament and armor, and was at war's end equal to any fleet in the world. After the war, Congress severely slashed its appropriations and the Navy declined perceptibly. In 1889, Secretary of the Navy Benjamin Franklin Tracy ranked the United States' fleet behind Britain, France, Russia, Germany, Holland, Spain, Turkey, China, Norway-Sweden, and the Austro-Hungarian Empire. Starved for funding, the United States' fleet gradually became obsolete and lost its technological edge.[12]

4. *Unilateral Decision.* This is a conscious, considered policy of self-imposed military restrictions or limitations that may stem from a variety of purposes and have various objectives.

In a self-imposed limitation, the Second Lateran Council in 1139, and subsequent councils, banned the use of crossbows between Christian forces, although they might be employed against pagans. In 1607, the Tokugawa shoguns imposed increasingly restrictive regulations upon gunsmiths and, within a century, the manufacture and use of guns virtually disappeared in Japan. In medieval Europe, the several "peace pacts"—the Peace and Truce of God—involved unilateral restrictions initially enforced by regional clerics and nobles.[13]

President Franklin D. Roosevelt declared, on June 8, 1943, that the United States would employ a "no-first-use policy" regarding chemical weapons, but promised "full and swift" retaliation should the Axis powers initiate their use. Japan's constitution (Art. 9) and Austria's peace treaty (1955) that restricted armaments to their national defensive needs—together with the West German chancellor's declaration (1954) not to manufacture atomic, biological, and chemical weapons—represent post–World War II self-imposed decisions.[14]

During the Cold War, the Soviet Union, United States, France, and the United Kingdom unilaterally pledged not to use strategic nuclear weapons against any state that was a party to the Non-Proliferation Treaty and did not possess nuclear arms. In November 1969, President Richard Nixon stated that the United States had decided, unilaterally, to renounce the use of bacteriological and biological weapons. In September 1991, President George H. W. Bush ordered the unilateral withdrawal from overseas of all land- and sea-based tactical nuclear weapons. Subsequently, the Soviet Union (1992) responded with its own unilateral nuclear reductions. (Many of the tactical nuclear weapons, however, remain in each nation's arsenal.)[15]

The post–Cold War years saw a continuation of unilateral decisions. In January 1992, President Boris Yeltsin unilaterally halted the production of strategic bombers and air-launched cruise missiles and indicated that Russia was going to shut down those nuclear reactors still producing weapons-grade plutonium. President Jacques Chirac announced in February 1996 that France was going to unilaterally reduce its nuclear weapons programs, including closing down its plants producing fissile materials for nuclear weapons and its Pacific test site.[16]

Reciprocal Measures

5. *Bilateral Negotiation.* By this traditional and frequently used method, two nations could seek to improve their security through arms control measures employing mutually acceptable terms.

The Anglo-French pact (1787), the Rush-Bagot agreement (1817), the Argentine-Chilean accord (1902), the Turko-Greek protocol (1930), the Turko-Soviet protocol (1931), and the Anglo-German treaty (1935) all involved placing restrictions on naval forces that were contributing to tensions between the involved parties. During the last half of the twentieth century, the United States and the Soviet Union negotiated and signed numerous bilateral treaties, including the SALT I and II, START I and II, and INF treaties. In 2002, the two nations added the SORT pact, which placed qualitative and quantitative restrictions on their strategic weapons systems. The two superpowers also concluded several other accords aimed at easing anxieties between Washington and Moscow.

> 6. *Multilateral Negotiation.* This common twentieth-century approach, as mili-
> tary-political problems became regional, if not global, sought arms control
> measures enhancing vital interests of several nations.

The Hague treaties (1899 and 1907) were products of multilateral negotiations involving several nations, most of which became signatories on various
emerging agreements. The leading naval powers negotiated the Washington naval pact (1922) and during the interwar years met at subsequent conferences.
During their deliberations, they also established qualitative and quantitative features that were incorporated in the League of Nations disarmament drafts. The
Latin American denuclearization treaty (1967), known as the Treaty of Tlatelolco, while negotiated by regional participants, called for and gained international concurrence.

During the decades following both world wars, the major powers were
almost constantly engaged in some form of multilateral negotiations dealing
with issues relating to weaponry under the auspices of the League of Nations
and, later, the United Nations. Among the most significant agreements emerging from League efforts, was the Geneva Protocol on Poisonous Gases (1925)
and from the UN were the Outer Space Treaty (1967), Non-Proliferation Treaty
(1968), the Biological Weapons Convention (1972), Convention on Chemical
Weapons (1993), and the Comprehensive Nuclear Test Ban Treaty (1996).[17]

TECHNIQUES AND CATEGORIES

Caught up as today's world is with the efforts to deal with "weapons of mass
destruction," it is easy to forget that buried in the recesses of the past were peoples—as described above—who confronted, and occasionally succumbed to,
the total eradication of their tribe or city-state. Not surprisingly then, many of
the earliest societies, even quite violent ones, gradually developed prohibitions
or taboos that restricted their use of specific weapons and tempered the intensity
of their conflicts. The arms control techniques and categories defined here, indirectly or directly, trace their lineage to many of these early examples. Modern
efforts to regulate weapons technology, limit the size of arsenals, and lessen the
destructiveness of warfare have tended to be much more specific and technical,
whether focused on the quantity of armaments and force strengths or on the
employment of certain weapons. In many cases, as with other types of treaties,
these instruments were short-lived as the political/military situations changed,
and treaty objectives were not adapted to the new circumstances. Those agreements that survived for any substantial length of time were found to require
modification to meet changing conditions.

Employing a historical perspective, this study divides arms control and disarmament proposals, treaties, and agreements into six descriptive categories or classifications, ranging from arms limitation/reduction to stabilizing the international environment. While a brief description of each category is presented here, the following six chapters introduce selected treaties and agreements that demonstrate each category's specific characteristics. However, the six categories are not exclusive since, for example, the outlawing of weapons has the same effect as the limiting of them, while a treaty that prohibits placing weapons of mass destruction in outer space is also an example of geographic demilitarization. Moreover, a single treaty may incorporate several arms control techniques: the Treaty of Versailles (1919) restricted the number of German arms and military personnel, demilitarized specific zones, and outlawed German manufacture of military aircraft, submarines, and tanks.

Nonetheless, the descriptive categories that are listed below, and are elaborated in subsequent chapters, should be useful in identifying and understanding the lineage of various types of arms control measures that historically have been employed.

1. *Limitation and Reduction of Armaments.* These negotiations, proposals and treaties place specified limits on the mobilization, possession, or construction of identified military personnel and weaponry—occasionally, their actual reduction. The restrictions may be qualitative, regulating weapons design and characteristics, as well as quantitative, limiting the total numbers of permitted personnel and weaponry.

2. *Demilitarization, Denuclearization, and Neutralization.* The first two types of accords or proposals involve removing or placing restrictions on military forces, weapons, and fortifications within a prescribed area of land, water, or airspace. Neutralization is a special status that guarantees political independence and territorial integrity, subject to a pledge that the neutralized state will not engage in hostilities except in self-defense. The essential feature of all three is the emphasis on restrictions for geographical areas.

3. *Regulating Use or Outlawing Specific Weapons.* These undertakings limit or prohibit the military use of or even the possession of specific weapons. Frequently the weapons involved are newly introduced and threaten the traditional patterns of warfare. The rationale for these limitations or prohibitions is that the parties involved consider that the unrestricted use—or often any use—of a particular weapon exceeds recognized "just use of force."

4. *Controlling Arms Manufacture and Traffic.* This approach usually involves restrictions on the sale or transfer by either private parties or governments of specific weaponry, delivery systems, and munitions; it may also seek to restrict or prohibit the manufacture of specific weapons. Although there have been many proposals, few formal bans have resulted. The post-1945 era found, however, various multilateral export control regimes to be quite useful in restricting the sale and delivery of certain proscribed technology and weaponry. Also included in this category are unilateral or multilateral embargoes of specific classes of weapons and munitions.

5. *Law of War.* These arms control measures—collectively know as the "law or customs of war"—have been designed to regulate military violence once armed conflict breaks out. These measures seek to protect noncombatants from military violence and, in the process, to define legitimate targets. Among the basic principles embodied in the customs and law of war are (a) the prohibition of weapons that cause unnecessary or disproportionate suffering; (b) the protection of historical treasures and the physical environment; (c) the realization that the demands of humanity should prevail over the necessities of combat; and (d) the treatment of prisoners of war.

6. *Stabilizing the International Environment.* The various pacts and proposals in this category seek to protect the environment—its people, animals, and vegetation—from lasting damage due to the testing or use of military technologies. Additionally, there are treaties that seek to find the means of lowering international tensions and preventing hostilities prompted by miscalculation. This involves efforts to lessen the possibility of a "cause célèbre" through misperception or accident by both improving communication and having an ongoing sharing of significant information between antagonistic parties.

The various treaties, agreements, and proposals cited in the categories below comprise an extensive sampling but should not be considered a complete list. A representative sampling of these treaties and agreements is included in the following brief narrative description.

OTHER TYPOLOGIES

Those analysts who find value in typologies have classified many of the same agreements treated above and below in a variety of different categories for the purpose of analysis. Two of these variations are pointed out here for those readers that may wish to investigate them or develop their own classifications. One criticism of my earlier typologies is that they have never been subjected to any systematic analytical evaluation. The reason for this was that when I began researching and writing about arms control issues in the late 1950s, most studies were limited to historical examples drawn from the interwar years. My initial effort resulted in a coauthored multi-volume study for the U.S. Arms Control and Disarmament Agency, *Disarmament in Perspective, 1919–1939* (1968), and launched several decades of studying the subject.

But subsequent research began to uncover and identify many other examples of arms control activities that were spread across a wide historical landscape. The sheer volume and differences of these examples called for some means of arranging them. Thus my typography grew out of attempting to classify these many and varied episodes—including their objectives, how they were arrived at, by what means were they verified, and their successes and failures—in order to draw attention on the historical lineage of the various categories.

Christopher Lamb apparently was aware of my efforts at classification, as he drew upon my *Arms Control and Disarmament: A Bibliography* (1977) to create his own "seven categories of disarmament" for the purpose of analysis. Employing historical examples, he suggested disarmament endeavors consisted of:

1. nuclear or nonnuclear activities;
2. voluntary or nonvoluntary methods;
3. partial or complete disarmament;
4. material or moral considerations;
5. unilateral achievement;
6. bilateral accomplishment; and/or
7. multilateral negotiation.

Lamb's basic objective was "to cut through the fog of confusion surrounding the controversies on arms control and disarmament" by providing simplified "alternative approaches without obscuring critical if subtle distinctions between them." His "tools" were designed to provide the means to "identify quickly the premises and assumptions of the principal competing schools of thought," related to security issues. To this end, his study was "designed to assist in the development of a sober sense of historical perspective. A sense of historical perspective on arms control means more than an awareness of past successes and failures. It means removing oneself from the current debate, abandoning ephemeral fervency and ideological consistency ... by comparing current historical trends with past experience."

In a more recent work, Stuart Croft has acknowledged my classifications, but chose to offer intriguing ones of his own. To flesh out his categories, Croft introduced a substantial number of historical agreements and treaties, many of which were referenced to volume three of my *Encyclopedia of Arms Control and Disarmament*. At the core of his study are the following five categories:

1. *Arms control at the conclusion of major conflicts* that employed either imposed and/or negotiated disarmament;
2. *Arms control to strengthen strategic stability*, which focused on pacts to control weaponry that has heightened tensions and to permit time for diplomacy to seek solutions;
3. *Arms control to create norms of behavior* that in times of conflict may limit military violence inflicted upon noncombatants, may outlaw certain weaponry as too destructive, and establish norms of behavior;
4. *Managing the proliferation of weapons* that included preventing weapons from reaching one's adversaries, embargoing weaponry to limit the danger of war or escalation, and efforts to halt proliferation of weaponry; and
5. *Arms control by international organization* that involved arms embargoes, UN peacekeepers, and efforts to enforce the laws of war.

After placing Cold War nuclear arms control from 1960–1990 in perspective, Croft suggests that these activities "were not unique, nor solely a product of the advent of nuclear weapons technology." Turning to the post–Cold War era, he poses an open-ended question: How have arms control activities changed? The answer, he argues, will be "not provided by judgments on whether arms control agreements have been 'successful' or not, but by reference to typologies of the objectives sought by the agreements, and by analyzing how both the objectives and scope of those agreements have evolved over time."[18]

1 ───────────────────────────────

Arms Limitations and/or Reductions

This basic arms control category—limitation and reduction—has involved specified limitations on the mobilization, possession, or acquisition of military personnel, the characteristics of military equipment, and/or the permissible units of specified military equipment. The restrictions specified in various accords have been qualitative, regulating a weapon's design, as well as quantitative, limiting the numbers of permitted personnel and weapons. Agreements may or may not result in the actual reduction of existing military forces and weaponry. This measure has been imposed upon vanquished foes, often together with heavy reparations payments that were specifically added to slow a defeated state's efforts to rebuild its military forces.

Negotiated, mutually acceptable arms limitation agreements that focus on military personnel or specific weaponry usually have emphasized the technical dimensions of the involved forces or armaments. As such, they can, at best, provide for a temporary stable political environment by diminishing the tensions that have arisen from actual or impending arms races or other threatening military activities. The arms limitation measures, by themselves, are not likely to resolve the threatening, contentious issues that originally prompted an arms build-up or mounting tensions. At most, these measures may allow political leaders and diplomats—in an atmosphere temporarily cleared of tensions inspired by uncurbed weaponry or threatening military actions—to come to terms with the vexing political, social, and economic differences.

Motivated by fear and anxiety, victors have imposed arms limitations and reductions upon their vanquished foes, as noted above, with the aim of preventing future hostilities. Imposed disarmament, as British historian Philip Towle has pointed out in his significant study, *Enforced Disarmament*, has not been without its drawbacks. The defeated foe may not forego its aggressive ambitions, and being disarmed may foster domestic discord among its statesmen, generals, and citizens. Popular opinion may become resentful and prompt the feeling of being discriminated against, and the public may look upon being disarmed as a humiliating denial of their sovereignty. A bitter and humiliated populace might welcome the opportunity to throw aside what they consider vindictive terms and unite to challenge the dominating power(s) when the opportunity arises.[1]

The Western democracies have disarmed their foes following their victories in World Wars I and II hoping to establish a stable, if not a peaceful, world. Other victors, such as Napoleon and Hitler, used imposed disarmament as an interim measure while they contemplated what to do with the countries they had defeated. In an earlier episode, Rome imposed disarmament terms upon a defeated Carthage in 202 BCE; yet, even these severe terms did not diminish the Romans' sense of insecurity and led to their decision to reopen hostilities and exterminate Carthage fifty years later.

Looking for its historical lineage, one finds relatively few examples of formal proposals and actual employment of arms limitations and/or reductions treaties from antiquity to the nineteenth century—and most of those few were imposed. If this technique became progressively more sophisticated in the arms control negotiations and treaties since World War I, the earlier conventional weaponry did not match the enormously destructive capabilities of the nuclear era. During the age of conventional warfare—up to and including World War II—the victors and vanquished, even those suffering enormous casualties and widespread devastation, still retained a basic infrastructure and could usually recover in a few decades. An arms control failure to halt an outbreak of hostilities could have serious consequences, but the basic fabric of each society would survive.

During the Cold War, with ever-increasing numbers of sophisticated nuclear weaponry and enhanced delivery systems, the superpowers achieved the capability to destroy entire societies, perhaps even to render the world's climatic conditions inhospitable to life. In American and Soviet strategic "command and control rooms," the bleakness of the situation became evident and the concept of "victory" became meaningless. This was demonstrated by the experience of former ambassador Thomas Watson, who at the request of President Jimmy Carter, participated in investigating the preparedness of the United States' nuclear triad and command status. According to the Soviet ambassador to Washington, Anatoly Dobrynin, Watson informed him how the Pentagon generals planned to conduct a nuclear war against the Soviet Union. "With huge maps and lighted charts lining the walls, they showed him more than a thousand targets on Soviet territory marked for destruction during the first hours of war. Soviet causalities would be more than one hundred million." Then Watson asked, "What about our casualties?" The generals responded that the death toll would be "about eighty million Americans and many major industries would be destroyed, just as in the Soviet Union." Watson persisted: "And what would you do after almost everything was destroyed? The generals looked at each other and did not have much to say." The pursuit of victory did not involve dealing with its consequences. In his memoirs, Dobrynin suggested that the Soviet military probably evaluated the prospect of nuclear war in similar fashion.[2]

Fortunately, however, a broad-based arms control "regime" comprised of various arrangements and prohibitions—most, but not all, formally structured—gradually lessened the danger of a nuclear confrontation. This consisted of a series of bilateral agreements that dealt with nuclear weapons and their delivery systems—from Strategic Arms Limitation Treaties (SALT I and II) to Strategic Arms Reduction Treaties (START I and II). These pacts reinforced a sense of strategic stability based on a crude superpower "parity" that, in turn, lent credence to an unstructured, but mutually understood, concept of deterrence. This stability was further enhanced by a series of agreements—such as the Hotline, Accidents Measures Agreement, Prevention of Incidents On and Over High Seas, Nuclear Risk Reduction Centers, and so on (see Chapter 6)—designed to prevent an unintended conflict.

Formal efforts to halt or prevent the spread of nuclear weapons also played a role in dampening down international fears. The Non-Proliferation Treaty (NPT), together with the International Atomic Energy Agency (IAEA), the Nuclear Suppliers Group, and the Missile Technology Control Regime, became a center point of this activity (see Chapter 4). Then, too, the Nuclear Weapons-Free Zones—such as Antarctic Treaty, Outer Space Treaty, Treaty of Tlatelolco (for Latin America)—assisted with diminishing the desire for nuclear weaponry (see Chapter 2).

Finally, along with a worldwide moral condemnation of nuclear warfare, there gradually developed among affected heads of state, an informal taboo against the first use of nuclear weapons (see Chapter 10). Arms control efforts, formal and informal, sought to protect the security of all parties while, at the same time, seeking to rein in the weapons technology that frequently proved unsettling and to prevent dangerous unanticipated scenarios from occurring.

What follows is a representative, chronological sampling, together with a brief narrative description, of the treaties and agreements that demonstrated the historical lineage of arms limitation and/or reductions.

FROM ANTIQUITY TO WORLD WAR I

Warfare during this era, especially during antiquity, was a particularly intimate and bloody affair. Even during this early time, people saw the need for restrictions on weapons. The victors occasionally imposed upon their defeated foes treaties requiring the reduction and limitation of armaments. The Romans employed this arms control strategy and enforced heavy reparations designed to limit their foe's ability to rebuild their military forces. At the same time, the Romans usually required political terms that bound the defeated state to assist imperial objectives in war and peace.

Over time, efforts to limit and reduce armies and navies gradually became more sophisticated, even though they retained some of these earlier elements. These arms control proposals and treaties usually comprised a more formal structure, although they often still might be combined with features such as general political settlements, imposed terms, and reparations.

Sparta-Athens, 404 BCE. At the end of the Peloponnesian War, the victorious Spartans considered various punishments, but settled on the surrender of all but twelve Athenian warships. To further weaken Athens, Sparta demanded that the Athenians dismantle their defensive Long Wall that connected the city to its port of Piraeus. It was not long before repairs to the wall began.

Rome-Carthage Treaty of Peace, 202 BCE. This imposed agreement, generally referred to as the Treaty of Zama, followed Rome's victory over Carthage in the Second Punic War. After some seventeen years of warfare—with campaigning ranging from Spain into Italy and, finally, North Africa—Hannibal's army was routed at the battle of Zama and Carthage sued for peace. Although some Romans urged the razing of Carthage, the prolonged, costly task of besieging the well-fortified city persuaded the victors to settle for drastic military terms that (1) required the destruction of all but ten warships; (2) prohibited Carthage's possession and training of elephants to be used in combat; (3) restricted Carthage's use of mercenary soldiers; and (4) barred Carthage from conducting military campaigns beyond its city limits. In addition, Carthage was subjected to heavy reparations payments and had to obtain permission from Rome before conducting any military operations even within its borders.

Ignoring the latter provision, five decades later the rearmed Carthage used force to retaliate against the Numidians for attacking the Carthaginian city of Oroscoa. The Romans used this episode to charge that the Carthaginians had violated their treaty obligations and, in 146 BCE, dispatched armies that captured and completely obliterated the city.

Peace of Apamea, 188 BCE. Another example of the Roman strategy of imposing severe military limitations on their defeated foes followed the defeat of the Seleucid kingdom. Antiochus III was forced to (1) turn over all but ten of his warships; (2) surrender his war elephants and no longer possess them; (3) halt the hiring of mercenary troops; and (4) desist from military campaigns in regions he had formerly controlled. Substantial reparations were also demanded.[3]

Austrian Proposal for Arms Reductions, 1766. Shortly after the Seven Years' War, Austrian officials sought negotiated military reductions. In 1766, Austrian Chancellor Prince Kaunitz proposed to emissaries of Frederick the Great of Prussia that the two countries reduce their standing armies by three-fourths in an effort to allow both states to reduce their military expenditures. Both countries' finances had been badly strained by the Seven Years' War. Frederick refused, however, to consider the offer. Joseph II of Austria renewed the offer in 1769, with Prussia again declining.[4]

Anglo-French Naval Limitation Pact, 1787. As British and French leaders sought to avoid being drawn into a civil war underway in Holland during June

1787, Prime Minister William Pitt proposed that France and England discontinue "warlike preparations ... until such time as notice might be given for their renewal." His earlier suggestion during 1785–1786 discussions for a commercial pact that the two nations reduce their warships in the East Indies was rebuffed. French foreign minister Count Montmorin, seeking to harmonize relations with London, accepted the current offer.

In a Reciprocal Declaration, the French and British monarchs each "agreed (1) to limit active naval forces to six ships-of-the-line; (2) to maintain naval armaments at a peacetime level, and should that change; (3) to resist augmenting their naval strength until the other party had been notified of their impending action." Three separate Declarations signed at Versailles on October 27, 1787, reaffirmed the naval limits. In early December, the two nations exchanged information on the strength of their naval home fleets as of January 1, 1987, with Pitt suggesting to the reluctant French that an on-site visit might verify the agreed-to reductions. Nothing came of the proposal. Five years later, the naval pact was pushed aside when revolutionary France declared war on Britain and Holland.[5]

Poland Disarmed and Dismembered, 1792, 1794. To resist dismemberment and assert its independence, the Poles managed to antagonize the Russians who, using questionable allegations, forced the Polish Diet in July 1972 to give up additional territory and demobilize its army. Refusing the latter demand, the Poles were defeated at the battle of Maciejowice in 1794. The Poles sought to negotiate only to be told by General Suvorov: "Treaties are not necessary. The soldiers must be disarmed, and all weapons handed over to the Russians." Warsaw surrendered in November 1794 and, with Austria demanding a share of the spoils, Poland was erased from the map until 1918.[6]

Franco-Prussian Treaty, 1808. After Napoleon defeated the Prussians at Tilsit in 1807, the Treaty of Paris (September 17, 1808) imposed military restrictions on Prussia. Napoleon apparently took "malicious satisfaction in emulating Prussian and Russian behavior towards their weaker neighbor [Poland]." In "Separate Articles" to the Paris Treaty, Professor William O. Shanahan writes,

> The size of the Prussian army was limited to 36,000 men: 22,000 infantry, and 8,000 cavalry, with 6,000 artillery and technical troops, to which might be added 6,000 men of the Royal Guard, making a total of 42,000 effectives. No extraordinary levy, militia, or civil guard, or other measure intended to augment this force was permitted.

Additionally, the original treaty called for 73 million francs in reparations, which Napoleon later raised to 140 million—a most difficult burden for 4.5 million Prussians.

Historians have suggested that the "Krümper" system of recruitment involving furloughing regular army soldiers and training reservists for a month, was established as a subterfuge for evading the treaty. Although contemporaries believed this evasion was taking place, Shanahan notes that the system, established in 1792, was never fully developed and argues that the fiscal drain of the indemnity significantly restricted the size of the Prussian army. With Napoleon's defeat in Russia, financial assistance from the British and the release of their prisoners-of-war, the Prussians abrogated the treaty on March 16, 1813, and participated in the final defeat of Napoleon.

Still, the Krümper myth had a serious impact on the 1919 Treaty of Versailles. Allied leaders Lloyd George, Balfour, and others, believed Germany had earlier evaded disarmament terms through the Krümper system and, therefore, sought to design the military terms of the Versailles Treaty to prevent this from occurring.

Franco-Austrian "Separate Articles," 1809. After the ill-fated decision to challenge Napoleon based upon an inflated view of its capabilities, Austria was defeated. At Schönbrunn on October 14, 1809, the Austrians agreed to a peace treaty with a separate disarmament arrangement similar, but with subtle differences, to one that was imposed upon the Prussians. It limited Austrian forces to 150,000 men and included reparations payments. The limitation of forces lasted for only a year, but a depleted economy restricted Austrian efforts to rebuild their military forces.[7]

Limitation of Egyptian Arms, 1841–1879. To maintain some control over its vassal in Egypt, the Ottoman Turks issued four Firmans (royal decrees) that imposed restrictions on Egypt's expanding military forces and demanded tribute as measures designed to impede that state's growing sense of independence. After British, French, and Russian fleets destroyed the Egyptian and Ottoman navies at Navarino in 1827 during the Greek war, the Egyptian governor, Muhammad Ali, with French assistance substantially enlarged his army and acquired modern warships. With the blessing of European nations who sought to preserve the Ottoman Empire, the Turks in 1841 limited Egypt's peacetime army to 18,000 men, required permission to build warships, especially ironclads, and appointed all general officers.

An Ottoman Firman of 1866 increased the number of allowable troops to 30,000; however, the prohibition against building ironclads remained. The new Egyptian Khedive (governor) paid a substantial price for this privilege as his tribute was raised to 600,000 pounds. London played a major role in the last two Firmans and, as a result, Egyptian aspirations for independence would be dampened by British intervention. In 1873, the restriction on the number of Egyptian troops was eliminated but the possession of ironclads was still prohibited. After the British purchase of Suez Canal company shares, the Anglo-Egyptian pact of 1877 promoted Britain as the "protector of Egyptian territorial interests." The Ottoman Firman of 1879—restoring limits on the Egyptian army to 18,000 and maintaining the restriction on ironclad warships—was directed by London.

Black Sea Naval Limitation, 1856. To ease tensions and provide a respite once again during a centuries-long contest, Russia and Turkey agreed to limit their naval forces in the Black Sea (see Chapter 2). The size of these forces could not be more than six steam-driven warships of 800 tons, and four light steam or sailing ships of 200 tons.[8]

The Hague Conferences of 1899/1907. Fearing an international arms race, Tsar Nicholas II of Russia invited the great powers to meet at The Hague. In early March 1899, the First Lord of the Admiralty, George J. Goschen, indicated that the British government was prepared to reduce naval building should the other powers do the same. However, at The Hague, Admiral John Fisher, the British naval delegate, worked closely with Captain Alfred T. Mahan, a senior U.S. delegate, to prevent any limitation of naval forces.

The Americans were opposed to any limitations on U.S. forces or restrictions on new weapons technologies. While President William McKinley said, "it behooves us as a nation to lend countenance and aid to the beneficent project," he declared that America's active military forces were "so conspicuously less" than other powers that "the question of limitations had little practical importance." Because of the opposition of most major powers, no limitation of arms or military budgets was agreed upon. However, the delegates did restrict the use of certain existing munitions, outlaw aerial "bombing," prohibit the use of submarines or similar engines of destruction, and revise and codify the laws of war (discussed further in Chapters 3 and 5).

Prior to the ill-fated second Hague conference (1907), President Theodore Roosevelt indicated that the United States might be willing to support naval limitations. Amid growing international rivalries, however, his offer was ignored. This rebuff did not deter the United States from continuing to inquire about naval limitations. In a move prompted by a desire to reduce military expenditures, both houses of Congress in June 1910 unanimously endorsed naval limitations. The proposal failed to gain support abroad but it did point to new limitation endeavors by the major sea powers more than a decade in the future.[9]

Argentina-Chile Naval Pact, 1902. A boundary dispute stimulated a naval arms race that was stressing Argentina and Chile's national budgets. To protect Britain's sizeable economic investments in both countries, British diplomats in Buenos Aires and Santiago and moderate elements in both countries aided in the resolution of the boundary dispute and the naval race. In three agreements of May 28, 1902, known as the Pactos de Mayo, Argentina and Chile pledged to arbitrate their differences, to not make further purchases nor take possession of warships under construction in Europe, and to not dispose of excess warships to potentially unfriendly countries. Furthermore, they agreed to reduce existing fleets to a reasonable parity, and not to increase their naval armaments for five years without advance notice. Meanwhile, Britain undertook to mediate their boundary dispute.

The naval agreement began to unravel in 1904, when Brazil ordered three battleships, three armored cruisers, and several smaller warships. The Argentines and Chileans promptly canceled the 1902 naval pact and scheduled construction programs; however, before a naval race emerged, fate intervened.

When the crews of two new Brazilian dreadnoughts mutinied in November 1910, the three alarmed civilian governments unilaterally reduced their naval armaments and cancelled their foreign contracts for new ships.[10]

INTERWAR YEARS—I: GERMANY, THE LEAGUE, AND OTHER TREATIES

The Allies imposed long-term arms restrictions on Germany and the other defeated Central Powers—limiting the size of armies and armaments, reducing navies to insignificance, prohibiting air forces, and eliminating compulsory service. Inter-Allied Commissions of Control were established in all of the defeated nations. The League of Nations assigned responsibility for long-term supervision of compliance.

The League of Nations, beginning with its Covenant and continuing at several conferences, sought unsuccessfully to persuade the major powers to limit and reduce their military arsenals. Most of the fundamental issues related to arms control were discussed, argued, and rebutted during these meetings. One of the most important lessons emerging from all of this talk, according to James Barros, was the realization that "at its core the fundamental determining factors in arms control and disarmament were political not technical."

Spurred by the League's efforts at disarmament and its own ideological convictions, the Danish Social Democratic Party in the 1920s sought to emphasize the nation's desire to maintain its neutrality by unilaterally reducing its army and navy. This was accomplished by legislation in 1922 and 1929 and driven by the desire to eliminate the military as a political foe, the fiscal crisis brought on by the depression and, finally, the realization that Denmark was incapable of creating a military force sufficient to defend itself single-handedly. Even though the Danes reversed the trend when Adolf Hitler assumed power, their revitalized forces could not prevent its occupation by Germany during World War II.

Other agreements appearing in this section deal with arms control activities in Central America (1923–) and the eastern Mediterranean (1930, 1931).

League of Nations Covenant, 1919. The fourth point of President Woodrow Wilson's famous Fourteen Points called for the reduction of armaments. Without much debate at the Paris Peace Conference, the substance of this idea reappeared in Article 1, which stated that any new League member must accept "such regulations" that the League might applied to its land, naval, and air forces and armaments. Developing the idea further, Article 8 stated that League members must recognize that maintaining world peace required "the reduction of national armaments to the lowest point consistent with national safety and the enforcement by common action of international obligations."

The Permanent Advisory Commission that was provided for under Article 8 and created in 1920 began examining the questions regarding arms control. Staffed largely by military professionals who focused on technical issues, the commission's performance was, as Barros points out, "at best, lackluster." In February 1921, the Temporary Mixed Commission, comprised of civilians, undertook a review of the basic issues but with only meager results.[11]

Treaty of Versailles, 1919. The Allies linked German arms restrictions to Article 8 of the League Covenant. Thus, the preamble of Part V to the Versailles Treaty held that: "In order to render possible the initiation of a general limitation of the armaments of all nations, Germany undertakes strictly to observe the military, naval and air clauses which follow." The Versailles Treaty demanded that by March 31, 1920, the German army be reduced to 100,000 men with 4,000 officers. Only 102,000 rifles and 1,134 light and 792 heavy machine guns were permitted. The navy was limited to 15,000 men, 8 battleships, and 42 destroyers. Manufacturing or possession of airplanes, battleships, submarines, tanks—offensive weapons—and poison gas were forbidden. The German General Staff was abolished and planning for mobilization was prohibited. The Rhineland was to be permanently demilitarized, other designated areas were to be demilitarized and defortified. France also insisted on heavy reparations as another means of keeping any German military ambitions in check.

Supervision of the treaty's many arms control clauses fell to various Inter-Allied Control Commissions. Subsequent German governments, although obliged to assist the Commissions, always viewed the inspectors as intruders and often hampered inspection efforts. When Allied inspectors entered Germany after World War I, there were still millions of men under arms, perhaps 25,000 factories capable of producing war munitions, and thousands of planes, warships, tanks, and artillery pieces in excess of permitted levels. The German military, civilian government, and general population were united in contempt for the treaty.

Even so, under the direction of a few hundred inspectors, the Germans destroyed unprecedented numbers of heavy weapons, small arms, military aircraft, and warships of all kinds, and shut down or converted most of their arms-producing factories. A high-ranking inspector claimed that more war material had been destroyed by 1923 than Germany possessed in 1914. While imperfect, the Inter-Allied Control Commissions' accomplishments in demobilizing the German armed forces and eliminating massive amounts of arms and munitions constituted a substantial achievement.

"Germany posed no military threat whatever to its neighbors at the end of control in 1927," Neal Petersen has concluded, "or when Hitler came to power in 1933 or indeed in 1935 when Germany unilaterally abrogated the main disarmament provisions of Versailles." In a broader assessment, British historian Philip Towle suggests that German evasions of the treaty were not nearly as significant in the short run as was "German industrial and demographic strength" for the future.

Towle faulted the British and Americans for failing to have "studied the problem of disarmament in depth or fully understood the implications of what they were doing." Consequently, the Allies failed to create a coherent policy to establish a stable, peaceful Germany—neither a foundation built on mutual arms limitations and reasonable reparations, nor a collective military force prepared to deal with German treaty evasions. On March 15, 1935, Chancellor Adolf Hitler formally announced German rearmament—the Versailles Treaty was dead.[12]

Central Powers Disarmed, 1919. The Peace Conference imposed severe military limits on Germany's allies. In the past, such terms were imposed on major powers, not minor states.

The Treaty of St. Germain with Austria, signed September 10, 1919, limited the central remnant of the former Austro-Hungarian Empire to an army of 30,000 men. Under the terms of the Treaty of Neuilly, November 27, 1919, the Bulgarian army was limited to 20,000 men and required to surrender most of its arms and war material. The Treaty of Trianon, June 4, 1920, reduced the army of Hungary to 35,000 men. The Treaty of Sevres with Turkey, August 20, 1920, was never implemented and was replaced by the Treaty of Lausanne in 1923, which demilitarized the straits (see Chapter 2).

These restrictions made it impossible for them to threaten their neighbors according to Towle. They "made it impossible for them to use force to regain their lost territories but also increased their bitterness." Violations of the treaty were generally minor, aimed at bolstering internal elements. After Benito Mussolini came to power in Italy, he was caught "red-handed" in 1928 attempting to supply "carloads of machine guns" to right-wing elements in Hungary. Mussolini has also been accused of supplying Prince Starhemberg's private army that would transform Austria into a fascist country in 1934.[13] By the mid-1930s, the treaty prohibitions had been largely ignored as general rearming was taking place.

Central American Arms Pact, 1923. To offset potential threats to the Panama Canal, U.S. officials proposed arms limitations to lower arms expenditures and contribute to regional stability. Five Central American nations agreed in principle to arms reduction, but disliked the proposal to replace standing armies—often arbiters in domestic affairs—with national guards. The United States prevailed and the size of each nation's standing army, including a national guard, was fixed for a five-year period—Guatemala, 5,200; El Salvador, 4,200; Honduras, 2,500; Nicaragua, 2,500; and Costa Rica, 2,000 men each. National constabularies were to work with existing armies in preserving public order.

Reflecting the region's political realities, the Salvadorans acknowledged arms limitation as an ultimate ideal, but argued it was not currently practical. Over the next five years, Costa Rica reported its military strength below the 1923 treaty provisions and Honduras indicated compliance. Guatemala maintained a larger army than allotted, while El Salvador and Nicaragua created national guards but did not eliminate their armies. With the exception of Costa Rica, military expenditures remained a major budgetary item in each country and various military units contributed to ongoing domestic unrest.[14]

Turko-Greek Naval Protocol, 1930. A potential naval race loomed in 1928 when Turkey announced plans to refurbish the former German battleship

Goeben, now rechristened the *Yavuz*. The appearance of a single capital ship in the Aegean Sea posed a serious problem to the area's equilibrium, given the 500-year history of animosity between these two states. Several factors figured in resolving the crisis: mediation by Italy, accommodating attitudes by both heads of state, especially Greece, and the limited financial resources of both governments. On October 30, the Protocol was signed at Ankara. Pointing to the desirability "of preventing any unnecessary increase in their expenditure on naval armaments," the Protocol stated that both parties must "undertake to effect no order, acquisition or construction of war units or armaments, without having notified the other Party six months previously."

Turko-Soviet Naval Protocol, 1931. The Turks were unhappy that the Soviets had shifted additional warships to the Black Sea, and the Soviets were alarmed at the possibility of a Franco-Italian naval pact. However, the newly signed Greco-Turkish protocol provided precedent and form to prevent a naval race and restore a naval balance. This Protocol, signed on March 7, stated that neither party would "lay down any naval fighting unit whatsoever." Also, neither party was able to strengthen its fleet in the Black Sea or any neighboring seas, "or to place orders for any such unit in foreign shipyards, or to take any other measure" to increase its present fleet in either sea "without having notified" the other party.[15]

Preparatory Commission's Draft Convention, 1930. Established by the League in 1925, the Preparatory Commission labored for five years to draft the outline of a general disarmament treaty to be presented to League members. The Commission largely focused on "technical aspects of the question [of arms reductions], especially methods and general guidelines." It avoided dealing with the obligations to be assumed by individual nations; this was postponed for the general disarmament conference. Among the various plans submitted to the Commission was the Soviet Union's draft Convention for Immediate, Complete and General Disarmament (1928)—a forerunner of its 1962 proposal.

The Disarmament Conference met on February 2, 1933, to consider the Preparatory Commission's Draft, and adjourned in mid-December to allow diplomats to resolve outstanding issues that arose. It reconvened in late January 1933. Unforeseen developments, however, did not create the best of climates for these discussions—the 1931 Manchurian crisis caused Japan to lose interest, the new German chancellor Hitler demanded military and political "equality," and France insisted on an ironclad supervisory system in any agreement. Given the unsettled international scene, the Conference eventually ended in a stalemate on June 11, 1934.[16]

INTERWAR YEARS—II: WASHINGTON NAVAL LIMITATION SYSTEM

The spring of 1921 witnessed a burgeoning arms race—before the year was out, more than 200 warships would be under construction. The Washington

Naval Treaty (1922) established a ratio system for the five major naval powers. Subsequently, a series of conferences and agreements—the "Washington naval system"—ultimately placed both quantitative and qualitative limits on most classes of warships. Since efforts to outlaw submarines were unsuccessful, in 1930, restrictions were established on submarine warfare (see Chapter 5). By the late 1930s, however, the looming prospect of hostilities prompted dropping the ratio system and employing a much different approach. (For an evaluation of differing compliance issues, see Chapter 9.)

Washington Naval Treaty, 1922. As a means of heading off an expensive naval arms race, the major naval powers—Britain, Japan, France, and Italy—gathered in Washington, DC, during the fall of 1921. Overruling his admirals, Secretary of State Charles Evans Hughes developed a detailed plan grounded on two themes: (1) an immediate halt of all capital-ship construction; and (2) the defining of national strategies in terms of "relative security." By formally presenting his proposal for capital-ship reductions and limitations at the opening session, Hughes seized the diplomatic initiative and gained widespread public support.

The Washington conference produced seven treaties and twelve resolutions, three of which introduced arms control provisions. The Five Power Naval Treaty of February 6, 1922, established: (1) a ten-year moratorium on the construction of battleships; (2) quantitative limits (or ratios—United States, 5: Britain, 5: Japan, 3) on capital ships and aircraft carriers; (3) qualitative restrictions on future naval construction; and (4) no further fortifications of stipulated Pacific regions. For the United States, Part 4 meant the Philippines, Guam, and Wake Island—but not Hawaii; for Japan, this included Formosa, the Pescadores, and other islands around Japan. (For the Pacific mandated islands, see Chapter 3.)

Naval limitations and reductions for all five signatories meant that seventy-one ships were scrapped. This number was realized because they were supported by the Four and Nine Power pacts that acknowledged current political realities between the Americans, British, and Japanese. The former terminated the 1902 Anglo-Japanese Treaty and urged the use of diplomacy to settle future disputes regarding the Pacific regions; while the later sought recognition of America's "open door" policy for China.

Since the limitation of smaller auxiliary warships was not achieved at Washington, various admiralties rushed to build large cruisers as close as possible to the ten-thousand-ton limit that defined capital ships. Faced with a renewed naval race, President Calvin Coolidge initiated the 1927 Geneva naval conference, seeking to place limits on auxiliary warships—cruisers, destroyers, and submarines. But efforts to extend the Washington treaty's capital-ship ratios (5:5:3) to auxiliary categories floundered amid technical arguments by naval professionals regarding the value of 6-inch guns vs. 8-inch guns, and 10,000-ton cruisers vs. smaller ones.

London Naval Treaty, 1930. At London, the five naval powers agreed not to build their capital-ship replacements authorized between 1931 and 1936. The Big Three agreed to scrap nine more capital ships that, by 1936, would leave the United States with 18 battleships (462,400 tons), Britain with 18 battleships (474,750 tons), and Japan with 9 battleships (266,070 tons). Aircraft carrier tonnage remained unchanged, despite attempts to lower it.

Having overcome the technical concerns that sank the Geneva Conference, the Big Three agreed to auxiliary tonnage limits. These were: (1) heavy cruisers—United States, 180,000 tons; Britain, 146,800; and Japan, 108,400; (2) light cruisers—United States, 143,500 tons; Britain, 192,200; and Japan, 100,450; (3) destroyers—United States and Britain, 150,000 tons; and Japan 105,000; and (4) submarines—each with 52,700 tons. The United States and Britain had resolved the problem of naval "equality." However, since France and Italy could not agree to limitations on their auxiliary ships, London insisted on a "safety value" clause that was designed to maintain Britain's two-power standard in European waters; that is, the British fleet would be equal to the combined French-Italian fleets.

Many senior Japanese naval officers strongly opposed the treaty, arguing that Japan's lower tonnage endangered its security and restricted its ambitions. The Japanese government reluctantly accepted the negotiated auxiliary ratios only to see their naval faction denounce the treaty and their prime minister and other government members assassinated by young fanatics.[17]

Anglo-German Naval Agreement, 1935. The controversial naval agreement of June 18, 1935, allowed Hitler's Germany to build a navy limited to 35 percent of the British fleet, with the option of submarine parity. Germany could complete 8 battleships, 21 cruisers, and 64 destroyers, yet by 1939, it had built only 2 capital ships, 11 cruisers, and 25 destroyers. In December 1938, Berlin notified London of its intention to exercise paragraph 2(f) of the 1935 understanding that allowed Germany "to build up to 100 per cent of the British submarine tonnage."

The lingering claim that Germany evaded the terms of the 1935 pact stems from the charges levied during the Nuremberg trials. It was charged that the Nazi government built more submarines and larger battleships than it was authorized. Admiral Eric Raeder was indicted for building 118 submarines prior to the denunciation of the agreement. Facts were hidden—such as the *Scharnhorst*, listed at 26,000 tons, which actually weighed 31,300 tons and the *Bismarck* and *Tirpitz*, listed at 35,000 tons, which actually had a displacement of 41,700 tons.

An erroneous reading of German records apparently substituted the 1942 projected figures for actual construction. In early 1935, the Germans possessed six 250-ton submarines, parts of which had been constructed between 1933 and 1935. Six slightly larger U-boats and two 750-ton submarines were under construction. At the outbreak of war, according to former British Prime Minister Winston Churchill's account, Germany had fifty-seven submarines, of which only twenty-seven were ready to operate in the Atlantic, which was on par with Britain. In the case of the *Scharnhorst*, *Bismarck*, and *Tirpitz*, the prosecutors failed to realize that battleship tonnage limits had been raised by agreement on June 30, 1938, to 45,000 tons, and that neither the *Bismarck* nor the *Tirpitz* were commissioned until well after that date. While Hitler ordered that the actual figures not be released to the British, Germany's total capital ship tonnage was less than allowed. Consequently, Admiral Raeder was exonerated of these charges.

Hitler denounced the pact on April 28, 1939. Because he had set a leisurely pace for naval construction, the German navy was not nearly as prepared for war as the army and air force. It was British historian D. C. Watt's conclusion—although Captain Stephen W. Roskill, Royal Navy, was less generous—that the 1935 pact "was more or less faithfully observed until its denunciation in April 1939."[18]

London Naval Treaty, 1936. The shifting political situations in the Far East and Europe brought an end to quantitative naval limits. Unrealistically, Washington steadfastly rejected Tokyo's demand for an end to naval ratios and parity of total tonnages, and clung to the hope for greater naval reductions. London officials—preoccupied with Hitler's revisionist demands and Franco-Italian disputes—argued for increased cruiser tonnage, an Anglo-American Pacific agreement, and replacement of ratios with qualitative restrictions. Japan's withdrawal from the second London naval conference and abrogation of the Washington naval system, effective December 31, 1936, brought about an arrangement that reflected Britain's desire for only qualitative restrictions that applied almost exclusively to European nations.

On March 25, 1936, the United States, Great Britain, and France agreed to restrictions on ship displacement, gun calibers by class, and an annual exchange of detailed information related to naval building and modernization programs. The pact also allowed for other nations to adhere to the treaty as bilateral parties with Great Britain. Germany, the Soviet Union, Italy, and eventually the Scandinavian countries accepted these qualitative limits.[19]

WORLD WAR II—AFTERMATH

The negotiations between the United States, Great Britain—later France—and the Soviet Union from 1945 to 1947 resulted in agreement on the initial disarmament terms to be implemented by the Allied occupation forces in Germany and Austria. Draft peace treaties were also arranged for Italy, Finland, Rumania, Bulgaria, and Hungary. By 1948, however, the Cold War was setting in and, subsequently, these terms were largely ignored as the North Atlantic Treaty Organization (NATO) and the Warsaw Pact focused on rebuilding their former military forces.

Berlin (Potsdam) Protocol, 1945. One result of the Big Three meeting at Potsdam in August 1945 was a general Allied consensus on disarmament terms to be imposed on occupied states. The Berlin Protocol stipulated that German military forces were to be completely disarmed and its armaments industry demilitarized. In addition to the abolition of "all German land, naval and air forces," the General Staff, Reserve Corps, and any semi-military organizations, the Protocol authorized the seizure and/or destruction of "all arms, ammunition and implements of war and all specialized facilities for their production."

The failure of the occupying powers in 1947 to agree to a peace treaty led to two Germanys, each of which was eventually urged to rearm. In the West, this process culminated in the Protocols to the Brussels Treaty (1954) that led to the limited rearmament of the Federal Republic of Germany and Italy to augment NATO ground, air, and naval forces. Washington argued that without German manpower which eventually reached 12 divisions, NATO could not match the Warsaw Pact force.[20]

Balkan Treaties, 1946. The American and British proposals for the other ex-enemy states also sought the imposition of specific arms limitations and Allied supervisory inspections. The Soviet draft, however, called for only a general disarmament clause rather than detailed limitation, arguing that these defeated states, unlike Italy, were small nations that had fought against only the USSR, and were incapable of supporting large armed forces. The Soviets subsequently relented and accepted stipulated limits: the Rumanian army would be limited to 120,000 soldiers; the air force to 150 aircraft and 8,000 personnel; and the navy to 15,000 tons and 5,000 sailors. The Bulgarian army was limited to 45,000 troops, 70 combat aircraft, and 5,200 personnel; the Hungarian army was allowed 65,000 soldiers, 70 combat aircraft, and 5,000 personnel.

Moscow refused to allow any Allied control or inspection agency for the Balkan states and, "from the beginning, the fulfillment of the Military Clauses of the Balkan Treaties was governed by Soviet wishes." When Italy was integrated into NATO, the Balkan military terms were ignored.[21]

Italian Peace Treaty, 1947. The imposed naval, military, and air clauses of the Italian Peace Treaty limited the army to 185,000 soldiers and 200 medium and heavy tanks, allowed the air force 200 combat planes, and restricted the navy to 106,756 tons and 25,000 personnel. All existing warships over the established limit were to be turned over to the victors or destroyed, and new naval construction was prohibited for five years. Italy was prohibited from storing guided missiles, atomic, bacteriological, and chemical arms; furthermore, it was forbidden to manufacture weapons for export. The Italian government and public were greatly disappointed with these restrictions; however, in 1951 when Italy became a member of the western alliance, the military limitations were gradually abolished.[22]

Finnish Peace Treaty, 1947. After being forced to cede one-ninth of its territory after the Winter War, 1939–1940, the Finns joined Germany in a joint assault upon the Soviet Union in June 1941. Confronted with a major Soviet offensive toward the end of the war, the Finns managed to stabilize, stall its advance, and avoid occupation. When the Allied (Soviet) Control Commission arrived in Helsinki after the Armistice agreement in October 1944, the Commission ordered that the Finnish military services, whose combat forces numbered some 450,000, be reduced to their prewar levels of less than 40,000 personnel, and their weapons and equipment stored in several depots.

The peace treaty limited the Finnish army to 34,400 troops, the navy to 4,500 personnel and 10,000 tons, and the air force to 3,000 personnel and 60 aircraft. Additionally, the Finns were prohibited from possessing atomic weapons, guided missiles, and certain sea mines and manufacturing weaponry in excess of that required by their military services. As many of the treaty's articles were imprecise and open to interpretation, the British took a strict position and the Soviets a permissive one. Ignoring the British position, the Finns were able to create an infrastructure that could mobilize an army of some 530,000 men and retained sufficient weapons to equip them.[23]

COLD WAR—I: NUCLEAR WEAPONS AND SYSTEMS

Bargaining over nuclear weaponry between the United States and the Soviet Union (later Russia) began in 1946 and, with few interruptions, continued past the turn of the century. These discussions sought initially to stabilize, limit offensive and defensive nuclear warheads and missile systems, and later to reduce them. An awareness of the extremely destructive nature of this weaponry prompted diplomats to seek much more complex controls than those required by earlier accords.

The first unsuccessful efforts sought to bring the entire range of nuclear weaponry under control—beginning with the Baruch Plan (1946), and continuing with Soviet and American proposals for General and Complete Disarmament (1962). As the "deterrent" effect of these weapons was gradually recognized, the focus shifted to a series of bilateral agreements. There was SALT I (1972)—the Interim Agreement on Strategic Offensive Weapons limiting missile systems, and the Anti-Ballistic Missile Treaty (1972). The SALT II Treaty (1979) placed limits on all strategic offensive systems; the INF agreement (1987) eliminated intermediate-range nuclear missiles; the START I Treaty (1991) reduced strategic offensive systems; START II (1993) reduced deployable strategic warheads; and SORT (2002) limited rather than reduced strategic warheads.

Baruch Plan, 1946. Bernard Baruch presented the United States' proposal to control atomic weapons at the initial meeting of the UN Atomic Energy Committee on June 14, 1946. The plan called for an International Atomic Development Authority that would control or own all activities associated with atomic energy, from raw materials to military applications, and would control, license, and inspect all other uses. It would foster peaceful uses of atomic energy by conducting research and development. With the Authority established, manufacturing of atomic bombs would cease and all existing weapons be destroyed. Baruch insisted that sanctions be imposed on nations possessing or building an atomic device without a license. Finally, he declared that "there must be no veto to protect those who violate their solemn agreement not to develop or use atomic energy for destructive purposes."[24]

From the outset, American and Soviet diplomats were at odds. The United States insisted on extensive safeguards, including on-site inspections, before destroying its atomic weapons or releasing information on their manufacture. The Soviets and others viewed the Americans as insincere since they held onto their atomic energy program, while expecting others to forego developing their own. Washington's continued insistence, beginning with the Baruch Plan, upon intrusive inspection systems to verify treaty compliance—which Moscow viewed as sanctioned espionage—figured prominently in stalemating various arms control endeavors.

Proposals for General and Complete Disarmament, 1955–1962. Proposals for eventually eliminating most military forces long have been put forward for a variety of reasons. Some of them were undoubtedly well intended; others were more for propaganda purposes, such as the Soviet's draft convention that was sent to the League of Nations in 1928; Premier Nikita Khrushchev's offer to the UN General Assembly in September 1959 and again in 1962; and President John F. Kennedy's 1962 counterproposal. This view has been confirmed by many participants, including Soviet ambassador to Washington Anatoly Dobrynin, who wrote that the Soviet proposals were "nothing more than a good piece of propaganda dating as far back as the League of Nations."

The post-1945 offers involved the reduction of armaments using a step-by-step arrangement. The United States' approach required international inspection to ensure that each stage had been carried out, while the Soviets downplayed such caution, relegating supervision to a later stage. The Soviets and Americans through the Zorin-McCloy agreement issued on September 20, 1961, established principles for renewed negotiations. As a result, the Eighteen-Nation Disarmament Committee in 1962 took under consideration the USSR's "Draft treaty on general and complete disarmament under strict international control" and the United States' "Outline of basic provisions of a treaty on general and complete disarmament in a peaceful world." Discussions continued on these proposals and their revisions over the following years without reaching a final agreement. The provisions that caused the most difficulty involved the stages of implementation, nuclear issues, and verification procedures. As it became apparent that general and complete disarmament was not going to be achieved through a single, comprehensive international instrument, arms control and arms limitation came to be seen as more viable and achievable.[25]

SALT I, 1972. The Interim Agreement on Strategic Offensive Weapons established, among other restrictions, a quantitative limit on both inter-continental ballistic missiles (ICBMs)—United States, 1,054 ICBMs, USSR, 1,618 operational and under construction—and submarine-launched ballistic missiles (SLBMs). Using a formula that exchanged dismantled ICBMs for SLBMs, the United States could possess up to 710 SLBMs on 44 submarines, the Soviets 950 SLBMs on 62 submarines. The Interim Agreement's limits focused on the numbers of missile or launchers rather than on warheads, and allowed deployment of multiple independently targeted reentry vehicles (MIRVs) that eventually expanded greatly the number of warheads in both nations' arsenals. The failure either to ban or restrict MIRVs prompted critics to argue that SALT I actually fueled the nuclear arms race. SALT I did not secure reductions and its ceilings were higher than existing forces, thereby allowing the deployment of additional ballistic missiles.

An informed observer believed Soviet behavior "did at times suggest a 'devil-may-care' attitude about strict compliance with treaty provisions.... While these episodes had no appreciable strategic significance—and none violated the letter of SALT I—they did tend to vitiate the 'spirit' of the agreement and cast Soviet motives in a bad light." There were, however, several problems associated with the ad hoc manner of drafting the pact, especially given the ambiguities that arose. During the ratification process, a persistent critic of the SALT process, Senator Henry M. Jackson, questioned the lack of agreed data on Soviet missile systems. He refused to accept Ambassador Gerald Smith's explanation that America's spy satellites could determine if the Soviets were violating the freeze on the number of ICBMs and heavy ICBM launchers. Jackson wanted Moscow to stipulate how many ICBM launchers it had. He also questioned the limits placed on increases in ICBM silo dimensions, pointing out that the 15 percent limit could be interpreted several different ways. Several issues arising from various ambiguities were finally resolved in the SALT II contract.[26]

In May 1986, the United States withdrew from the SALT I Interim Agreement and commitment but agreed to abide by the unratified but theretofore upheld SALT II Treaty, citing Soviet violations of these and other arms control accords as its reason for withdrawal.

Anti-Ballistic Missile Treaty, 1972. Negotiated concurrently with SALT I, the Anti-Ballistic Missile (ABM) Treaty stipulated that each side could deploy up to 100 ABM interceptors at each of two sites, later reduced to one site. Although both parties had spent substantial time and funds to develop defensive systems, their efforts bore little fruit because of the ever-increasing numbers of offensive weapons, especially MIRVed missiles, and doubtful operational technology. Later, President Ronald Reagan's Strategic Defense Initiative (SDI), known to critics as Star Wars, gradually challenged the constraints of the ABM pact, especially when it became embedded in the Republican Party's list of goals.

Surveillance satellites in 1983 caught the Soviets building a large radar station at Krasnoyarsk (Abalakovo), Siberia, in violation of the ABM restrictions. The Reagan administration used this discovery as evidence of the natural tendencies of the "evil empire." In October 1987, Mikhail Gorbachev initiated a one-year freeze on construction at Krasnoyarsk, and some six months later admitted that it had violated geographic limitations in the ABM treaty on radars. In September 1989, Soviet Foreign Minister Edvard Shevardnadze informed Secretary of State James Baker that the Soviet Union would unilaterally dismantle the disputed radar.

President George W. Bush abrogated the ABM Treaty in 2002, despite protests from Moscow and some members of Congress. He subsequently ordered the deployment of anti-ballistic missile systems in Alaska and California, even though their effectiveness in stopping incoming ICBMs was unproven.[27]

SALT II, 1979. President Jimmy Carter hoped to conclude a treaty that included "deep cuts," but the Soviets rejected his proposal because it changed the formula previously agreed to by President Gerald Ford and General Secretary Leonid Brezhnev at Vladivostok in November 1974. The SALT II agreement, finally signed in Vienna on April 18, 1979, was a mix of an engineering document and a lawyer's brief—the text was extraordinarily complex with extensive definitions and elaborate "counting rules" appended.

The treaty limited each side to 2,400 ICBMs, SLBMs, and heavy bombers, to be reached within six months after the treaty entered into force, followed by a further reduction to 2,250 strategic nuclear launch vehicles by 1981. Each side was limited within this ceiling to no more than 1,320 ICBMs, SLBMs, and long-range bombers equipped with MIRVs or multiple cruise missiles. Each party could build and deploy only one new type of ICBM, and they agreed that the 1972 ABM Treaty was to remain in effect. The 78-page treaty required both parties to dismantle some systems to make room for new deployments, and it included an extensive list of qualitative restrictions.

After Soviet military forces intervened in Afghanistan, President Carter failed to press for Senate ratification of the treaty; nevertheless, the administration continued to honor its terms. In 1985, some arms control experts feared that the Reagan administration would exceed the SALT II limits when the United States launched a new Trident submarine armed with 24 missiles. On June 10, however, the president ordered the dismantling of one Poseidon with 16 nuclear missiles to keep the United States under the 1,200 multiple warhead agreement. A year later the Reagan administration was again embroiled in a fierce struggle over whether or not to ignore the SALT II treaty limits. Caspar Weinberger and William Casey insisted that alleged Soviet noncompliance of the pact demanded a response—a decision that caused a loud outcry in Congress, dismay among allied leaders, and a public uproar. Discussions of the alledged evasions within the Standing Consultative Commission had collapsed and efforts to use diplomatic channels to resolve differences failed.

Even though State Department officials and Admiral William Crowe, the head of the Joint Chiefs of Staff, argued that there was no operational reason for going over SALT limits, President Reagan announced on May 27, 1986, that the United States would no longer be bound by the SALT II ceilings. The United States exceeded the SALT II limits on November 28, 1986, with the mounting of cruise missiles on some of its B-52s.[28]

INF Treaty, 1987. The intermediate nuclear forces (INF) controversy arose as the result of a NATO decision, late in Carter's administration, to deploy 108

Pershing II and 464 ground-launched cruise missiles to West Germany, Belgium, Britain, the Netherlands, and Italy to offset the Soviet Union's new intermediate nuclear force, especially the SS-20s. Under pressure in late 1981 from anti-nuclear protesters in NATO countries and the "nuclear freeze" movement at home, the Reagan administration offered the Soviets a "zero option" concept—the United States would cancel its scheduled deployment if the Soviets removed their SS-20s, with their 1,100 warheads—which they correctly surmised the Soviets would reject.

Later, Soviet Secretary General Mikhail Gorbachev stunned NATO and Washington by accepting the "zero-option" with its disproportionate reductions in 1986, and agreeing to extensive verification demands. Signed on December 8, 1987, the INF treaty eliminated 1,836 Soviet missiles with ranges from 1,000 to 5,000 kilometers and 859 U.S. missiles. By 1991, it had been verified that the missiles had been removed from Europe and Asia.

In Moscow, several Russian military analysts during 2007 noted that other countries around the Russian periphery had been acquiring intermediate-range missiles—China, North Korea, and Iran—and urged the country withdraw from the INF Treaty. Others have pointed out that building more strategic missiles would alleviate any security issues.[29]

START I, 1991. Washington initially offered Moscow a two-stage "practical phased reduction" of strategic nuclear weapons, but it was so one-sided that analysts considered it to be nonnegotiable. The Soviets promptly rejected it. At the Reykjavik summit on October 10–11, 1986, President Reagan suggested the elimination all of ballistic missiles within 10 years, and Soviet leader Gorbachev immediately countered with the elimination of all Soviet and U.S. strategic nuclear weapons within 10 years and research limits on Reagan's Strategic Defense Initiative. Reagan refused to accept any restrictions on his Star Wars system and these radical arms reduction proposals were dropped—much to the relief of U.S. military leaders, NATO ministers and, undoubtedly, to senior Soviet marshals. There were tentative understandings reached on numbers of strategic delivery systems and warheads that were formalized in a long-delayed pact.

At the December 1989 Malta Summit, Presidents George H. W. Bush and Gorbachev revitalized negotiations on START I. Bush and Gorbachev finally signed the complex 750-page START I treaty on July 31, 1991. It limited each side to the deployment of 1,600 ballistic missiles and long-range bombers, carrying 6,000 "accountable" warheads by December 5, 2001, and established further sub-limits—4,900 warheads on deployed ballistic missiles, including no more than 1,100 warheads on deployed mobile ICBM systems, and 1,100 "accountable" bomber weapons. In addition, START I incorporated the INF treaty's verification system that provided access to telemetry data and permitted on-site inspections. This was the first agreement that called for each side to significantly reduce its strategic arsenal. Some 25 to 35 percent of the nuclear warheads carried on ballistic missiles were to be eliminated.

After the dissolution of the Soviet Union, the Lisbon Protocol, signed on May 23, 1992, created a five-state START I regime joining Belarus, Kazakhstan, Russia, Ukraine, and the United States. Belarus, Kazakhstan, and Ukraine agreed to turn over the strategic nuclear weapons based in their territories to Russia. By December 4, 2001, the START I reductions were completed.[30]

South African Nuclear Disarmament, 1990. In March 1993, South African President F. W. de Klerk formally discussed his nation's 1974 decision to develop "a limited nuclear deterrent capability." This was undertaken, according to de Klerk, because of the Soviet Union's "expansionist" activities in Africa, especially the introduction of Cuban military forces into Angola during 1975. Denying that South Africa ever conducted a nuclear test, he did acknowledge that the program had assembled six nuclear bombs. Following the collapse of the Soviet Union, the South African government closed its enrichment plant in 1989 and the following year, unilaterally dismantled its six bombs and returned the nuclear materials to civilian usage. An additional incentive for this decision was South Africa's participation in the continent's regional control of proliferation (see Chapters 2 and 4).[31]

UNSC Resolution 687 [Iraq], 1991. Following Iraq's defeat in the Gulf War of 1991, the United Nations Security Council decreed that Iraq must eliminate all of its biological, chemical, and nuclear weapons programs, as well as all of its ballistic missiles capable of flying more than 150 kilometers. A special commission, the United Nations Special Commission on Iraq (UNSCOM), and the International Atomic Energy Agency (IAEA) were mandated to oversee the destruction of these weapons. The Security Council also placed economic sanctions against Iraq that were to remain in effect until that nation had met its disarmament pledge. As with most imposed arms control arrangements, the inspection process encountered various types of domestic resistance. A subsequent UN Security Council Resolution (715) in September 1991 took the Baghdad officials to task for obstructing the inspection process and ordered them to "cooperate fully" with the weapons inspectors. Despite various obstacles, the UN teams were "remarkably successful in their efforts to disarm Iraq of its weapons of mass destruction."

In spite of the inspectors' reports that Iraq had been largely disarmed by the mid-1990s, Washington and London officials later refused to believe them. President George W. Bush, Prime Minister Tony Blair, and their spokesmen insisted throughout the fall of 2002 and early 2003 that Iraq was expanding and improving its biological and chemical weapons facilities, working on an unmanned aerial vehicle to deliver these weapons, stepping up its quest for nuclear weapons, and rebuilding "much" of its missile production infrastructure.

Following the capture of Baghdad in 2003 by U.S.-led forces, the Bush administration rushed two groups of inspectors to Iraq charged with uncovering Saddam Hussein's caches of banned weaponry, but they found nothing. In October 2004, the Iraqi Survey Group headed by Charles Duefler confirmed that Iraq's illicit arms had been indeed destroyed during the early 1990s as reported by UN and IAEA inspectors. Iraq may have desired to reconstitute its programs to develop the banned weaponry, but Duefler said that there was no evidence that any such programs had been undertaken. This entire episode demonstrates how a very selective use of intelligence and verification reports can be used to develop popular support for predetermined objectives.[32]

Unilateral Presidential Nuclear Initiatives, 1991. President George H. W. Bush's unilateral "presidential nuclear initiative" (PNI) of September 27, 1991 stated that the United States would unilaterally begin withdrawing all of its land-based tactical nuclear weapons from overseas bases, and its sea-based tactical nuclear weapons from U.S. ships, submarines, and aircraft. Moreover, the country would remove all strategic bombers from day-to-day alert status and return weapons to storage areas, halt development of the rail garrison and mobile ICBM project, and cancel the short-range attack missile (SRAM-II) for heavy bombers.

President Gorbachev responded on October 5, 1991, with a unilateral PNI ordering all strategic bombers to stand down from daily alert status and store their weapons, removing from alert 503 ICBMs, including 134 MIRVed missiles, and halting the construction of rail-based ICBMs and returning them to permanent stations. Finally, he cancelled development of a small mobile ICBM and a short-range attack missile for heavy bombers. On January 27, 1992, Russian President Boris Yeltsin unilaterally halted production of strategic bombers and air-launched cruise missiles and ceased replacing tactical nuclear warheads. All remaining nuclear reactors that produced weapons-grade plutonium were to be closed by the year 2000.

President Jacques Chirac announced on February 22–23, 1996, that France intended unilaterally to reduce its nuclear weapons activities. He closed French facilities producing fissile materials for nuclear weapons and its Pacific test site. Chirac also declared that four rather than five nuclear powered ballistic missile submarines would be deployed, and that the two surface-to-surface missile systems, the 18 S3Ds and at 30 Hades, were to be withdrawn and dismantled.[33]

START II, 1993. With the end of the Cold War, the Reduction and Limitation of Strategic Offensive Arms (START II) treaty was put in place on January 3, 1993; however, ratification was delayed—the United States took three years and Russia took nearly seven years. This agreement placed the number of strategic nuclear warheads to be held by each party on January 1, 2003, to no more than 3,000 to 3,500 each. To persuade the Russian Duma to ratify SALT II, Clinton and Yeltsin met in Helsinki during March 1997 and drew-up the so-called Helsinki Initiatives (Protocol to START II). It included, among other things, amendments to various SALT I terms designed to alleviate the Duma's fears that since Russia could not afford to replace all its aging missiles, it would lose parity with U.S. forces.

Most significantly, SALT II banned all land-based MIRVed strategic ballistic missiles, eliminating what most experts considered to be a destabilizing technology. The treaty also called for the destruction of all Russian SS-18 "heavy" (i.e., large throw-weight) missiles and a sub-limit of 1,700 to 1,750 submarine-launched ballistic missile warheads, which was a reduction of about one-half the SLBM warheads allotted to the United States under START I. Although its verification procedures were built upon START I, some additional measures were added, most significantly increasing the number of on-site inspections. Compliance was to be governed by the new Bilateral Implementation Commission located in Geneva, Switzerland.

Agreement in principle was reached to an outline for START III that would stipulate even deeper cuts, but this framework was subsequently ignored. At a March 21, 1997, summit, Presidents William Clinton and Boris Yeltsin agreed to extend the time for reduction of strategic nuclear warheads to between 2,000 and 2,500 for each side by December 31, 2007.[34]

SORT, 2002. President George W. Bush initially sought to implement strategic offensive weapons reductions with unilateral declarations and a handshake, but Russian President Vladimir Putin insisted upon a more formal arrangement. The brief May 24, 2002, treaty, in the tradition of the early Cold War treaties, called more for limits than reductions. The United States and Russia each agreed to deploy no more than 1,700 to 2,200 strategic warheads by the end of 2012—when the treaty expired—ignoring the earlier goals projected for START III.

While SORT, also known as the Moscow Treaty, stipulates deployed warhead limits, it does not restrict the number of permitted delivery vehicles that can be retained—as long as neither party exceeds the START I limits. But SORT does not provide strict counting rules; hence, a MIRVed nose cone might contain a single warhead and be counted as a single warhead, although it could quickly be loaded with nine additional warheads. Nor did warheads in excess of the stipulated limits have to be dismantled or destroyed; they could be stored. The Bush administration stated that it planned to maintain at least 2,400 warheads in ready reserve. SORT did not provide for its own verification, thus adding to its unpredictability. START I would remain in force until the end of 2009, but whether its extensive verification regime would continue to monitor SORT was unclear.

The Bush administration frequently demonstrated a dislike for traditional arms control agreements. As a reflection of this attitude, the Strategic Offensive Reductions Treaty of 2002, according to an early assessment, "totals less than 500 words [and] repudiates key arms control principles and achievements, eschewing predictability and compounding the proliferation dangers from Russia's unsecured nuclear weapons complex."[35]

COLD WAR—II: CONVENTIONAL WEAPONS SYSTEMS

To offset the Soviet Union's large number of conventional forces, especially in Central Europe, the United States maintained a substantial conventional presence in bordering NATO countries. By the late 1960s, some Americans began to question the costs and necessity of this deployment. Negotiations seeking to limit conventional military forces in Europe, launched in the early 1970s, went on for nearly twenty years, ending finally in comprehensive agreement.

Mutual and Balanced Force Reductions Talks, 1973–1989. The Nixon administration launched these negotiations on conventional forces because it was being pressured by Congress to reduce its forces in Europe and it felt that a reciprocal withdrawal, by both superpowers, would be better policy than unilateral action. The mutual and balanced force reduction (MBFR) talks were part of a two-pronged diplomatic effort: the American-instigated MBFR and the Soviet-inspired Conference on Security and Cooperation in Europe (CSCE).

The imbalance between the much greater Soviet and Warsaw Pact forces and the U.S. and NATO forces meant that Moscow was reluctant to offer concessions. Under these circumstances, a CSCE measure adopted in the Helsinki Final Act of 1975—that called for providing advance notice of major military exercises to avert fear of a surprise attack, (see Chapter 6)—was more easily achieved than arms limitations. Although no agreement was reached during the MBFR discussions, many participants believed that the negotiations, including those of the CSCE, set the stage for reaching a final agreement to limit conventional forces in Europe.

Conventional Forces in Europe, 1990. Negotiations between 1989 and 1990 finally resulted in the Conventional Forces in Europe (CFE) agreement. Several factors contributed to success: France joined the talks; Soviet leader Mikhail Gorbachev unilaterally withdrew troops and equipment from forward areas; the Warsaw Pact disintegrated; and a reunited Germany agreed to troop limitations.

The November 11, 1990, agreement's bloc limits for NATO and the Warsaw Pact applied to five categories of conventional armaments stationed in Europe from the Atlantic Ocean to the Ural Mountains. These included three categories of ground equipment (tanks, artillery, and armored combat vehicles), aircraft, and helicopters. Formal limitations on personnel were set aside for follow-up negotiations. The verification process included a full of sharing of conventional arms information among all parties, followed by three categories of inspections and a Joint Consultative Group to iron out differences. By 1998, more than 3,000 on-site inspections had been carried out, and the dismantling of 58,000 pieces of armaments and equipment had been verified.

No sooner was the conventional arms treaty signed than negotiations began to establish military personnel limits and resolve or clarify other issues. A CFE 1 Adapted Treaty was signed on July 10, 1992, at Helsinki, Finland, which eliminated the bloc limits and spelled out national weapons and personnel limits, including restricting the United States to 250,000 personnel in Europe. Another parallel agreement to facilitate verification was formalizing the "Open Skies" accord of 1992 (see Chapter 6).[36]

Originally, 30 parties joined the treaty, but subsequently 22 NATO countries have refused to ratify the Adopted CFE Treaty, linking such action to Russia's withdrawal of military units from Georgia and Moldova. Moscow refuses to acknowledge such linkage and, irritated by the U.S. efforts to deploy its missile defense system to nearby countries, indicated in 2008 that it would unilaterally alter portions of the CFE accords—including suspension of treaty inspection rights.

For the various forms of negotiations employed, the various types of verifications that were adopted, and the problems of compliance or non-compliance that were encountered, see Part II.

Demilitarization, Denuclearization, and Neutralization

Demilitarization involves prohibitions against the maintenance of troops or other military components, including fortifications, within a specified geographical area. It may also involve restrictions on the construction of various strategic installations such as airports, highways, railroads, communications centers, or harbor facilities. While the general concept of demilitarization is quite broad, the terms of individual agreements have tended to be more limited. The essential objective of most agreements has been to stabilize a potentially troublesome area by removing and/or limiting military forces and establishments in specific areas. Closely linked to demilitarization is "defortification," the stipulated razing of existing fortifications and installations. These forms of arms control/disarmament, as a result of negotiation, unilateral declaration, or imposition, have been frequently employed in past centuries, as well as in the modern era.

Denuclearization—creating nuclear weapons–free zones—is a form of demilitarization that is directly linked to modern weapons technology within a stipulated geographical area. While there is no authoritative definition of a nuclear weapons–free zone, there are certain accepted elements implicit in the concept. These include: (1) no manufacture or production of nuclear weapons within the zone; (2) no importation of nuclear weapons by nations within the zone; (3) no stationing or storing of nuclear weapons in nations within the zone; and, preferably and when obtainable, (4) a pledge by nuclear weapons states not to use or to threaten to use nuclear weapons against non-nuclear nations within the zone. Additionally, the agreements were to be in force indefinitely and none of the parties was to be permitted special conditions. Each nation agrees to comprehensive safeguards established by the International Atomic Energy Agency (IAEA), to verify that the treaty members were not acquiring illicit nuclear weaponry.

Neutrality, which may or may not involve demilitarization, has its own obligations. International law recognizes a unilateral declaration of neutrality *only* if it is acknowledged in some fashion by other nations. While a neutral state may possess military fortifications and forces, it is prohibited from participating in any international conflicts, military alliances, or allowing other states to use its territory for military activities. If neutrality places obligations on a neutral state, it also carries responsibilities for the states guaranteeing its neutrality. The guarantors pledge to respect the status and integrity of the neutral state, and they may be called upon to come to the aid of such a state if its neutrality is being threatened.

On at least two occasions, neutrality and demilitarization were connected. The treaty that neutralized Luxembourg (1867) also called for the Duchy to be demilitarized. Later, at the end of World War II, Austria was initially demilitarized and the subsequent Austrian State Treaty (1955) neutralized that nation. In another example of combined techniques, the Antarctic Treaty (1959) is not only an example of demilitarization, but also of a nuclear weapons–free zone.

One reason why demilitarization and neutrality were frequently employed is that these methods were relatively uncomplicated. Demilitarization pacts or "geographic disarmament" were just as easy to negotiate as their consequences were to assess. They also might be valuable tools for assuring political stability, given appropriate conditions and when they were employed in a manner that was equitable and was perceived as equitable. In such instances, they were able to defuse flashpoints and establish a climate of trust. When such arrangements were imposed, however, they were inevitably short-lived. Neutrality involved a completely different set of factors, in particular, the desire and steadfastness of the government and population seeking recognition for its neutrality. As examples below indicate, it was not easily achieved.

A particularly useful, often short-lived, arms control technique has been the separation of opposing forces at the termination of hostilities. The Treaty of Guayaquil in 1829 between Colombia and Peru, for example, provided that frontier forces were to be reduced to that "consistent with the preservation of order and security." Another approach has been to create a temporary "neutral zone" that separated antagonistic parties' military forces. Subsequent political settlements occasionally attempted to formalize a previously temporary agreement, by creating a permanent demilitarized or neutral zone. If a continuing hostile political environment resulted in a failure to agree on a formal peace treaty, a temporary demilitarized measure could be extended for decades.

Armistices. There have been many armistices where belligerent forces have withdrawn a stipulated distance from one another. For example, the 1859 armistice between Austria and France (and Sardinia), provided for a neutral space between the two belligerent armies. In the armistice convention following the Franco-Prussian War (1870), the two belligerent armies and their advance posts were kept at least 10 kilometers apart. The Treaty of Portsmouth that ended the Russo-Japanese War of 1905 established a zone between the forward military positions of the opposing forces.

The armistice that ended World War I called for a scheduled withdrawal of German forces from specified areas, so that after 31 days, the Germans had evacuated all territory on the left bank of the Rhine, and retired to a neutral zone on the right bank of the river. Somewhat similar terms were set down in the Protocol of Armistice between the Allied powers and Austria-Hungary.

Neutral Zones. Between the world wars numerous neutralized zones were created to defuse frontier disputes or assist in the termination of hostilities; however, the results were mixed. The League of Nations' attempt to establish a neutral zone during a border dispute between Poland and Lithuania in 1920 failed when the Poles simply disregarded it and seized the territory in contention. But in 1921 a "zone of demarcation" reduced tensions while Yugoslavia and Albania settled their border dispute. The League Council persuaded Greece and Bulgaria to separate their forces when a border war threatened in 1925. Hostilities between Chinese and Japanese troops were interrupted by an armistice in 1932, and again in 1933, when the Chinese troops created a demilitarized zone by withdrawing to a line running roughly from Tientsin to Peking (Beijing), while Japanese forces withdrew north of the Great Wall. These measures established a demilitarized zone between Japanese-dominated Manchuria and China that ameliorated friction for a time, but eventually hostilities engulfed the zone.

Another use of a demilitarized zone occurred in 1934, when the League of Nations sought to end the protracted Gran Chaco War between Bolivia and Paraguay. The League, in accordance with Article 15 of the Covenant, proposed an armistice and the separation of the two forces by least 100 kilometers when hostilities ceased. Within that zone no offensive or defensive military works could be established, nor were the troops to be re-equipped. The League stressed that these proposals were only temporary and were not designed to prejudge the territorial issues between the parties. Hostilities ended in June 1935 and the demilitarized zone appeared to have been a useful contribution.

Demilitarized Zones. When the First Indochina War ended in 1954, a demilitarized zone (DMZ) was established at the Geneva conference (1954). It temporarily divided North and South Vietnam along the Song Ben Hai River near the 17th parallel, pending final efforts at the reunification of Vietnam. The DMZ consisted of a 10-kilometer-wide (6-mile) demilitarized area and, with gradual U.S. economic, political, and military intervention, it came to be seen as a de facto border. Once the Second Indochina War was fully underway in 1966–1967, the zone gradually became a battlefield once more.

The Korean War ended with a ceasefire and an armistice in 1953 that established a demilitarized zone between the North and South. The DMZ was approximately 20 miles wide, with the southern boundary generally following the 38th parallel. The Military Armistice Commission established to supervise the terms of the armistice was usually unable to resolve the many, many claims and counterclaims regarding violations of the DMZ. Nevertheless, the Commission's role was viewed to "have value as a conduit for communication between the commanders in times of crisis to prevent miscalculation." Although it was intended to be a temporary condition, a formal peace treaty was not forthcoming and, although it has been violated several times, the DMZ has remained for more than five decades.[1]

Compliance Issues. Agreements that endured for a substantial length of time usually required that signatories heed changing circumstances and seek modifications to maintain their viability. The Rush-Bagot agreement, noted below, is a prime example of successfully adjusting to shifting political environments. The IAEA's responsibilities in verifying nuclear weapons–free zones have shifted over time in response to technological innovations and mounting dangers posed by possible secret conversion of civil nuclear programs into weapons facilities. Demilitarized zones that separate hostile forces, as noted, have had mixed success with frequent charges of noncompliance.

Short-term successes, as well as outright failures, usually can be found where terms were imposed. Honoring their pledge to Sparta, the Athenians razed their Great Wall and did not rebuild it—for a decade. Those treaties imposing defortification at Dunkirk (1713–1783) were frequently evaded by the French. Belgium's neutrality was ignored when, during World War I, Germany's invasion repudiated the 1831 treaty guarantees. The Versailles Treaty's demilitarization/neutralization of the Rhineland failed in 1936 when Germany reoccupied the region. Similar clauses for other regions were ignored after Adolf Hitler unilaterally denounced the Versailles Treaty in 1935.

What follows is a representative, chronological sampling, together with a brief narrative description of the treaties and agreements that demonstrated the historical lineage of defortification, demilitarization, neutrality, and denuclearization—nuclear weapons–free zones.

DEFORTIFICATION

There are numerous examples regarding the removal of a specific fortification being written into general peace treaties, with the aim to improve the security and stability of a particular region. For example, the Congress of Vienna (1815), acting on a Swiss request to enhance their neutrality, ordered that the fortress of Huningen in Upper Alsace (on the Eastern border of France) be razed. The Treaty of Versailles mandated that the German fortifications on Heligoland, an island in the North Sea, be dismantled as part of a program of demilitarization.

Sparta-Athens, 404 BCE. Victorious at the end of the lengthy Peloponnesian War, the Spartans in 404 BCE contemplated the total destruction of Athens, but decided instead on the destruction of the Long Wall—that connected the city of Athens to its port of Piraeus—and the surrender of all but twelve Athenian warships. The Athenians complied for nearly a decade, before enlisting help from the Persians in 393 to rebuild the Long Wall and again challenge the Spartans.

Azov Fortifications, 1605. Further east, the expansionist Russian and declining Ottoman Empires were frequently engaged in hostilities. A continuing point of contention, beginning in 1605, was the fortifications at Azov that ensured Russian access to the inland seas; consequently, the Russians built fortifications when victorious, while the Turks insisted on razing them when they won. The Turks also sought to establish a demilitarized zone that would encompass the region and separate the two military forces; however, by the 1770s the Russians had gained permanent control of Azov.

Dunkirk, 1713–1783. During the English and French wars of the eighteenth century, British officials viewed the fortifications at Dunkirk to be a serious threat to their navigation of the English Channel. After France's defeat in 1713, the Treaty of Utrecht insisted "that all the fortifications of the city of Dunkirk be razed" and the harbor be filled. The impact of the latter imposed a severe penalty on the surrounding civilian economy. Not surprisingly, each subsequent conflict during this century found the French striving to rebuild the fortifications and open the port, while each time the British prevailed the peace treaty imposed a clause demanding destruction of Dunkirk's fortifications. This interplay continued from the Treaty of Utrecht (1713) until the Treaty of Paris (1783).[2]

DEMILITARIZATION

Among the oldest forms of arms control, this technique was used frequently to reduce or eliminate a possible "flash point" that might launch unanticipated and undesired hostilities. Demilitarization arrangements have taken several forms—some were anticipated to have a long lifespan, others were employed as temporary measures. Then, too, an often-troubled region may have spawned a series of such understandings. One group of such similar agreements and treaties that focuses on a specific region is in the section, "Turkish Straits, Black Sea, and Suez Canal."

Peace of Callias, 460s BCE. Although historical evidence is sketchy, this bilateral agreement between the Athenians and Persians was essentially a multi-year truce for acknowledging spheres of influence. In recognition of the imperial interests of the two states, it provided for demilitarized buffer zones around the Aegean Sea into which neither Athens nor Persia could send military, especially naval, forces.[3]

Rush-Bagot Agreement, 1817. Demilitarization was the major feature of the Rush-Bagot agreement. The War of 1812 had demonstrated the strategic importance of the Great Lakes to the United States and Britain's eastern Canadian provinces. By the war's end, the British flagship on the lakes was a three-decker more powerful than Admiral Nelson's *Victory*. Two even larger vessels were being built at Kingston. In response, the Americans had begun constructing two warships that would be the largest in the world.

After the conflict ended, however, the U.S. Congress began an economy drive. On February 27, 1815, the president was authorized "to cause all armed vessels of the United States on the lakes to be sold or laid up, except such as he may deem necessary to enforce proper execution of revenue laws." Building was stopped on the two huge U.S. warships, but their hulls were "housed." The other U.S. warships on the lakes apparently were laid up or dismantled except for an 18-gun brig. Economies also prompted the British to curtail construction and begin dismantling its warships. Washington feared, however, that a series of small, unpleasant incidents between the Canadians and Americans might lead to a renewed naval race on the lakes.[4]

In November 1815, Secretary of State James Monroe approached the British to limit the number of armed ships on the lakes, fearing that, should building warships begin again, a "vast expence will be incurred" that might lead to "the danger of [a] collision" between the two countries. Lord Castlereagh agreed that such a naval race was "ridiculous and absurd." The agreement of April 29, 1817, limited the naval forces of each party "on Lake Ontario, to one vessel, not exceeding one hundred tons burden, and armed with one eighteen pound cannon. On the upper lakes, to two vessels, not exceeding like burden each, and armed with like force," and "on the waters of Lake Champlain, to one vessel not exceeding like burden, and armed with like force." However, the pact did not end competitive armaments in the Great Lakes region, as the construction of fortifications continued along the border until the Treaty of Washington (1871), after which the "unguarded frontier" with Canada gradually emerged.

The British authorized outfitting armed vessels in excess of the stipulated number to intercept American assistance to rebels during the Canadian Rebellions of 1837–1838. Washington protested but took no action after London explained that the vessels were for defensive purposes only and that they would "be discontinued at the earliest possible" date. By 1843, the British force was reduced to its Rush-Bagot quota, but the United States had launched the *Michigan,* which exceeded the authorized tonnage and carried more cannons than allowed. This time, the British protested.

On at least two other occasions, issues arose regarding compliance: during the U.S. Civil War and during the 1920s Prohibition era. In both of these episodes, the United States declared that it required additional naval forces to maintain the security of its borders and, each time, the Canadians acquiesced. In spite of these obstacles, the Rush-Bagot pact was sustained and remained one of the world's most successful arms control undertakings, certainly its most enduring.[5]

The Panama Canal, 1850–1903. Negotiations preceding the construction of the canal often considered neutralization and even demilitarization. The Clayton-Bulwer Treaty (1950) between the United States and Britain provided that neither would erect nor maintain any fortifications commanding such a canal, nor occupy, fortify, colonize, or assume control over any part of Central America. It also provided that neither of these countries would seek exclusive control over the proposed canal. Fifty years later, the first Hay-Pauncefote Treaty granted the United States the sole right to construct and control the canal. Neutrality was maintained by adopting the same rules found in the Constantinople

Convention of 1888 for the Suez Canal. No fortifications that commanded the canal or adjacent waters were allowed. However, the United States could police the canal "to protect it against lawlessness and disorder." In the Torrijos-Carter treaties (1999), the U.S. had the right to defend the neutrality of the canal, while Panama was responsible for its defense.

A second Hay-Pauncefote Treaty (1902) removed the non-fortification clause, but suggested that the new canal would be neutralized and that the canal "should never be blockaded or any act of hostility be committed within it." The Hay-Bunau-Varilla Treaty (1903) provided the United States with the perpetual and unrestricted use, occupation, and control of a 10-mile-wide canal zone and employment of its armed forces to protect the canal.

The Straits of Magellan, 1881. To the south, Chile and Argentina quarreled over their boundary line. When, in 1843, Chile claimed the Straits, Patagonia, and Tierra del Fuego, the Argentines were too involved with the Paraguayan War to do more than issue a protest. By 1870, however, the situation had changed and Argentina began pursuing its interests in the area. Accepting the mediation of the United States in 1881, Argentina gained control of Patagonia and Chile was granted sovereignty over the Straits of Magellan. The territory of Tierra del Fuego was to be divided.

On June 6 after several telegraphic exchanges, demilitarization of the Straits emerged. Argentine telegraphed Chile its version of Article V of the proposed treaty: "The Straits of Magellan are to be neutralized forever and their free navigation [e]nsured to the flags of all nations; and it will be forbidden to raise on either side of their coast fortifications or military establishments." The Chileans countered with their position: "The waters of the Straits are neutralized and free navigation therein [e]nsured to the Flags of all nations; no works of defense will be allowed to be raised that may impede ... free passage through the canal." They feared that the Argentine's language might prevent constructing defenses for Chilean settlers near the Straits, but which would not impede the free navigation of the Straits. The treaty signed on July 23, 1881, conformed closely to the Chilean version. Article V has withstood the test of time—there has been no proof of violations.

Convention of Karlstadt, 1905. This Scandinavian agreement was arrived at during negotiations aimed at preventing or eliminating the possibility of hostilities. The Norwegians, resentful of being united under the Swedish crown, insisted upon their independence and had earlier demonstrated their frustrations by building fortifications along the frontier to close off possible invasion routes from the east. This activity irritated Stockholm officials who demanded these fortifications be demolished. The political separation of Norway from Sweden took place peacefully; however, the Norwegian fortifications took on new significance. Although the Swedish government chose not to fortify its new frontier, there was some concern that differences might lead to conflict. Negotiations relating to the new frontier, consequently, began immediately.

When the Norwegians refused Sweden's demand to dismantle their fortifications, the parties agreed to create a demilitarized zone, averaging about

10 miles, on each side of the border. Reassured, Norway dismantled three fortresses, which were of limited military value, within the zone. The zone was defined as permanent and absolute: no military operations could be conducted within it; no military forces could be concentrated there. Throughout its long history, no evidence of violations have been reported.[6]

Treaty of Versailles, 1919. Germany was forbidden to maintain or construct any fortifications on the left bank of the Rhine, nor on the right bank west of a line drawn 50 kilometers east of the river. Nor could Germany keep any troops in this area, permanently or temporarily, conduct maneuvers there, or maintain any mobilization facilities. All fortified works, fortresses, or field works within this zone were to be dismantled. The Treaty also permanently prohibited German fortifications and armed forces within the Rhineland area. Likewise, the Saar Basin was to be demilitarized; however, Germany's fortifications on its eastern and southern borders could be maintained in their existing state.

Spitsbergen Treaty, 1920. Although no military action took place there during World War I, military strategists thought the Arctic islands would provide an ideal naval base, especially for submarines. The treaty of February 9, 1920, resolved a dispute between Norway, Sweden, Holland, and England over possession of the islands, by awarding them to Norway on the condition that they be permanently demilitarized. The treaty held that Norway "undertakes not to create nor to allow the establishment of any naval base in the territories ... and not to construct any fortification in said territories, which may never be used for warlike purpose."

Despite the lack of international supervisory machinery, the arms control provisions were apparently upheld during the interwar years. No *official* complaints of evasion were ever submitted and the press reported no violations of the arms control provisions. One post–World War II study noted: "For a quarter of a century Norway has scrupulously honored the Treaty. No fortifications have been built in Svalbard [Spitsbergen]." However, during World War II, the Germans did attempt to establish a naval base in the islands and, early in the Cold War, the Americans were suspicious of Russian "economic" missions and "commercial" endeavors on the islands.

Aland Islands Convention, 1856, 1921. The Convention was one of the more successful League of Nations efforts in demilitarization. These islands, a Swedish possession for hundreds of years, were ceded to Russia. Following its defeat in the Crimean War, Russia agreed in the Treaty of Paris in 1856 to neither fortify these islands, nor maintain any military or naval establishment there. During World War I, Czarist Russian forces occupied the islands and constructed fortifications, intending to maintain this status after the war. In the Treaty of Brest-Litovsk, however, the weak Soviet government gave up all claims to the islands and agreed to demolish the fortifications, but Germany's defeat annulled the terms of the Brest-Litovsk pact.

The League Council awarded the islands to Finland in 1921, on the condition that they be demilitarized and neutralized. No military, naval, or air installations or fortifications could be established on the islands, nor could any troops be stationed there. If domestic circumstances demanded it, Finland could send troops into the archipelago, but they had to be withdrawn once order was restored. The Convention prohibited the manufacture, import, transport, and re-export of arms in this demilitarized area. It also provided that no other power's military, naval, or air force units could enter the demilitarized zone.

Additionally, in time of war the islands would be considered a neutral zone and were not to be used, either directly or indirectly for any purpose connected with military operations. To preserve that neutrality, Finland was given the right, in the event of war affecting the Baltic Sea, to lay mines temporarily in Aland Islands waters. In 1938, the Finns and Swedes urged, subject to the approval of the other signatories to the 1921 Convention and interested parties, the refortification and remilitarization of the Islands. Although the signatories granted their approval, the USSR, an interested party, on May 31, 1939, formally opposed refortification. In spite of the Russo-Finnish War, the subsequent German invasion of the USSR and the Finnish entry into the war on the side of Germany, the neutrality of the islands apparently was honored during the World War II. No *official* complaints of evasion were submitted and the media reported no violations of the arms control provisions.[7]

Pacific Mandated Islands, 1920–1939. Two agreements regulated Japanese activities, to varying degrees, in their newly acquired mandated islands—the former German possessions of the Marianas, Carolines, and Marshalls. The League of Nation's mandate arrangement with Japan was restated in the bilateral United States–Japanese Convention of February 11, 1922.

Tokyo's December 17, 1920, pledge to the League relative to military policies in their mandates, embodied three points: (1) the Japanese would rigorously control all "traffic in arms and ammunition" in accordance with the League's September 10, 1919, Convention—the so-called Treaty of St. Germain; (2) they would limit the military training of natives to "purposes of internal police and the local defense of the territory"; and (3) they would abstain from erecting military installations in the mandates—"no military or naval bases shall be established or fortifications erected in the territory." Finally, Tokyo agreed to "make to the Council of the League of Nations an annual report to the satisfaction of the Council, containing full information with regard to the territory, and indicating the measures taken to carry out the obligations assumed." (For a discussion of compliance, see Chapter 9.)

Washington Naval Treaty, 1922. Article XIX of the Washington Naval Treaty insisted that the status quo be maintained with respect to the fortifications and naval bases of the United States, the British Empire, and Japan in the Pacific Ocean. There were exceptions: for the United States, these were the islands adjacent to the U.S. coast, Alaska, the Panama Canal Zone, and the Hawaiian Islands; and for Britain these were the islands adjacent to the coast of Canada, the Commonwealth of Australia and its territories, and New Zealand. The status quo limitation applied to the rest of the United States' insular Pacific possessions. For Britain, the limitation applied to Hong Kong and its insular possessions in the Pacific east of the meridian of 110° east longitude. The status quo was specified for Japan's Kurile Islands, the Bonin Islands, Amami-Oshima, the Loochoo Islands, Formosa, and the Pescadores.[8]

Turkish Straits, Black Sea, and Suez Canal

Great power rivalry in nineteenth-century Europe often revolved around the so-called Eastern Question—the competition for power, influence, trade, and often territory in the Middle East at expense of the declining Ottoman Empire. A major focal point of the contest was the "Turkish Straits"—the Dardanelles, the Sea of Marmora, and the Bosporus—that connected the Mediterranean to the Black Sea. The Russians sought to control passage through the straits, while other powers wanted unrestricted access to the Black Sea. The British, more-over, wanted to keep the Russians out of the eastern Mediterranean in order to guarantee the security of the Suez Canal and their lines of communication with the empire. Two arms control techniques—neutralization and demilitarization—were employed regarding the straits to promote one or the other of these objectives.

Given the relationship of the Straits to Great Britain's, France's, and Russia's interests and to Turkey's national security, it is not surprising that efforts at demilitarization met with only moderate success and duration. Yet the various Straits regimes were perceived as reassuring at the time and contributing to stability in the region.[9]

Straits Conventions, 1833, 1841. The czar's government, following an Egyptian victory over Turkish forces, persuaded the Turks to sign an agreement closing the Dardanelles to all foreign warships, except Russian vessels. Known as the Treaty of Hunkiar Iskelesi (1833), this treaty signaled Russia's temporary dominance in the region, rendered the Black Sea a virtual *mare clausum*, a closed sea, and provided its warships access to the Mediterranean.

Other European powers exerted heavy diplomatic pressure to gain a new Straits Convention, signed in London on July 13, 1841, which provided that the Straits would be closed to all warships, so long as Turkey was at peace. But, since Turkey had regained control of the Straits, should it become involved in a conflict, the Turks had the option to open the Straits to foreign warships. This system lasted for a decade and half.[10]

Black Sea Convention, 1856. With the Treaty of Paris of March 30, 1856, that ended the Crimean War, a new regime was instituted that not only aimed to neutralize the Black Sea, but to demilitarize its Russian and Turkish shores as well. The neutralized and demilitarized status of the Straits, established by the treaty, advanced the interests of the victors, particularly Great Britain. With Russia's influence over Turkey diminished, Britain achieved its objective of opening the Straits to commercial shipping. The restrictions of the Treaty of Paris, from a Russian standpoint, constituted an infringement of its sovereign rights. Thus, Czar Alexander II seized upon France's defeat in the Franco-Prussian War unilaterally to repudiate the treaty in 1870.[11]

Pontus Treaty, 1871. A Conference of the Powers, in the so-called Pontus Treaty, established yet another policy for the Straits. Now the Straits were closed to all foreign warships but open to all merchant shipping. Russia and Turkey were permitted to refortify their Black Sea coasts and each might have an unlimited number of warships on the Black Sea; however, the Black Sea fleets were prohibited from passing through the Straits. This denied Russia operational access to the Mediterranean but the results would prove to be a mixed benefit.

Closure of the Straits prevented Russia's Black Sea fleet from participating in the Russo-Japanese War; but during World War I, when England, France, and Russia were allied, the British had reason to regret the 1871 treaty. A member of the Central Powers, Turkey closed the Straits to commercial as well as military shipping, thus blocking British and French efforts to ship supplies to Russia's southern ports. Allied military attempts to force open the Straits failed and their inability to supply Russia contributed to its ultimate collapse in World War I.

The Suez Canal, 1888. Efforts by European powers to "internationalize" the canal began as early as 1882. The French assembled a commission in Paris comprised of representatives from major nations during 1885. Subsequently, an international convention was signed at Constantinople that attempted to neutralize the Suez Canal by declaring that the canal would always be free and open in war or peace to all commercial vessels. The canal would not be subjected to the right of blockade. Furthermore, it would remain open in time of war to the warships of combatants. Even if the Ottoman Empire were one of the belligerents, no act of hostility or act designed to obstruct its free navigation was permitted in the canal or in, or near, its ports of access.

A 1904 Franco-British agreement appeared to modify the 1888 pact's provisions, since it recognized Britain's responsibility for protecting the Suez Canal Zone and guaranteeing free navigation of the canal. In 1922, London extended this commitment in its declaration that the British Empire's line of communications required them to preserve, at their discretion, the canal's security. During both world wars, consequently, Britain insisted that the necessities of the canal's defense took priority over the right of passage.

Treaty of Sevres, 1919. Forced to capitulate with the collapse of the Central Powers in World War I, the Turkish public became infuriated by the imposed Treaty of Sevres. The treaty called for the Straits to be internationalized, the adjoining territory demilitarized, and allied occupation made permanent. An International Straits Commission—composed of representatives from Britain, France, Italy, and Turkey—was to supervise carrying out of the terms. Not surprisingly, Turkish nationalists led by Mustafa Kemal Pasha, later known as Kemal Ataturk, rejected the treaty, organized a new government, and launched a diplomatic and military offensive. They won Soviet disavowal of Sevres, gained Italian and French withdrawals from Turkish territory, and drove the Greeks off the Anatolian mainland. Subsequently, the major powers invited Greece and Turkey to a conference that would draft a new treaty.

Treaty of Lausanne, 1923. In a more conciliatory mood, the former Allies renegotiated, rather than imposed, an agreement that provided for free sea and air transit of the Straits in time of peace. The same rules would apply in wartime if Turkey remained neutral. If the Turks were at war, they must allow passage of neutral merchant ships and civil aircraft, provided these did not carry contraband, but they could prevent enemy vessels from using the Straits. Both shores of the Dardanelles and the Bosporus were to be demilitarized, as were the islands off the entrance to the Dardanelles and all islands in the Sea of Marmora except one known as Emir Ali Adasi. Allied maritime powers, signatories to the Lausanne convention, guaranteed the security of the Straits under the League of Nations.

The International Straits Commission, retained from the earlier Sevres treaty, reported to the Council of the League of Nations. The Commission was charged with defining the precise boundaries of the demilitarized zones and verifying the destruction of fortifications within the zones. Once these conditions were met, the demilitarization terms were to be mutually enforced, that is, the nations affected—Turkey, Greece, and Bulgaria—were responsible for continued fulfillment of their pledges. The Commission informed the Council on November 16, 1925, that the initial demilitarization of the Straits had been accomplished.

A decade later, the Turkish government sought revision of the demilitarization terms. In marked contrast to Italy and Germany, who undertook revisions unilaterally, Turkey formally requested the Lausanne signatory states and the League to allow the Turks to fortify the Dardanelles. Consequently, a July 1936 international conference at Montreux, Switzerland, approved a new convention allowing Turkey to proceed immediately with the fortification of the Straits, as well as its Thracian frontier and its Aegean islands. The Straits Commission was disbanded as the Turkish government assumed its functions.[12]

NEUTRALITY

The nineteenth-century legal concept of neutrality implied several responsibilities. A neutral country may maintain armed forces, but may only employ them in self-defense. Moreover, a neutral state may not engage in military alliances nor allow its territory to be used by foreign belligerents. In wartime, neutral countries may not undertake provocative political activities that encourage hostilities, nor may they aid any contending parties. Other states are expected to honor a country's declared and recognized neutral status, although this is not always the case.

From an earlier standpoint, Rome employed a form of neutralization on its frontiers to reduce tensions and potential conflict with powerful neighbors. In 20 BCE, Rome established a 70-mile stretch of the Nile Valley, south of the present Aswân High Dam as a neutral zone. By following a Ptolemaic precedent of assigning the title of this zone to the temple of Isis, Rome was able to reach a peace settlement with the central Sudanese kingdom of Meroë. More significant was the Roman Empire's creation of the neutral buffer state of Armenia on its eastern frontier to appease at first the Parthians and, after the third century CE, the Sassanid Persians. Kings related to the Parthian royal family ruled Armenia but they were approved and crowned by Rome.[13]

Centuries later, there were attempts to create neutralized "city-states." The city of Cracow, in Poland, was declared to be a neutral city in the treaty signed at Vienna in 1815 and it was to be protected by Russia, Prussia, and Austria. Cracow's neutral status lasted 31 years until 1846, when it was disavowed by Austria on the grounds that the city had become a center of revolutionary activity. The city and its surrounding territory were absorbed by Austria.

Switzerland, 1648–. The most widely recognized modern example of neutrality is Switzerland. The Swiss experience led to the formulation of two parallel concepts: (1) that a community or nation could elect not to take part in any external conflict; and (2) that a specific geographic area or region could be exempt from military hostilities. By the fourteenth century, the Swiss realized that their mountains provided the means of avoiding military conflicts. In 1309, the city of Zürich persuaded the ruling Austrian dukes to exempt its nearby valley floor from any hostilities. Later in 1393, Zürich and Austria each agreed that it would remain neutral and impartial during any military conflict.

The Swiss later sought to avoid being caught up in the recurring wars between France and the various states, primarily German, of the Holy Roman Empire. Threatened during the Thirty Years' War, Switzerland in 1647 called up an army of 36,000 men to defend its territory. After the Peace of Westphalia (1648), the Swiss confederation unilaterally proclaimed its neutrality that was generally recognized, if not always respected. The Swiss subsequently became entangled in the Napoleonic Wars; however, the Act of Paris (1815) at the Congress of Vienna ended their unilateral neutrality and granted them an international guarantee. By its terms, France, Britain, Prussia, Russia, and Austria declared "their formal and authentic Acknowledgement of the perpetual Neutrality of Switzerland; and they Guarantee to that country the Integrity and Inviolability of its Territory." This pledge was restated in the Treaty of Versailles (1919). As a condition for the acknowledgment of their neutrality, the Swiss were expressly required by the Congress of Vienna to maintain it. Consequently, the Swiss developed a unique form of volunteer military forces, and avoided becoming militarily involved in both World War I and II.

Belgium, 1831. Neutralizing Belgium was mentioned at the Congress of Vienna (1815), but occurred only after Belgians broke away from Dutch control in 1830. Since major European powers desired Belgium as a barrier against the

French, a treaty of 1831 recognized Belgium's independence and declared it a "perpetually Neutral State." After eight years of negotiations a treaty was finalized and again Britain, France, Russia, Prussia, and Austria agreed to recognize Belgium's independence and guarantee its unenthusiastic neutralization.

In 1914, Germany invaded Belgium, ignoring its neutrality, as Berlin dismissed the 1831 treaty as "a scrap of paper." The Treaty of Versailles formally terminated the 1831 pact that many Belgians felt impinged upon their sovereignty; however, Belgium's army was unable to provide for its security during World War II.

Luxembourg, 1867. The neutrality of Luxembourg differed from that of Belgium and Switzerland. A very small state, the Grand Duchy of Luxembourg occupied a strategic position flanking the northeastern approaches to France by way of the Meuse and Moselle valleys. Its neutrality was guaranteed by treaty in 1867, at the end of a war between Prussia and Austria. The same five signatories that guaranteed the neutrality of Belgium signed the treaty, but under different circumstances. Britain maintained that the guarantee was collective only, and that the guarantor states were not individually responsible to defend Luxembourg's neutrality. The other guarantor states did not share this opinion. Secondly, Luxembourg was demilitarized as well as neutralized; indeed, Luxembourg may be the only example of a demilitarized state in nineteenth-century Europe.

Luxembourg was occupied in the German advance during 1914, but the occupation primarily was involved with facilitating the rail transit of troops and supplies to the Western Front. Ironically, the Grand Duchy did not consider its neutrality to have been violated and, therefore, did not break relations with Germany. Luxembourg was not a participant at the 1919 peace conference, and it did not recognize the abrogation of the 1867 treaty provided for in the Versailles Treaty. It considered its neutrality to be in force at the beginning of World War II, but later abandoned that position.[14]

Austrian State Treaty, 1955. After World War II, a Four-Power Allied Council was responsible for the demilitarization of Austria. Military training and activities were prohibited and equipment was destroyed, removed from Austria, or controlled by the Allied powers. Military installations were dismantled or used by the occupying forces, while military factories were catalogued and destroyed or switched to civilian enterprises. The production, acquisition, and development of military equipment and ammunition was also prohibited. The initial demilitarization was essentially completed by 1947.

The April 1955 Moscow Memorandum between Austria and the Soviet Union stated that Austria was "to adhere to a policy of permanent neutrality on the Swiss model." As with the Swiss, the initial concept of Austrian neutrality was based on the nineteenth-century legal concept. But in several respects, Austrian neutrality developed independently, for Austria undertook an active role in the international arena. It joined the United Nations in 1955 and the European Community at a time when the Community was moving toward increased cooperation in political and security areas that would strain Austria's neutral position. Austria has participated in UN peacekeeping forces, but it never contemplated conducting its own defense as has Switzerland, and has never become a member of the western alliance, NATO, or participated in the Conventional Armed Forces in Europe Treaty. One year after the signing of the 1955 treaty, only 6,000 men were under arms; after two years, that number had increased to 30,000. Eventually, active Austrian armed forces slightly exceeded an initially proposed limit of 53,000, and ready reserves surpassed 240,000. In contrast, more than 200,000 Austrians died fighting with the German armed forces in the Second World War.[15]

DENUCLEARIZATION

Nuclear Weapons–Free Zones

Early proposals such as the Rapacki Proposals (1957, 1962) by the Polish Foreign Minister sought to prevent nuclear weapons from being stationed in Poland, Czechoslovakia, West Germany, and East Germany. They were caught up in the Cold War rivalry and came to naught. Yet the Rapacki concept did serve as a model for the nuclear weapons–free zones that eventually emerged. The Soviet Union was generally supportive of the program but the United States was more skeptical, viewing it as an effort to neutralize West Germany and split it off from NATO. Multilateral agreements that prohibited nuclear weapons in a specific, non-populated area—Antarctica, outer space, and the seabed—succeeded in gaining general approval and are essentially nuclear weapons–free zones. There apparently have been no reported violations of these agreements.

Each designated zone discussed below includes the entire territory of all of its parties. Territory is understood to include all land holdings, internal waters, territorial seas, and archipelagic waters. Each member state also adopted comprehensive safeguards that were administered by the International Atomic Energy Agency, which is charged with verifying that the member states were not pursuing illicit nuclear activities.

The territorial clauses have caused some differences. The Latin American treaty, for example, claims to extend hundreds of kilometers from the signatories' territories into the Pacific and Atlantic Oceans. Consequently, the nuclear-weapon states, citing their freedom at sea, assert that these limits do not apply to their ships and aircraft that might be carrying nuclear weapons. The Rarotonga Treaty (1985) posed a similar freedom of the seas issue for Washington. The inclusion of the Chagos Archipelago, which includes the U.S. military base at Diego Garcia in the Indian Ocean, as part of the African nuclear weapon–free zone, prompted another dispute. Neither the United States nor the United Kingdom accepted the claim that Diego Garcia was subject to the restrictions stipulated in the Pelindaba Treaty (1996). The Treaty of Tlatelolco (1967), which sought to denuclearize Latin America, initially had to face the Brazilian military's efforts to develop nuclear weapons. However, the Bilateral Agreement for the Exclusively Peaceful Uses of Nuclear Energy between Brazil and Argentina, signed in July 1991, acknowledged these two nations' adherence to the Tlatelolco pact.[16]

The Antarctic Treaty, 1959. While this multilateral treaty has been frequently denigrated, critics overlook the fact that it excluded a specific geographical area from strategic competition and, at the same time, provided a measure of confidence among nuclear states for future negotiations. In addition to assuring that the continent would be set aside for peaceful uses, Article 1 prohibits all types of military activities and Article 5 specifically prohibits any nuclear explosions or the disposal of nuclear wastes without international agreement. Together these articles are viewed as creating a de facto nuclear weapons–free zone. There were, in 2007, 45 parties to the treaty that entered into force on October 10, 1961.

The demilitarization of the Antarctic was accomplished, however, with the full understanding and agreement of the parties involved to the concept of prohibiting *all* weapons, most assuredly nuclear ones, on the continent. Signatory "compliance with the disarmament mandate throughout the Antarctic has clearly been met," Christopher Joyner has noted. "Since 1961, the Antarctic Treaty system has functioned exceedingly well as the institutional framework for preserving peace and stability, fostering scientific cooperation, and promoting standards for environmental preservation and conservation." The Antarctic Treaty has been successfully monitored because of stipulated total prohibition rather than ceilings or ratios.[17]

Outer Space Treaty, 1967. This agreement emerged from nearly two decades of UN-sponsored, multilateral disarmament discussions. In September 1960, President Dwight Eisenhower suggested a similar proposal, but the Soviets were not interested. UN Resolution #1884 (October 17, 1963) responded to a renewed interest in an outer space weapons ban. U.S. Pentagon officials—desiring to keep options open for possible military activities in outer space—reacted negatively to the proposal insisting on the need for "inspection and control" mechanisms. President John F. Kennedy likely could have obtained a pact in 1963 but refrained because he thought it "would excite controversy." Washington's attitude brings to mind Lord Salisbury's ironic 1891 observation that "if you believe the soldiers, nothing is safe.... If they were allowed full scope they would soon insist upon the garrisoning of the moon to protect us from Mars." By 2007, 107 states had signed the treaty that entered into force October 10, 1967.

The Outer Space Treaty dealt with many aspects of activities in outer space. Article IV committed signatories "not to place in orbit around the Earth any objects carrying nuclear weapons or any other kinds of weapons of mass destruction, install such weapons on celestial bodies, or station such weapons in outer space in any other manner." In addition, the article prohibited "the establishment of military bases, installations and fortifications, the testing of any type of weapons and the conduct of military maneuvers on celestial bodies." However, employment of military personnel and any equipment or facility needed in the pursuit of peaceful purposes is permitted.

In December 1979, the UN sponsored an elaborate pact that sought to augment the demilitarization of "the moon and other celestial bodies." It proposed to do this by prohibiting the placing in orbit of "objects carrying nuclear weapons or any other kinds of weapons of mass destruction or place or use such weapons on or in the moon." Also forbidden was the establishment of any military installations, fortifications, or testing of military devices on the moon.

The Outer Space Treaty is the basic arms control agreement governing outer space, but the nuclear test ban accords—and the abrogated ABM treaty (1972–2002)—have added constraints against testing various weapons in outer space. The ABM, SALT, and START treaties prohibited interference with national technical means of verification, thereby permitting the use of reconnaissance satellites. However, anti-satellite weapons were not banned by any of these treaties and pose a serious, continuing concern.[18]

Seabed Treaty, 1971. The objective of this treaty was to prevent the installation of nuclear weapons on the ocean floor beyond national territorial waters. As no nation was contemplating any such deployment, the proposal met with little opposition. Article 1 prohibits treaty parties from introducing nuclear weapons or weapons of mass destruction on the seabed beyond the 12-mile limit. The treaty also called for continued negotiations aimed at the complete demilitarization of the seabed and ocean floor. By 2007, 94 states had signed the treaty that entered into force May 18, 1972.

Procedures for verification include individual observation via national technical means, followed by consultations with other parties should a violation be suspected. Any serious, unresolved violation could be referred to the UN Security Council.[19]

The Treaty of Tlatelolco, 1967. After the Cuban missile crisis, this pact was designed, in part, to persuade Latin American and Caribbean countries not to seek nuclear weapons. In all, 33 nations of Latin America have signed and ratified the treaty pledging not to test, develop, or import nuclear weapons; and not to permit foreign-controlled nuclear weapon bases in the region. Compliance with the treaty obligations is overseen by the Agency for the Prohibition of Nuclear Weapons in Latin America and the Caribbean (OPANAL), based in Mexico City. Each signatory must also conclude safeguard agreements with the IAEA, creating a rather complicated system.

Later, two additional protocols were added to the treaty. Protocol I asked nations having territorial interests in the region "to apply the status of denuclearization in respect to warlike purposes" to these territories. Protocol II required nuclear weapon states "not to use or threaten to use, nuclear weapons against" Treaty of Tlatelolco signatories or to engage in any activities that might lead to treaty violations.

Argentina, Brazil, and Chile initially had shown varying interest in joining the nuclear weapons club; however, in July 1991 Argentina and Brazil signed the Bilateral Agreement for the Exclusively Peaceful Uses of Nuclear Energy. By 1994 these three states had signed and ratified the agreement and later joined the Treaty of Tlatelolco.[20] In 2007, 33 states were parties to the basic Treaty that had entered into force; however, there were several nations who had not ratified the added protocols.

The Treaty of Rarotonga, 1985. The signatories, including Australia and New Zealand, along with nearby island states, modeled this pact after the Tlatelolco treaty. The treaty also allows regional ports to prohibit the entry of ships carrying nuclear weapons, and prohibits nuclear testing and waste disposal in the region. The principle motivation for the treaty was to pressure France into halting nuclear tests on the Mururoa Atoll in the Tuamoto Archipelago, which ended in 1996, and to prevent radioactive-waste disposal in the region. In addition to the Tlatelolco prohibitions, Rarotonga relies on the IAEA to verify that any nuclear materials present in the area are covered by the treaty. A South Pacific Forum may, in case of a suspected violation, authorize a special inspection. In 2007, 13 states were party to the treaty that entered into force November 12, 1986.

Washington feared that Rarotonga might encourage additional nuclear weapons–free zones in the South Pacific, which would restrict the navy's freedom of movement. Consequently, the United States signed but delayed ratification of the agreement. The Reagan administration's talk of waging and winning a nuclear conflict earlier prompted New Zealand, in February 1984, to ban a U.S. destroyer from its ports because the United States refused to say whether or not it carried nuclear weapons. The episode caused a rift between the two countries, prompting the United States to sever diplomatic contacts with New Zealand in 1985. Normal diplomatic relations were reestablished in February 1993.[21]

The Treaty of Bangkok, 1995. The search for a Southeast Asia Nuclear Weapons–Free Zone dated from November 27, 1971, when the Association of Southeast Asian Nations (ASEAN) issued a Declaration on a Zone of Peace, Freedom, and Neutrality. By 2007, there were 10 parties to the Treaty, which had entered into force March 27, 1997. Signatories to the treaty pledged

> not to develop, manufacture or otherwise acquire, possess or have control over nuclear weapons; station nuclear weapons; or test or use nuclear weapons anywhere inside or outside the treaty zone; not to seek or receive any assistance in this; not to take any action to assist or encourage the manufacture or acquisition of any nuclear explosive device by any state; not to provide source or special fissionable materials or equipment to any non-nuclear weapon state (NNWS).

In addition to IAEA safeguards, verification would be accomplished through reports and the exchange of information among the member states, and overseen by a Commission for the Southeast Asia Nuclear Weapons–Free zone.

Refusing to sign the attached protocols, the United States and France objected to the unequivocal security pledges and to the definitions of the area covered. Washington has argued that the Treaty of Bangkok's provisions regarding the innocent passage of its warships and aircraft were "too restrictive" and has insisted on modifications.

The Pelindaba Treaty, 1996. The African pact, signed by 49 of the 53 members of the Organization of African Unity (OAU), came 32 years after the OAU formally declared its aim to create a nuclear-free Africa. South Africa had unilaterally dismantled its nuclear bombs in 1990 in order to play a leading role in the non-proliferation movement (see Chapter 1). The signatories pledged not to conduct research on, develop, test, or stockpile nuclear explosive devices; to prohibit the stationing of nuclear devices on their territory; to maintain the highest standards of protection of nuclear materials, facilities, and equipment; and to prohibit the dumping of radioactive waste. The pact also created an African Commission on Nuclear Energy. By 2007, 21 signatories had ratified the treaty; however, it was awaiting several additional ratifications before entering into force.

Five nuclear weapons states—the United States, Russia France, Britain, and China—pledged their cooperation by signing two protocols attached to the treaty. Protocol I declared that the nuclear weapons states agree "not to use or threaten to use nuclear weapons" within these zones or against any treaty parties. The United States, United Kingdom, and Russia signed the pact but held back on ratifying their pledges under Protocol I and II. UN General Assembly resolutions in 1997 (twice), 1999, 2001, 2003, and 2005 have called upon those African states that have not yet done so to sign and ratify the treaty promptly so that it may enter into force, and for states noted in Protocol III to ensure its speedy application.

A serious obstacle to completion of the pact is the status of Diego Garcia, a large island in the Indian Ocean, which Mauritius claims as part of the Chagos Archipelago. The island is administered by London and is employed as a military base by Washington; consequently, neither nuclear power recognized Diego Garcia as being within the area covered by the treaty. Russia refused to ratify the agreement until the status of Diego Garcia had been resolved.[22]

Treaty of Semipalatinsk, 2006. The Central Asian States of Kazakhstan, Kyrgyzstan, Tajikistan, Turkmenistan, and Uzbekistan agreed on September 27, 2002, to create a nuclear weapons–free zone. In the past these states had nuclear weapons stationed on their territories and they continue to "live in a nuclear-armed neighborhood" that consists of Russia, China, Pakistan, India, and Israel. Additionally, Russia and the United States have military facilities in the Central Asian states.

Disagreement between the nuclear weapons states and the Central Asian nations, and among the Central Asian states themselves, stalled signing the formal agreement until September 8, 2006. The two major hurdles prolonged discussions: (1) how would the treaty regard the possible transit of nuclear weapons through the zone; and (2) how could the treaty reconcile the relationship of existing security treaties. Kazakhstan, Kyrgyzstan, and Tajikistan were successful in preserving an implied provision for nuclear weapons transit through some ambiguous language and in maintaining their security pacts with Russia.

While Russia and China accepted the final agreement's provisions, the United States, the United Kingdom, and France have been critical of several provisions of the treaty and have indicated that they would not sign the protocols unless their concerns were resolved.[23]

For the various forms of negotiations employed, the several types of verification adopted, and problems of compliance or non-compliance, see Part II.

Regulating Use/Outlawing Weapons and War

Several attempts to limit or prohibit the military use, manufacture, and/or possession of specific weaponry, such as poison, chemical agents, fire, and so on, may be found scattered throughout history. They began in preliterate societies and are recorded in their traditions and customs. The Romans, for example, imposed the prohibition of war elephants upon defeated enemy states. During the medieval ages, the weaponry that had been recently introduced often found their use regulated or outlawed because such implements were seen as threatening the traditional patterns of warfare. New weapons such as crossbows often were banned because they were perceived as threats to the position of the warrior class. The same revulsion appeared later against the introduction of firearms spread throughout Europe. Various ordinances were issued against their use and, in some cases, captured gunners were not treated as prisoners of war but were executed as outlaws. These actions were, obviously, of little avail.

Ancient and medieval prohibitions against the use of certain "weapons" met a decidedly mixed reception. Despite the Koran's admonition against the use of fire, designated Islamic military units employed a terrifyingly effective "liquid fire"—especially when fighting the Crusaders. Medieval Roman Catholic Church officials banned the use of crossbows, but the prohibition was often ignored when secular leaders found mercenaries so armed to be useful for their purposes. Laws were issued throughout Europe in an effort to prevent the use of firearms, but these too failed and were soon renounced. One of the few successful examples was the Japanese suppression of the warrior class's use of firearms from the mid-seventeenth to the mid-nineteenth centuries. Yet, the arrival of Matthew Perry's black ships in 1853 launched the reintroduction of modern weaponry.

As weapons became much more destructive in modern times, their potential to inflict extensive casualties among combatants and noncombatants sparked new attempts at formal restrictions and prohibitions. The rationale for these limitations or prohibitions was that the parties involved considered the unrestricted use—or often any use—of a designated weapon to exceed the recognized "just use of force." There is a close relationship between treaties that prohibit possession or use of specific weapons, and the law of war's restraints or limits placed on their usage (see Chapter 5). The St. Petersburg Declaration (1868), for example, outlawed the military use of "dum-dum" or hollow-point bullets. Seventeen European nations signed the Declaration, which was the first formal, modern agreement prohibiting the use of certain weapons in war.

Post-9/11 media concern about weapons in the hands of terrorists that could have disastrous consequences has given rise to the popular usage of a term that had been relatively dormant since appearing in the late 1940s—"weapons of mass destruction" (WMD). This term refers to deadly biological and chemical agents, in addition to various nuclear devices. The fear of these weapons and, correspondingly, arms control mechanisms to contain this threat are not new.

Ignoring The Hague prohibition against employing chemical agents during World War I resulted from outrage over the use of "poison gas." To a considerable extent, the Geneva Protocol (1925) and subsequent no-first-use policies prevented the use of such agents in World War II. Yet chemical and biological weapons (CBW) were slow to become matters of serious concern in the post-1945 era. During the first two decades of the Cold War, both the United States and the Soviet Union accumulated large stocks of various chemical weapons and integrated them into their military planning. When the UN General Assembly in 1966 tried to add herbicides and riot-control agents to augment the 1925 Protocol, Washington immediately objected. The Senate finally ratified the Geneva Protocol in January 1975—50 years after signing it—with the reservations that it did not apply to riot-control agents or herbicides, being widely used by the United States in Vietnam. The United States also reserved the right to retaliate in kind should an enemy violate the protocol.

If attempts have been made frequently since ancient times to prohibit poison, biochemical, and combustible weapons on moral and legal grounds, it was because they were seen as inhumane devices. An interesting example of eighteenth-century humanists exerting "moral" pressure against "inhumane" weaponry may be found during the Seven Years' War and, later, during the early years of the French Revolution. In 1759, during the Seven Years' War, a Parisian jeweler claimed to have rediscovered the secret of Greek fire—a burning-liquid weapon used by the Byzantine Greeks, Arabs, Chinese, and Mongols. Despite its potential military advantage, Louis XV expressed his desire that the secret be allowed to remain "forgotten." Thirty years later, in 1790, the French Academy of Science was asked to investigate the claims of a man who insisted that he had invented an incendiary bullet. The investigating commission reported that the device might achieve even greater destruction than was claimed. However, harkening back to Louis XV's decision regarding Greek fire, the commission concluded that "faithful to its principles and to those of humanity," it could not even make experiments on the cartridge without an expressed order of the government.

The government of the Terror later sanctioned the development of an incendiary bullet. There is no evidence, however, of it becoming an accepted or decisive weapon at the time. Yet the decision to proceed might be construed as the beginning of the divorce between science and morality as justified by the German philosopher Immanuel Kant. One may also infer that the revolutionary government was less "humane" than Louis XV or that, in 1793, France was in greater peril than it was during the Seven Years' War. More probably, it might simply be considered as an inevitable concomitant aspect of the first *total war* in modern history.

Attempts to outlaw war grew slowly in the Western world, perhaps reaching their peak during the interwar years (1919–1930s). Early efforts to curtail "private" hostilities between various European nobles and principalities were instigated by the clergy in the Middle Ages with the Peace of God in the tenth century and culminated in the secular Peace of Lands of the fifteenth century (see Chapter 5). The rise of national monarchies ended the right of local nobles to wage their own wars. It was the Peace of Lands that Professor Kunz referred to when he wrote, "Private war could be successfully forbidden in the Holy Roman Empire in 1492, when compulsory courts with sheriffs and a legislature had been firmly established."[1]

In the early fourteenth century, the "grand schemes" of Pierre Dubois's *De Recuperatione Terre Sancte* (c. 1306), Dante Alighieri, *De Monarchia* (c. 1310–1311), and Marsilius of Padua, *Defensor Pacis* (1324) "revived the utopian tradition of pursuing peace through perfect political design." Later the idea of the "superstate" came to epitomize "the utopian position that the solution to war is a more inclusive society...." This concept was further refined in conjunction with the "perpetual peace" theories of the Duc de Sully, Emeric Crucé, William Penn, and the Abbé de Saint-Pierre and, in the wake of the Enlightenment, Jean-Jacques Rousseau, Immanuel Kant, and Jeremy Bentham.

Pacifists and international lawyers continued the search and achieved their greatest successes in the League of Nations Covenant (1919), which urged collective security as a means of halting hostilities and, of course, in the Kellogg-Briand Pact (1928). Unfortunately, these efforts met with few positive results.[2]

What follows is a representative, chronological sampling, together with a brief narrative description, of the treaties and agreements that demonstrated the historical lineage of regulating use and outlawing weapons and war.

PROHIBITIONS ON SPECIFIC WEAPONRY

Some nonliterate societies prohibited the use of specific weapons or restricted the way that a particular weapon could be used in combat. For example, on the Small Islands, adjacent to Malekula in the New Hebrides, where conflicts between villages led to ceremonial battles, it was agreed that spears would not be used—only clubs and stones. However, when these same villagers fought with warriors from other islands, there were no restrictions on weapons. When the Kapauku Papuans of western New Guinea met in ritualized battle, "they fought exclusively with bows and arrows, using no hand weapons such as clubs."[3]

Ancient Hindus were recorded in the *Book of Manu* to have prohibited the use of barbed, poisonous, and flaming projectiles. A treaty dating to the late eighth or early seventh century BCE is believed to have prohibited the use of missile weapons—presumably slings and bows and arrows—on the Greek island of Euboea. The Chinese, who invented gunpowder, decided in the tenth century not to use it for warlike purposes. Bans on crossbows in late medieval Europe and on firearms in early modern Japan were prohibitions that sought to protect the social order by insulating the aristocracy from the threat posed by the emergence of lower class military personnel armed with effective weaponry.[4]

Treaty of Zama/Peace of Apamea. When the Second Punic War between Rome and Carthage ended, the victorious Romans sought to make sure that their opponent would not be able to employ elephants in future combat. In the imposed Carthage-Rome [Zama] Treaty of Peace (202 BCE), Carthage's envoys had to agree that "... all the trained elephants in their possession were to be handed over and no more to be trained." Later, in 188 BCE, the victorious Romans stripped King Antiochus of his war elephants. Polybius described the treaty in some detail, noting that the king had to "surrender all the elephants now in Apamea and not keep any in [the] future."[5]

Koran's Prohibition on Use of Fire, 632 CE. According to several accounts, Muslims supposedly prohibited, among other weapons, the use of fire in warfare against other Muslims. Islamic scholar Hamza Yuset contends that later Islamic traditions—based upon the compilation of Muhammad's deeds and sayings after his death in 632—"prohibited using fire as a means to kill another being." Historians have indicated, however, that the early Islamic scholars were often at odds over what were permissible weapons, for despite the Koran's prohibition against the use of fire as a weapon, it did allow its use against nonbelievers. "Perhaps because of bans on poisoning water or air," Adrienne Mayor suggests, "Muslims apparently refrained from adding toxins to their incendiaries, as were common in ancient Chinese and Indian recipes."

During Muhammad's time, petrochemical incendiaries were frequently employed in siege-craft; indeed, in 683, Muslim attackers used catapults to launch burning petroleum upon rival Muslims holding Mecca. Several centuries later, designated Islamic military units employed a terrifyingly effective liquid-fire—especially when fighting the Crusaders.[6]

Lateran Councils Ban Crossbows, 1139. Medieval church leaders, apparently prodded by nobles, barred the use of crossbows in wars among Christians, although their use could be permitted in conflicts with infidels and heretics. Employed by relatively untrained lower-class combatants, often mercenaries, crossbows were among the most lethal weapons of the twelfth century. Since their arrows could achieve considerable accuracy and penetrate armor, and were frequently laced with various toxic or infectious substances, knights and noblemen of the time felt the use of crossbows to be vulgar and unfair.

The Second Lateran Council issued a ban (Canon 29) in 1139: "We forbid under penalty of anathema that the deadly and God-detested art of slingers and archers be in the future exercised against Christians and Catholics." The ban was reaffirmed several times but with limited effect.[7]

King Henry VII/VIII Bans Wheel Locks, 1485. Since firearms might contribute to social disorder, every ruler in Europe restricted their use and availability. In England, for example, laws appeared during the reign of Henry VII (1485–1509), who worried that the wheel lock—the first firearm that used a spark to ignite the powder when a wheel struck a piece of iron—might enhance the power of the lower classes. Thus, Henry VII and Henry VIII both outlawed wheel locks. Henry VIII sought to restrict the possession and use of firearms to the aristocracy. In 1541, an act of Parliament decreed that only nobility and freeholders who received at least £100 from property—some fifty times more income than a freeholder needed to vote in county elections—could possess firearms.

These regulations were easily enforced because it required frequent practice to become proficient in the use of these early firearms. Such activity required powder and shot and constant maintenance by skilled artisans, all of which could only be found in shops regulated by the government.[8]

Japan Restricts Firearms, 1540s. Guns had been introduced by the Europeans in the 1540s and for the next hundred years were widely manufactured and used throughout the nation. After suppressing a Christian rebellion in 1637, Japanese authorities turned away from firearms. The informal abolition of firearms was "an extremely slow series of cutbacks, with no one point at which one might say: At this moment the Japanese gave up guns." With centralization underway and with the army ceasing to purchase firearms, the manufacturing and use of guns disappeared within a century.

Five reasons have been suggested for this policy. First, Japan's large elite warrior class, some 7 to 10 percent of the population, equated the sword with prestige. Second, the Japanese were feared warriors and their islands were most difficult to invade. Third, the Japanese sword—far superior to any Western blade—was seen as "the only embodiment of honor," as its exquisitely crafted handle and guard signaled its owner's rank. The fourth reason was Japan's general rejection of Western ideas—especially Christianity and European business practices. And, perhaps most curious of all, the final reason was the sword's aesthetic value as a far more graceful weapon than a gun.

The arrival of the U.S. Navy's Commodore Matthew Perry and his "black ships" in 1853 near the capital was instrumental in initiating the Meiji Restoration and the reintroduction of modern weapons technology.[9] The new government hired British specialists to assist in creating a new navy, as well as German military experts to help train the new army.

The Hague Prohibition on "Bombing," 1899. There had been free-flying hot-air balloons for the previous 115 years and two attempts to use them as weapons. The Russians in 1812 sent a balloon carrying explosives against Napoleon as his forces advanced on Moscow, and the Austrians in 1849 tried to employ balloons to "bomb" Venice. Neither attempt was successful. In 1899, the delegates to The Hague conference were aware that heavier-than-air vehicles were being developed, but did not know yet what their military use might be. One of the restrictions achieved on July 29, 1899, at the first Hague meeting, prohibited the launching of projectiles and explosives from balloons or by other new methods of similar nature.

Representatives from the lesser states had argued for "an absolute prohibition," but those from the United States, Britain, France, and Germany were opposed to any restrictions. The American delegate, Captain William Crozier, arranged a compromise that limited the prohibition to five years. When the delegates met at The Hague in 1907, France, Germany, Russia, and Italy had begun production of military dirigibles, while Great Britain and the United States had not. America and Britain, consequently, reversed themselves and asked for an extension of the ban but failed.

The ban was rescinded and, four years later, an Italian aircraft dropped the first bombs during the Italo-Turkish War in 1911–1912. The targets were Arab villagers.[10] During World War I, aerial bombardment entered modern warfare. The Hague rules had failed to provide a mechanism that would allow restrictions to stay abreast of advancing weapons technology.

Submarine Protocols, 1922, 1930, 1936. In 1799, the American inventor Robert Fulton tried to persuade Napoleon's Directory to adopt his plans for the submarine *Nautilus*. With a request for a contract, he enclosed an essay on "Observations on the Moral Effects of the *Nautilus* Should It Be Employed with Success" seeking "to defend the submarine as a humane weapon and enhance his reputation as a humane inventor." Viewing a demonstration of the submarine's effectiveness, naval minister Pierre Forfait in rejecting Fulton's proposal concluded that "the *Nautilus* infringed on the laws of war." When a submarine sank a surface ship during the American Civil War, the unconventional attack raised moral and legal issues. The debate, which continued at the 1899 Hague conference, found many naval officers and political leaders convinced of the submarine's utility, and the likelihood of its progressive refinement as an instrument of war. Germany's use of submarines during World War I, believed by some states to be unlawful and immoral, stimulated efforts either to abolish the submarine or to regulate its employment consistent with the existing rules governing naval warfare.

A code of conduct restricting submarine operations was placed in the failed Submarine and Poison Gas Treaty of 1922, but was resurrected and incorporated into the London Naval Treaty of 1930. Part IV of the 1930 London treaty declared that submarines "must conform to the rules of international law to which surface vessels are subject." Thus, "except in the case of persistent refusal to stop … or of active resistance to visit and search, a warship, whether surface vessel or submarine, may not sink or render incapable of navigation a merchant vessel without having first placed passengers, crew, and ship's papers in a place of safety."

The submarine code was to "remain in force without limit of time"; however, when the first London treaty expired in 1936, the code was recast as a separate instrument (a *process-verbal*) and extended by the United States, Great Britain, France, Italy, and Japan to include other sea powers. In all, more than 30 nations, including Germany, agreed to abide by the regulations relating to submarine warfare.

These rules had an ephemeral and controversial existence. They gained legal identity only to become victims of wartime realities with the outbreak of World War II, with Germany gradually, and the United States immediately, choosing to ignore the 1936 protocol. The Nuremberg Tribunal questioned whether Germany's Grand Admiral Erich Raeder and Fleet Admiral Karl Doenitz had violated the protocol. After considerable testimony, the tribunal concluded that— since the British Admiralty had integrated the merchant vessels with its fighting forces and the U.S. Navy had from the first day carried on unrestricted submarine warfare in the Pacific—only Doenitz was guilty. He was not given credit for attempting to create a "rescue zone of immunity" in September 1942, when a U-156 sank the troop ship *Laconia* carrying 1,800 Italian POWs. Immediately, the submarine commander and companion U-boats, approved by Admiral Doenitz, initiated rescue operations; however, the next day a U.S. Army B-24 circled the subs towing lifeboats and flying a white flag and, upon orders, dropped bombs on the U-156. After this episode, Doenitz instructed his U-boats to stop rescue efforts.[11]

Efforts to Ban Aerial Bombing, 1922–1932. The interwar aviation arms control discussions touched upon several areas, but one major focus was defining legitimate targets an aircraft could bomb. This was because urban areas and villages had been indiscriminately bombed during World War I, and national air forces were developing and their strategists were contemplating even more intense bombings in the future.

The Hague Commission of Jurists (1922–1923) initially sought to devise rules on aerial bombing, but faced the persistent vexing issue of civilian and military targets. The final report urged rules that prohibited the bombing of urban areas, but no formal actions followed (see Chapter 5). The issue moved on to the League's Preparatory Commission (1925–1930), which, despite four years of discussions, failed to recommend restrictions on the bombing of civilian targets. In 1927, the German delegate Count von Bernstorff proposed that all aerial bombardment should be prohibited—no offensive weapons could be launched from aircraft, including unpiloted ones. Despite President Herbert Hoover's desire to prohibit bombing, the U.S. representative Hugh Gibson stated during the 1929 debate, that the bombing of civilians was a "complicated and endless problem" and it was impractical to consider it currently. The

French delegate René Massigli also opposed Bernstorff's suggestion, claiming some nations needed bombers for defensive, not offensive purposes; this thereby raised the central—and irresolvable—problem that plagued many arms control proposals at that time and in the future negotiations: how to distinguish between offensive and defensive weapons.

Because of the controversy, the 1930 draft convention of the Preparatory Commission did not mention aerial bombing. Belatedly, on June 22, 1932, Gibson presented Hoover's proposal to abolish all offensive armaments and prohibit aerial bombing to the General Disarmament Conference (1932–1934). Hoover's idea was endorsed by Italy, Germany, and the Soviet Union but was found to be unacceptable by Great Britain, France, and Japan.

Adenauer's Unilateral Declaration, 1954. In Paris on October 23, 1954, the Chancellor of the Federal Republic (West Germany at the time) Konrad Adenauer unilaterally declared that his state would not manufacture weapons of mass destruction. "The Federal Chancellor declares: that the Federal Republic undertakes not to manufacture in its territory any atomic weapons, chemical weapons or biological weapons." It was attached to the Protocols of the 1948 Brussels Treaty of Collaboration and Collective Self-Defence Among Western European States that entered into force on May 6, 1955. At the time, Adenauer did not rule out obtaining nuclear weapons in the future; however, he gradually came to understand that while "nuclear war is possible, ... it is also improbable."

The West German public reacted negatively to nuclear weapons generally, and particularly to having them stationed in their country. In a speech on September 3, 1968, to the Conference of Non-Nuclear States in Geneva, Foreign Minister Willy Brandt reiterated Adenauer's original pledge: "The Federal Government has given an understanding to its allies not to manufacture nuclear weapons and has subjected itself to appropriate international controls. It does not seek any national control over nuclear weapons nor national possession of such weapons."[12]

Certain Conventional Weapons (CCW). On October 1, 1980, the Convention on Prohibitions or Restrictions on the Use of Certain Conventional Weapons which May be Deemed to be Excessively Injurious or to Have Indiscriminate Effects (also known as the "Inhumane Weapons" Convention) concluded in Geneva. The initial Convention was comprised of three Protocols: (I) restricting non-detectable fragmentation weapons; (II) restricting mines, booby traps, and certain other explosive devices; and (III) restricting incendiary weapons. Nations could become party to the Convention after ratifying at least two of the protocols. Later, two other Protocols were added: (IV) restrictions on blinding laser weapons (adopted on October 13, 1995, in Vienna) and (V) setting of obligations and best practices for the clearance of explosive remnants of war (adopted on November 28, 2003, in Geneva). As of 2007, the number of states party to the protocols were: I (102); II (89); III (96); IV (87); and V (35). Some of those countries (including the United States) initially adopted only two of the five protocols, the minimum required of a signatory.

Protocol II was amended in 1996 to extend the restrictions on landmine use to internal conflicts; establishing reliability standards for remotely delivered mines; and prohibiting the use of non-detectable fragments in antipersonnel landmines (APL). The failure of nations to agree to a *total* ban on landmines led to the Ottawa Treaty.

Ottawa Land Mines Convention, 1997. Popular efforts to outlaw APLs gained a major boost with the first Non-Governmental Organizations (NGO) International Conference on Land Mines held at London in May 1993. In 1996, the Organization of American States adopted a resolution that was aimed at "the global elimination of antipersonnel land mines and conversion of the Western Hemisphere into an antipersonnel mine-free zone." The resolution urged the declaration of a moratorium on the production, use and transfer of antipersonnel mines and joining the CCW.

At Ottawa, Canada, in October 1996, the 50 participating nations agreed that "urgent action on the part of the international community to ban and eliminate this type of weapon" was needed. The UN General Assembly endorsed a land-mine ban in December 1996 calling for "an effective, legally binding international agreement to ban the use, stockpiling, production and transfer of antipersonnel land mines with a view to completing the negotiation as soon as possible." One hundred and fifty-five countries endorsed the resolution and the Canadian government hosted a treaty-signing conference for a total ban in December 1997. The convention was signed by 121 nations at Ottawa, Canada in December 1997, with the United States declining. The convention entered into force on March 1, 1999, and, by 2008, 156 countries had joined the treaty.

The United States announced in January 1997 that it would ban the export and transfer of landmines and cap its own inventory at current levels; but wanted the Conference on Disarmament to devise a worldwide ban. The United States argued that the focus should be on eliminating "dumb" mines and, later, unilaterally promised to cease using landmines beyond South Korea by 2003. Moreover, a U.S.-led "Demining 2010 Initiative" hoped to remove all land-mines from at least 64 countries by the year 2010.

At the second "review conference" in September 2000, parties to the convention reported that more than twenty signatories had completed destruction of stockpiled antipersonnel mines, and twenty-three signatories were in the process of destroying their stockpiles. In January 2008, the UN's Mine Action Service reported that since 1999 more than four million antipersonnel mines, one million anti-vehicle mines, and eight million pieces of unexploded munitions had been removed. In 2006 alone, the program cleared more than 450 square kilometers of contaminated land of 217,000 antipersonnel mines. Emphasis on mine risk education reached more than thirty million people in some sixty nations with dramatic results—the annual casualties in 1999 were estimated at 26,000; by 2006 they had been reduced to 5,751. However, thirty-nine nations outside the treaty currently stored more than 160 million antipersonnel mines—the vast majority held by China, Russia, the United States, Pakistan, and India.

Convention on Cluster Munitions, 2008. When the United States, Russia, and other state parties to the Convention on Certain Conventional Weapons foiled efforts to abolish cluster munitions, Norway stated in 2006 that it would seek to obtain a new convention. More than 100 states agreed to a draft treaty, after two weeks of discussions at Dublin, Ireland. States would be able to officially become signatories to the accord in December 2008 and, when 30 states submit ratification documents, it will enter into force.

This accord requires the destruction of all banned cluster munitions within 8 years, and the removal of unexploded cluster munitions from affected areas within 10 years. Parties to the accord may only retain cluster munitions for use during hostilities if they meet certain requirements, such as self-destructive devices that reduce the lingering risks to noncombatants.[13]

POISON AND CHEMICAL/BACTERIOLOGICAL WEAPONS

The customs and traditions of early peoples occasionally banned or restricted the use of poisons. By the end of the medieval period, the prohibition against poison had become a principle of customary international law. In recent times, this principle has been extended to prohibit the use of poison gases and bacteriological/biological agents in warfare. Additionally, chemicals used to create weapons employing lethal "fire"—such as napalm—aroused protests. In 1994, Washington announced that it was unilaterally destroying all of its remaining supply of napalm. Since the 1970s, the United States had stored some 10.4 million kg of the extremely flammable jelly.[14]

Prohibition of Poison. Even before 300 BCE, precedents had emerged leading to generally accepted customs defining certain forbidden "military" usages. Among the prohibited practices was the poisoning of weapons, wells, and food. These prohibitions were acknowledged in different civilizations, although they were not always followed. In India, the *Atharva Veda* (c. 1500–500 BCE) and the Hindu *Laws of Manu* (c. 200 BCE–200 CE) condemned the use of poisoned arrows or fire; but the *Laws* allowed the Brahman rulers to "continually spoil the grass and water" of a foe under siege.

Customs or taboos of some non-literate societies placed prohibitions on poisoned weapons. The Tangale, an ethnic group in North-Eastern Nigeria, for example, poisoned their weapons for hunting elephants, but did not use poison in their warfare. The Nagas, inhabitants of the highland region near the Indian-Burma border, seldom employed poisoned arrows in combat because they thought that it failed to show respect for the opposing warriors. Since they did not recognize noncombatancy, the Nagas might use poisoned arrows on women.[15]

The ancient Greeks and Romans, who engaged in savage warfare, held that the use of poison was a violation of *jus gentium*, the law of nations. (An obscure passage of the *Odyssey* apparently condemned the use of poisoned weapons.) However, this prohibition did not cover the use of smoke and incendiaries, as evidenced by the Spartan siege of Platea (429 BCE) and the Boetian siege of Delium (424/423 BCE). Nor did it prohibit the use of the mysterious "Greek fire," a burning-liquid weapon—the secret of which is still a matter of speculation.

Marcus Tullius Cicero (106–43 BCE) explained the Roman view of the prohibition of using poison in his account, *De Officiis* (On Duty). He notes that Fabius Fabricus and the Roman Senate ordered a deserter, who offered to poison their foe Pyrrhus, be returned to their enemy's camp. "Thus they stamped with their disapproval the treacherous murder even of an enemy who was at once powerful, unprovoked, aggressive and successful." The Koran also restricted Muslim use of poison in warfare. As Islamic scholar Yuset suggests, based on the gathering together of Muhammad's actions and sayings in the seventh century, Islamic tradition "clearly prohibited ... poisoning wells."[16]

Formal decisions to prohibit the use of poisoned weapons began with the Treaty of Strassburg (1675), between the French and Germans. It was incorporated into the "Lieber Code" (1863) which governed the U.S. Army during the Civil War, and was repeated in The Declaration of Brussels (1874), and The Hague declaration on "Laws and Customs of War on Land" (1899). Article LXX of the Lieber Code put it quite succinctly: "The use of poison in any manner, be it to poison wells, or food, or arms, is wholly excluded from modern warfare."[17] Despite occasional violations, the prohibition on the use of poison has remained during the evolution of the law of war through custom, definition, and codification.

The Hague "Poison" Gases Conventions, 1899/1907. Concern that nineteenth-century developments in synthetic chemistry could lead to new weapons prompted the delegates to The Hague Conference of 1899 to ban the use of asphyxiating or "poison" gases. The special Declaration concerning Asphyxiating Gases (July 29, 1899) stated, "The contracting Powers agree to abstain from the use of projectiles the sole object of which is the diffusion of asphyxiating or deleterious gases." A similar pledge was signed at the 1907 Hague Conference. The United States and Great Britain did not sign the special declaration; however, the British later agreed to abide by its terms.

All of the World War I European belligerents were signatories, including Germany, who employed a toxic gas in April 1915. Initially, the Germans did not technically violate The Hague ban for they released chlorine from thousands of 100 kg containers deployed near the enemy's trenches. The British and French immediately retaliated, with the latter apparently the first to employ shells and cartridges to deliver toxic gas. Various toxic gases delivered by "projectiles" became a regular element of battlefield tactics in World War I, but neither side gained any significant military advantage from their usage, although there were roughly a million gas casualties in WWI. The use of toxic agents, therefore, gained a reputation as a dangerous weapon that in the future might be used against civilians as well as combatants.

Shortly after the war, a popular demand arose to prohibit its future use—leading to the Geneva Protocol of 1925.[18]

Versailles Treaty "Poison Gas" Ban, 1919. Article 171 of the imposed Treaty of Versailles prohibited the defeated Germans from having "asphyxiating, poisonous or other gases, and all analogous liquids, materials or devices." Moreover, "their manufacture and importation" was also strictly banned, as well as any "materials specially intended for the manufacture, storage and use of said products or devices."

While there were many confirmed evasions of the Versailles treaty, it appears that there were few clandestine efforts to experiment or produce chemical weapons prior to the mid-1930s—except perhaps some experiments in the Soviet Union.

Washington Treaty on Use of Gases, 1922. An advisory committee to the U.S. delegation warned that future use of toxic gases against cities could result in "the depopulation of large sections of the country" and could threaten the basic elements of civilized society. The five major naval powers at the Washington Conference in 1922 signed a separate pact—reinforcing The Hague 1899 and 1907 pledges—banning all deleterious gases. Unfortunately, this agreement was combined with the restrictions on submarine warfare that the French rejected, and thus killed both endeavors.[19]

Geneva Protocol of 1925. A step universalizing the prohibition against chemical and bacteriological weapons was taken on June 17, 1925. Signatories to the "Protocol for the Prohibition of the Use in War of Asphyxiating, Poisonous, or Other Gases, and of Bacteriological Methods of Warfare," acknowledged that "the use in war of asphyxiating, poisonous or other gases, and of all analogous liquids, materials or devices, has been justly condemned by the general opinion of the civilized world; and ... this prohibition shall be universally accepted as a part of International Law, binding alike the conscience and the practice of nations." The prohibition of bacteriological weapons was added at the urging of the Polish representative, who argued, quite persuasively, that the horrors of bacteriological warfare could surpass those of chemical warfare. (Literally speaking, the term *bacteriological* covered only bacterial agents since microbiological organisms, such as viruses, were unknown in 1925. The 1972 Biological and Toxin Weapons Convention expanded this prohibition.)

If the protocol provided a more comprehensive definition of chemical warfare, it suffered from attached reservations that usually insisted on the right of retaliation; thus, the Geneva Protocol was essentially a "no-first-use" pledge. The protocol allowed a state to douse its own citizens with non-lethal riot control agents, but disagreement arose over whether these could be used in international hostilities. Some nations reserved the right, in limited circumstances, to use riot-control agents on a battlefield, arguing that their use would save lives. Before the outbreak of World War II, 43 nations had ratified the protocol establishing it as "part of customary international law." Among the signatories that initially refusing to ratify the protocol were Japan and the United States—

subsequently Japan ratified the protocol in 1970 and the United States in 1975. By 2007, 134 states had signed the protocol.

During World War II, even though the European warring parties possessed chemical weapons including deadly nerve gases, they were not employed. In all probability, this was due more to the fear of retaliation and prevailing winds than the legal document. A party to The Hague Declaration and the 1925 Protocol, Japan employed chemical agents, anthrax, typhoid, and plague in several attacks after 1937 upon Chinese towns and cities. Doctors in the infamous Japanese Army Unit 731 used Chinese and other prisoners of war, including Americans, in experiments to see how biological agents were spread. After the war, nine Japanese doctors and nurses were convicted of having vivisected eight captured U.S. airmen; however, no senior Japanese official was charged. In fact, the U.S. granted immunity to the head of Unit 731 and several members, in exchange for the extensive records of their germ warfare experiments.[20]

There have been other violations of the protocol. Italy signed in 1928, but it used poison gas against Ethiopia (a party) in 1936. Egypt also signed in 1928, but used poison gas against Yemen (a party) in 1967; and Iraq, a signatory since 1931, used chemical agents in its war with Iran (a party) in the 1980s and Iran, of course, responded in kind. The Communist Chinese and the Soviets charged the United States with employing bacteriological and chemical agents during the Korean War, which American officials vigorously denied. Sheldon Harris summarizes the various allegations, which remain unresolved. Also, Cuba accused the United States of spreading crop and animal diseases, which was also denied by Washington.

"No-First-Use" Gas Policies, 1939, 1943, 1969. At the outbreak of World War II in 1939, Berlin acknowledged Britain's request to abide by the Geneva Protocol. "The German Government will observe during the War the prohibitions which form the subject of the Geneva protocol of June 17, 1925.... She reserves complete freedom of action in the event that the provisions of the protocol are violated on the part of the enemy." Adolf Hitler's personal aversion to gas warfare after his own experience in the trench warfare during WWI, a lack of readiness, and a fear of retaliation prevented Germany from employing this weapon. During the last days of the Third Reich, Hitler apparently ordered its use against the Allies, but "saner minds prevented implementation" of his instructions.[21]

President Franklin D. Roosevelt, responding to reports that the Japanese had used gas against the Chinese, declared on June 5, 1942, that, "if Japan persists in this inhuman form of warfare against China or against any other of the United Nations, such action will be regarded by this Government as though taken against the United States, and retaliation in kind and in full measure will be meted out." On June 8, 1943, Roosevelt stated a no-first-use policy that restricted the United States' freedom of action: "I state categorically that we shall under no circumstances resort to the use of such weapons unless they are first used by our enemies."[22]

With the focus on nuclear weaponry during the early Cold War years, few multilateral attempts were made to deal with chemical/biological (C/B) weapons. On November 25, 1969, President Richard Nixon restated the chemical warfare no-first-use policy. "As to our chemical warfare programs, the United States reaffirms its oft-repeated renunciation of the first use of lethal chemical weapons [and] extends this renunciation to the first use of incapacitating chemicals."[23]

Biological Convention, 1972. Western nations apparently believed the elimination of chemical weapons was a much more difficult problem than abolishing biological weapons (BW); therefore, they believed a less complex BW regime could suffice. This assessment was reflected in the United States' unilateral declaration of November 1969 that it was renouncing bacteriological or biological methods of warfare, was closing all facilities engaged in the production of these agents for offensive purposes, and was destroying its stockpiles of biological weapons and agents. Only research to develop defensive measures would continue—a position that would subsequently again bring up the offensive/defensive issue. Other countries followed suit—Canada, Sweden, and the United Kingdom announced that they had neither biological weapons nor plans to produce them. There was considerable doubt as to effectiveness of BWs on the battlefield that lessened concern at the time.

To supplement unilateral actions, the Soviet Union in March 1971 sent a draft dealing with biological and toxin weapons to the United Nations. The General Assembly endorsed the revised draft, agreed to by Moscow and Washington, in December 1971. President Nixon called it "the first international agreement since World War II to provide for the actual elimination of an entire class of weapons from the arsenals of nations."[24] By 2007, 155 nations had signed the treaty.

The Convention on the Prohibition of the Development, Production and Stockpiling of Bacteriological (Biological) and Toxin Weapons and on Their Destruction (BWC) basically committed the signatories never to develop, produce, stockpile, acquire, or retain microbial or other biological agents or toxins in quantities that have no justification for peaceful purposes. They were not to possess for hostile purposes weapons, equipment, or delivery systems for these agents or toxins. Additionally, the parties were to destroy or convert those weapons to peaceful purposes, and not to transfer any prohibited items in their possession, and to take necessary measures to insure that these provisions were observed. The initial handling of complaints about compliance would take place through consultations among the parties with the ultimate recourse being the UN Security Council. There were also provisions for providing assistance to parties that may be endangered by violations of the convention, and for exchanges of scientific and technical information relating to biological agents.

Later it was learned that the Soviet Union had systematically violated the pact with an elaborate BW research program (see Chapter 9). Meanwhile, South Africa, also a signatory to the BW Convention, had established a secret chemical and germ warfare program that was aimed at apartheid foes. This arsenal consisted of anthrax, botulinum toxin, Ebola, Marburg, and a human immunodeficiency virus—the cause of AIDS. Devices such as poison-tipped umbrellas and a walking stick capable of firing toxic pellets were developed. Chocolates, beer, and sugar also were laced with various agents resulting in the deaths "of many lives." "This paramilitary application of official apartheid policy aimed, quite clearly, at the selective injury or death of native blacks," according to Jacques Richardson, "while leaving the white part of the population untouched: governmental terrorism in a failing state." The program ended in 1994 when Nelson Mandela became president.

In 1975, U.S. congressional investigators turned up a Central Intelligence Agency cache of "pathogens, germ toxins, and biological poisons that were strong enough to sicken or kill millions of people." In violation of President Richard Nixon's orders and the terms of the 1972 pact, the small stockpile containing a wide variety of agents was housed at Fort Detrick, Maryland. During the 1980s, the Reagan administration viewed research on biodefense projects as permissible and funding was substantially expanded. "We are doing research in genetic engineering and related disciplines to understand what's possible," Richard L. Wagoner, an assistant secretary of defense stated. "But it's for the purpose of understanding how to design a defense, not to design an offense." Yet, a narrow line separates biological agents for defense and offense. According to a review of Pentagon research activities between 1980 and 1986, there were "fifty-one projects aimed at making novel pathogens, thirty-two at boosting toxin production, twenty-three at defeating vaccines, fourteen at inhibiting diagnosis, and three at outwitting protective drugs."[25]

Convention on Chemical Weapons, 1993. Following inconclusive bilateral negotiations from 1977 to 1980, a ban on chemical weapons was finally signed in January 1993. By 2007, there were 181 signatories for the Convention that entered into force April 29, 1997. According to Allan Krass, reaching agreement on the "details of the managed access regime was one of the most difficult challenges" of completing the pact. The Convention on Chemical Weapons (CWC) eliminated an entire class of weapons and established the most elaborate verification regime in history. The Organization for the Prohibition of Chemical Weapons was created to collect declarations as to a nation's stockpiles and to oversee their destruction. The organization will also maintain records and make reports to the parties, conduct inspections, and serve as the point of receipt for complaints lodged by one party against another. In April 1997, the U.S. Senate finally granted ratification. As of 2008, the number of nations that were party to the CWC increased from 87 at entry into force to 183 with five states needing ratification and only seven states that have neither signed nor ratified it. It is very near universal membership.

A most complicated arms control measure, the CWC impinges on one of the world's basic industries as well as on sensitive national security interests. Yet, the chemical industry for the most part accepted the terms. The current version of the text contains some 200 pages of detailed provisions for destroying chemical weapons and production facilities, the order of destruction and disposition of discovered war munitions, the criteria for determining toxicity, definitions of "precursors," reports on the production of certain chemicals, and many other details. It also incorporates provisions for assistance and protection against chemical weapons attack, sanctions against violators, and economic and technological development for signatories.

The task of destroying the world's chemical weapons has been full of surprises. For example, in 2005, the Albanian government discovered a hidden bunker containing hundreds of canisters of lethal military chemicals that were purchased from China in the 1970s. Meanwhile, China complained about 700,000 chemical munitions left behind by retreating Japanese forces. France also has a problem as it unearths each year some 30–50 tons of chemical weapons left over from World War I. In February 2008, a cache of WWI chemical shells were removed from a hasty burial area in the midst of what is now an upscale residential area of northwest Washington, DC.

The considerable expense involved in reducing chemical stocks has required several nations to extend the deadlines to complete the required destruction of their chemical arsenals.[26]

OUTLAWING WAR

The decades between world wars witnessed several efforts to eliminate war, often stimulated by discussions arising in the League of Nations. According to Article 12 of the Covenant of the League, members "agree in no case to resort to war" until three months after an award of arbitrators or a decision of the Council and they "will not go to war with any party to the dispute which complies with the recommendations of the report" (Article 15). The interwar efforts to declare wars "illegal" and employ international tribunals to settle differences between nations failed. The Gondra Treaty (1923), ratified by most Latin American states including the combatants, failed to halt the bloody Chaco War (1932–1935), a prolonged conflict between Bolivia and Paraguay. The Argentine Anti-War Pact (1933) also was unable to halt the Chaco War.

Obviously, the Kellogg-Briand Pact failed to halt the outbreak of World War II. An appraisal of the agreement might examine its influence on international law as the Nuremberg Tribunal found the major Axis war criminals guilty of, among other charges, violation of the Kellogg-Briand treaty of which Germany was a signatory state.

The Gondra Treaty, 1923. Drawing on suggestions by Paraguayan statesman M. Gondra, the treaty was formulated at the Fifth Pan American Conference at Santiago, Chile, in May 1923. Formally known as the Inter-American Treaty to Avoid or Prevent Conflicts Between American States, the pact drew upon ideas formulated at The Hague Conferences of 1899 and 1907. The pact had the added obligation that in the event of hostilities, all parties were immediately to renounce the use of force as soon as one of them requested an investigating commission. The Treaty was ratified by all Latin American nations except Argentina.[27]

The Kellogg-Briand Pact, 1928. Also known as the Pact of Paris for the Renunciation of War, the Kellogg-Briand Pact renounced offensive war as "an instrument" of national policy. It called on nations to settle their differences by pacific means. The idea originated with a Chicago lawyer, Salmon O. Levinson, who argued that international law should declare war illegal and a criminal act. While this concept appeared utopian, many opponents of the League's search for collective security, and other demands for political-military commitments, hoped to substitute the movement to outlaw war.

The Kellogg-Briand Pact emerged as the Coolidge administration sought to alter Paris' insistence that its security needed to be enhanced by British or U.S. political-military commitments before France would agree to arms limitations. Secretary of State Frank B. Kellogg's offer to outlaw war rested on the notion that the "moral force" of public opinion would be a sufficient means of enforcement. Acknowledging the virtue of world opinion, French Foreign Minister Aristide Briand was realistic enough to know that the U.S. Senate, the American people, and citizens of most other nations would not employ the necessary military-political power should public opinion fail to end aggression. Critics have condemned the pact for failing to provide any substantive means for enforcement—but, of course, that would probably have meant going to war.

Any reappraisal of the Kellogg-Briand Pact also should take into consideration that it did not abolish "defensive" war, and that the United States and other nations stated various reservations upon signing.[28]

The Argentine Anti-War Pact, 1933. Drafted by Foreign Minister Carlos Saavedra Lamas, the Anti-War Treaty on Non-Aggression and Conciliation was signed by six South American countries at Rio de Janeiro in October 1933, and by all of the American countries at the Seventh Pan-American Conference at Montevideo two months later. A year later, Lamas presented the Anti-War Pact to the League of Nations where it was well received and signed by eleven countries.

The pact offered four basic propositions: (1) the renunciation of war; (2) a pledge to use means of pacific resolution in all cases; (3) a pledge to remain neutral and present a united front with other neutrals should war break out; and (4) non-recognition of the victors' gains—"Victory gives no rights."[29]

Japan Outlaws War, 1947. After World War II, Japan was totally disarmed and adopted a "peace constitution" that unilaterally renounced participation in any future war, and spelled out a unique form of neutralism. Article 9 declared "the Japanese people forever renounce war as a sovereign right of the nation and the threat or use of force as a means of settling international disputes. In order to accomplish the aim of the preceding paragraph, land, sea, and air forces, as well as other war potential, will never be maintained. The right of belligerency of the state will not be recognized."

Continuing broad public support for Article 9 can be viewed as both as a tacit repudiation of Japan's past aggressive policies and as a means of preventing the return to power of those, civilian and military, who might seek a militaristic society. At the urging of the United States during the Korean War, nevertheless, Tokyo had reestablished a limited self-defense capability. Since the 1970s, Japan has progressively expanded the size and capability of its Self-Defense Forces (SDF).

The Japanese public has acquiesced in a gradual shift away from a narrow interpretation of the Article 9. In the 1980s, the Nakasone government agreed to defend the sea approaches to Japan out to 1,000 nautical miles toward the Philippines and Guam, upgrade its defenses to interdiction of Soviet long-range bombers and to participate in the Reagan administration's Strategic Defense Initiative (SDI). Responding to a subsequent threat, since 2002, of North Korean ballistic missiles and possible nuclear warheads, Tokyo dramatically increased its missile defense program. Japan has launched satellites via ballistic missiles that could be adapted to carry nuclear weapons. It relies more on nuclear power than any other country except France and Germany and subsequent plans to reprocess plutonium and construct breeder reactors for a new generation of plutonium-fueled power plants have produced more criticism outside Japan than inside.

Since the mid-1990s, the Japanese appeared to be moving toward the idea—increasingly suggested by younger politicians—that Japan should become a "normal" power with the freedom to maintain multipurpose defense forces and participate in international peacekeeping activities. A small number of self-defense personnel did join the postwar rehabilitation efforts in Iraq during 2003–2004, and questions arose as to whether it would accelerate that nation's break from pacifism.[30]

For the various forms of negotiations employed, the several types of verification adopted and problems of compliance or noncompliance, see Part II.

4

Regulating Arms Manufacture, Trade, and Traffic

National and international attempts to restrict the traffic in weaponry—that included ammunition, arms, and, later, delivery systems—have been undertaken throughout history, seeking to achieve a variety of political, military, and economic goals. The two most prominent reasons for controlling this activity were to restrict actual or potential foes from obtaining specific arms, and to restrict the spread of new and sophisticated weapons technologies, including the knowledge to produce them. In both ancient and modern times several different unilateral and multilateral approaches—such as embargoing arms shipments, regulating arms manufacturing and sales, and preventing weapons technology diffusion—were employed to accomplish these goals. Some attempts were successful, some partially so, and some failed.

"The ability to buy and sell weapons has almost been considered by states to be a sovereign right," political scientists Keith Krause and Mary K. MacDonald have written. "This, coupled with the uneven process of military technology innovation and diffusion (which produces gaps in the weaponry available to different states), generates a constant struggle between the military haves and have-nots to maintain or improve their relative position." Consequently, "the same set of forces that gave rise to the arms trade also generated attempts from the beginning to regulate and control it."[1]

Early attempts to curtail the arms traffic usually rested on a state's ability to curb its own tradesmen through licenses, embargoes, and other internal restraints. One can imagine that illicit trade, to varying degrees, took place depending upon the state's willingness and ability to prohibit the traffic. There were a few early formal multilateral attempts at curtailing the arms traffic; however, during the Middle Ages some Christian nations of Europe informally banned selling arms to the "infidel" Turks. When these understandings were periodically broken, their leaders expressed outrage but, apparently, no sanctions were imposed.

The development of cannon and firearms, during 1400 to 1650, accelerated the arms trade and, at the same time, intensified efforts to control it. These weapons were produced wherever sufficient concentrations of technological know-how, raw materials and market demand existed. Technological innovations meant that differences in the quality of weapons had emerged and political officials quickly became sensitive to the problems posed by an uncontrolled arms trade. They recognized that even more important than restricting the sale of arms was preventing the diffusion of the new weapons technology. Consequently, three types of unilateral national regulations appeared, usually involving restrictions on exports of arms and technology.

1. Some restrictions were aimed at controlling exports in order to retain the state's limited stock of weapons. France, Spain, and Portugal, for example, instituted stringent regulations on arms exports because of their chronic shortage of weapons.
2. Other measures were designed to maintain the state's technological advantages. With new manufacturing techniques, *surplus* production became a problem. Trade in arms might be permitted; however, there was fear that the transfer of the new techniques could strengthen one's competitors. This concern, by such leading producers such as Milan, Liège, and England, resulted in severe penalties for the transfer of such information.
3. The final type of controls, seeking to prevent the arming of a potential or actual foe, regulated arms sales to warring or adversarial states.

In addition to unilateral efforts, there were a few examples of temporary multilateral restraints.

The modern era, as indicated below, often featured unilateral or multilateral embargoes on specified weapons and munitions designed to restrict the flow of weapons across borders, as well as unilateral attempts by states to regulate their own arms exports. In addition to the reasons mentioned above, these activities were also aimed at reducing the availability of the implements of war, thus lessening a state's ability to engage in aggressive military actions. These efforts usually involved restrictions on the sale or transfer by either private parties or governments of specific weapons, munitions, and delivery systems. It might also seek to restrict or prohibit the manufacture of various weapons either by private parties or governments.

Great Britain passed the Exportation of Arms Act in 1900, for example, thereby allowing officials "to prohibit the export of arms and war materials ... to any specific country or place whenever necessary to prevent such materials from being used against the forces of Great Britain or her allies." Using this broad authority, London embargoed arms to China during the Boxer Rebellion. In other efforts to curtail civil strife, U.S. Presidents Theodore Roosevelt and Woodrow Wilson embargoed arms exports to the Dominican Republic in 1905 and to Mexico in 1912. France, along with other European suppliers, used restrictions on loans to slow or halt foreign arms imports—such was the case during the tense relationship between Argentina and Chile in 1902 (see Chapter 1).

Following World War I, there were several international attempts to control arms trafficking. These largely unsuccessful activities included imposed restraints in the peace treaties following the war, negotiations on multilateral treaties sponsored by the League of Nations, coordinated—but not negotiated—embargoes on arms transfers to specific war zones, and national efforts to regulate arms production and export policies. Most efforts explicitly addressed the transfer of weapons themselves, but some also attempted to control the transfer of machinery and materials that could be used to produce arms or to impose international restrictions on arms production.

One reason for the difficulty in placing controls on the arms trade after World War II was the absence of any consensus on the nature of the "problem" to be solved. To begin, given the tensions raised by the Cold War, there was disagreement over whether the arms trade was a global problem that could only be tackled with broad international treaties to restrict the transfer of certain types of weapons or a regional problem directly connected with particular conflicts. Most analysts agreed that arms transfers should be evaluated in their specific regional context—for example, transferring advanced fighter aircraft might seem "normal" in the Middle East, yet be seriously destabilizing in Latin America. The idea of discriminatory controls, however, had difficulty in obtaining support. As the sale of arms was often a test of a patron-client relationship, suppliers were unwilling to discriminate between clients on the grounds that refusing to supply an ally with weapons that another nation, friend or foe, had already received would be a major diplomatic and political snub. Likewise, there was no agreement over whether the arms traffic contributed to regional conflicts or whether it was merely a symptom of regional tensions, in which case the underlying insecurities needed to be addressed first.

There were also different justifications for controlling the arms trade, none of which were shared by all suppliers and recipients. Perhaps the broadest justification was the desire to make war less likely, or less destructive should it occur, by restricting the volume and sophistication of transferred weapons. But arms transfers have been often justified on the grounds that possessing the means to make war makes war less likely by creating a military balance or stalemate between potential foes.[2]

The Non-Proliferation Treaty (1968) emerged during the Cold War to become the cornerstone of a regime—including nuclear test bans, nuclear weapon–free zones, and International Atomic Energy Agency (IAEA)—that sought to prevent the manufacture and transfer of nuclear weapons and their technology. The Vienna-based IAEA was created in 1957—as the coordinating body for President Eisenhower's Atoms for Peace project—to promote and safeguard peaceful uses of atomic energy, while maintaining a system of international safeguards aimed at preventing nuclear materials from being diverted to military uses.

The Cold War, and the decades after, has witnessed a proliferation of multilateral export control groups, beginning with the secretive Coordinating Committee (1949–1994), designed to restrict the proliferation or diffusion of various weaponry and technology. They include a Nuclear Suppliers Group (1971–), established in London, to further ensure that nuclear materials, equipment, and technology would not be used in weapons production. Also, the Missile Technology Control Regime, (1987–) restricts transfer of ballistic missiles, the Wassenaar Arrangement (1996–) focuses on conventional weaponry, and the Proliferation Security Initiative (2003–) interdicts shipments of unconventional weapons.

What follows is a representative, chronological sampling, together with a brief narrative description, of the treaties and agreements that demonstrated the historical lineage of regulating arms manufacture, trade, and traffic.

ANCIENT-MEDIEVAL WORLD

Attempts to reduce ancient people's ability to wage war by imposing formal restraints on war-marking capacity were minimal. One known example is the ban on iron working and indirectly restricting the possession of iron weapons, which was imposed in the eleventh century BCE on the Israelites by the Philistines. According to 1 Samuel 13: "No blacksmith was to be found in the whole of Israel, for the Philistines were determined to prevent the Hebrews from making swords and spears. The Israelites had to go down to the Philistines for their plowshares, mattocks, axes, and sickles to be sharpened.... So when war broke out none of the followers of Saul and Jonathan had either sword or spear; only Saul and Jonathan carried arms." However, the primitive nature of ancient Near Eastern weaponry, primarily cutting and concussion weapons, and the rudimentary technology and resources necessary to produce such weapons, made it difficult to impose a prohibition for any length of time.

During the Roman Imperial period, arms production was controlled by the state, and no interstate arms trade existed. The laws of the Roman Empire forbade any transfer of arms to "barbarians." Rome also sought to employ unilateral arms control measures, most notably by limiting the military capacity of less economically developed peoples beyond the Roman frontiers, through strict export controls on products such as iron and bronze that were valuable in producing arms and armor.

The earliest documented regulations restricting arms traffic date from Charlemagne's era (768–814). The Franks sought to maintain their superior military position by prohibiting the export of Frankish armor that was much in demand across Europe. Later, the struggle during the Crusades for supremacy in the Balkans and eastern Mediterranean, saw attempts by Christian rulers to restrict the transfer of weapons to Muslims. In 971, the Doge of Venice banned the sale of arms to the Saracens, who were constantly battling various Balkan rulers.

The Third Lateran Council (1179) extended the prohibition on the sale of arms, ships, and material for weapons—such as iron—to the Saracens, on pain of excommunication or imprisonment. The Fourth Lateran Council (1215), the General Council of Lyon (1245), and Popes Innocent III and Benedict XI repeated this ban. Under pressure from the Church, Venice and Genoa, who had a brisk trade with Egypt, also prohibited their citizens from transporting arms to the "infidels."[3]

EARLY NATIONAL STATES

The political and military rivalries of competing European states between the tenth and fifteen centuries prompted new unilateral and bilateral restrictions on the trade in arms, as medieval religious injunctions were slowly replaced by agreements between secular rulers. The cooperative British and Portuguese embargos were indicative of this change. As manufacturers rarely had a surplus of weapons, since they responded largely on orders for various rulers, there was little urgency for systematic regulations of, or restrictions on, the arms market.

British and Danish Restraints, 1315–1487. Here are three of the more prominent examples of these controls. The English King, Edward II, engaged with the rebellious Scots, banned English and foreign suppliers in 1315 from selling weapons to Scotland. In an early example of a series of negotiated bilateral restraints, Edward III of England obtained an agreement (1370) with Flanders, Bruges, and Ypres to prevent the sale of arms and military materials to his foes. The initial pact stipulated, "that none of the subjects of the Count of Flanders will bring, or will have brought, by sea, any arms, artillery or supplies for the aid and comfort of the enemies of the King of England."[4]

While Denmark was at war with Sweden (1460–1487), the Danes negotiated a similar agreement with the Hanseatic cities to ban arms exports to the Swedes.

French, Spanish, and Portuguese Regulations, 1454–1572. Despite repeated attempts to create a robust domestic arms industry, France suffered from a shortage of armaments until the seventeenth century. The government, meanwhile, virtually banned the export of arms, as noted in its 1572 regulation that incorporated previous restrictions:

> Because the founding [i.e., casting] of cannon and ball and the gathering and manufacture of the materials for gunpowder are a sovereign right, belonging to the King alone for the safeguard and defence of the realm, "no subject whatsoever was to make or seek to sell such war material without license from those deputed to act" in the interest of the prince and of the public good.[5]

Spain had adopted similar restrictions in 1488 to prevent external sales of military equipment, including cannons, handguns, crossbows, and armor. These regulations were altered in 1570 to permit exports, only if previous royal orders for arms had been fulfilled. Because of London's weak export regulations,

France and Spain used various means to import English cannon. Portugal too confronted serious shortages of weapons, and from the fifteenth to the seventeenth centuries relied on imports to meet its needs. In part because of its diminished stocks, Portugal gladly endorsed a 1454 papal injunction banning the exportation of weapons to "infidels."

The migration of skilled workers posed a threat to several manufacturing communities. Milan and Liège, for example, repeatedly placed legal restrictions on such migrations, even threatening imprisonment, but with little success. When some of their military craftsmen migrated to Russia and refused to return home, the Poles and Livonians even executed a few. German and Southern European states, however, did not attempt to halt the migration of workers who supplied technical knowledge to those nations, such as Turkey and Hungary, which possessed limited local manufacturing capabilities.

When England did impose controls, its restrictions extended beyond arms and technological transfer, to the limiting of local weapons production for export. After the Privy Council was told that the export of guns from England ensured that their foe's ships were better armed than English vessels, Elizabeth I in 1574 restricted gun production to the amount needed "for the only use of the realm," and imposed heavy fines on unauthorized exports.[6]

Anti-Russian Arms Embargo, 1558–1583. An early example of multilateral controls was the attempt by Northern European states—especially Poland, Livonia, the Hanseatic League, and, to a lesser extent, England—to prevent arms from reaching Ivan IV (the Terrible), as he sought a Russian foothold on the Baltic. The perceived threat to Europe was summed up in an oft-quoted letter from the Duke of Alba to the Frankfurt Diet in 1571. In this letter, he asked for a ban on the sale of weapons to Ivan IV because, "if one day the Muscovites succeed in acquiring the military discipline and methods of Europe, they will pose a danger for all of Christendom."[7]

Colonial Americas. Although serious questions have been raised about the advantage of primitive European firearms over bows and arrows, attempts were made to prevent the trading of guns to the Indians. These measures often could be found in formal edicts issued by European monarchs and in colonial legislation. The Spanish and initially the French maintained a policy of not trading guns to the Indians.

In 1622, a proclamation by King James I of England complained that:

Wherefore, having received certaine information of many and intolerable abuses offered by sundry interlopers, irregular and disobedient persons ... [who] did not forebeare to barter away to the Savages, Swords, Pikes, Muskets, Fowling peeces, Match, Powder, Shot, and other warlike weapons, and teach them the use thereof; not only to their owne present punishment [others of them being shortly after slain by the same Savages, who they had so taught, and with the weapons which they had furnished them withal] but also hazard of the lives of Our good subjects already planted there.

The proclamation continued with a prohibition on the trade in such weapons under "pain of Our high indignation," and established penalties such as confiscation and forfeitures.[8]

In Virginia during 1619, one of the initial pieces of legislation that was passed by the House of Burgesses decreed, "no man do sell or give any Indians any piece of shott, or pouder, or any other armes offensive or defensive upon paine of being held a traitor to the colony & of being hanged." Subsequently, Connecticut and Massachusetts passed laws prohibiting Indians from possessing guns; while Rhode Island, for example, rejected such a ban. However, the French, the Spanish and even some British traders, undercut the colonial efforts to keep arms out of the hands of Indians. Some colonial governments in trafficking arms sought to make a distinction between friendly and hostile Indians with at best modest success. In the American-Russian Convention of 1824 the parties agreed to prohibit the sale of "fire-arms, other arms, powder, and munitions of war of every kind" to natives on the Northwest coast of North America.[9] The prohibitions of arms sales to Indians persisted in the United States well past the Civil War with little success.

THE NINETEENTH CENTURY

Embargoes played a major role in several efforts to control arms shipments during the late eighteenth and early nineteenth centuries. At the outbreak of the American Revolution, for example, London persuaded other European nations to ban the export of arms and ammunition to the colonies, but with little success. France provided substantial quantities of arms to the American forces. Most belligerents also imposed arms restrictions during the Napoleonic wars. Interest in restricting the arms trade grew slowly during the following decades, as major suppliers struggled to gain control over the weapons traffic.

British-Spain Arms Transfer Pact, 1814. Both London and Madrid were concerned with the spreading rebellion in the Americas against Spanish authorities. The British wanted this unfortunate situation to "cease, and the Subjects of those Provinces" to obey "their lawful Sovereign." To assist in bringing the rebels to heel, London agreed, "to take the most effectual measures" to prevent its merchants "from furnishing Arms, Ammunition, or any other warlike article" to the insurgents.

Russian-American Convention, 1824. In the agreement between Russia and the United States regarding joint occupation of a portion of the northwest coast of North America, the parties attempted to prevent Indian attacks upon their settlements. The article that defined trade arrangements with indigenous peoples declared, "fire-arms, other arms, powder, and munitions of war of every kind, are always to be excepted from the same commerce permitted: the two powers engage, reciprocally, neither to sell, nor suffer them to be sold, to the natives by their respective citizens and subjects."[10]

Brussels Act of 1890. The Brussels Act was the first significant multilateral agreement for the purpose of controlling the arms trade. The act or convention, designed to suppress the slave trade and to restrict the import of arms into Africa, was signed by 13 European states, the United States, Persia, Zanzibar, and the Congo Free State. The link between the illegal slave trade and the arms trade was established by Article 8, which declared that experience had shown "the pernicious and preponderating part played by firearms in operations connected with the slave trade as well as internal wars between the native tribes." The arms traffic was substantial: more than 100,000 firearms a year were imported along the East coast of Africa (Zanzibar and Kenya), while just prior to the Brussels conference, 600,000 rifles were being readied for shipment to Africa.

The Act prohibited the importation of firearms—especially accurate weapons—as well as powder and ammunition into the area between the 20th parallel North and the 22nd parallel South. This covered an area extending from the mid-Saharan desert to present day Namibia and Zimbabwe, including the coasts and islands of Africa. Problems with the agreement arose because its geographic demarcation did not correspond to existing frontiers, and thus, made enforcement difficult. It also was found difficult to define and enforce the Act's distinction between advanced—breech loading, rifled, percussion shells—and primitive weapons. Further limiting the Act's effectiveness was that suppliers such as Sweden and the United States failed to ratify it. A continent-wide, total ban on firearms imports might have been less difficult to manage.

Opposition to even the Act's limited application was substantial. However, the British public, which firmly linked the arms trade to slavery, pressured London for an international commitment in support of the convention with widespread meetings and protests. This was an early example of public influence on the formulation of arms control policy.

Despite not having any verification or enforcement powers, the Brussels Act did somewhat restrain the importation of arms into Africa, especially into interior and sub-Saharan regions. In some areas, such as Ethiopia, Djibouti, and Somalia, however, control measures were only weakly applied. It did, however, stimulate *national* legislation to control the colonial arms trade, and led to several regional joint efforts—between Italy and Britain in Somalia; Germany, Italy, and Britain in the Congo Basin; France, Italy, and Britain in the Horn of Africa—to restrict the import of arms. Also, Egypt moved to control export of arms to neighboring regions. Most importantly, the Act laid the basis for post–World War I initiatives to control the arms trade.[11]

INTERWAR YEARS, 1919–1939

Even though the decision to buy or sell weapons has been considered by nations to be a sovereign right, it is not true—although widely believed—that before World War II, arms were traded as freely as other commodities. In fact, most restrictions on the arms trade took the form of unilateral national regulations prohibiting the export of weapons or materials of war—"contraband"— for various reasons. Only for relatively brief periods has the arms trade been uncontrolled.

The initial efforts for international control of the arms trade appeared in the League of Nations Covenant and in the imposed peace treaties. Article 8, paragraph 5, of the Covenant stated, "the manufacture by private enterprise of munitions and implements of war is open to grave objections." Article 23, paragraph 4, of the Covenant entrusted members of the League "with the general supervision of the trade in arms and ammunition with the countries in which the control of this traffic is necessary in the common interest." But there were few examples of successful formal bilateral or multilateral international agreements to control the arms trade during these two decades.

Allied Peace Treaties with Central Powers, 1919–1920. The Allied-imposed treaties following World War I with Germany (Versailles, Article 170), Austria (St. Germain, Article 134), Hungary (Trianon, Article 118), Turkey (Sévres, Article 175) and Bulgaria (Neuilly, Article 81) contained similar restrictions dealing with arms trade. Each nation was explicitly prohibited "the importation ... of arms, munitions and war material of all kinds ... [and] the manufacture for foreign countries and the exportation of arms, munitions and war material."

It was initially hoped that these harsh restrictions would be combined with a broader multilateral pact that regulated international arms traffic; however, the attempts at a general agreement failed.

St. Germain Convention, 1919. The Convention for Control of the Trade in Arms and Ammunition was an ill-starred attempt to establish comprehensive controls of arms transfers as a supplement to the Versailles Peace Treaty and the League of Nations Covenant. The Allies' immediate objective was to prevent the large supply of weaponry existing at the end of the war from reaching undesirable groups. Based on the provisions of the 1890 Brussels Act, the St. Germain Convention called for national licensing and publicity of arms exports under the supervision of the League. It never gained much support as smaller nations felt it discriminated against them, but most significantly, Washington refused to endorse the convention on the grounds that it conflicted with the Monroe Doctrine and the United States' traditional laissez-faire approach to private business.[12]

China Arms Traffic Convention, 1919. Twelve nations agreed initially to restrict arms exports to the various warring factions in China, in an attempt to bring the disastrous civil strife to an end and to help establish a viable central government. The U.S. Minister to Peking, Paul S. Reinsch, initiated the talks with representatives of other nations aimed at stopping arms importation. When the Japanese suspended further arms shipments in March 1919, the diplomatic corps in Peking adopted an embargo and called upon the weak Chinese government's Customs Service to enforce it. The American and British diplomats who pressed the embargo, as historian Noel Pugach put it, attempted unsuccessfully to marry idealism with realism.

Weapons were supplied not only by the Soviet Union and the supposedly restricted Germany—two major non-signatories—but by France, the United States, Britain, Denmark, Norway, and Japan. The agreement was marred by endless disputes over definitions of armaments and war materials, with "military aircraft transferred in the guise of commercial craft and explosives as industrial chemicals." The embargo remained in effect until 1929, but after 10 fruitless years, hostilities continued to rage unabated and the pact was dissolved because of the numerous evasions. Pugach argues that for all its many faults, it should not be regarded as a total failure because it did discourage a more massive flow of weaponry into China.

Other observers, however, believe that the embargo "turned into a complete fiasco so much so that it appears to have produced widespread cynicism which may in turn have affected subsequent attempts elsewhere."[13]

Geneva Traffic Convention, 1925. The convention to control the International Trade in Arms, Munitions, and Implements of War grew out of continuing League discussions. It reintroduced a system of national licensing and provided transparency to national arms trafficking; but without the verification system of the St. Germain Convention. Again, "the nonproducers of arms objected, noting that their arms acquisitions, mostly from foreign sources, would be monitored while those of the producers would not."

The only accomplishment emerging from these negotiations was the League's *Armaments Year Book.* This annual provided important information on the interwar weapons trade, but it suffered from underreporting by some nations and lack of data on major weapons systems. Supporters hoped that by highlighting major arms dealers, international public opinion would inhibit their activities.

Chaco War Embargo, 1934. The 1932–1935 Chaco War between Bolivia and Paraguay was the subject of a series of unsuccessful League resolutions and conciliation efforts. At the onset of the conflict, at least 30 nations announced support for an arms embargo but, without any mechanism to enforce or regulate the arms traffic, there were wholesale violations. International arms cartels sought to evade the embargo and those governments that endorsed the embargo failed to stop their shipments. Even so, the embargo may have had some influence on bringing the two parties to a settlement, although both nations had reached the point of fiscal and military exhaustion.

Overall, however, efforts to fulfill the intent of the embargo proved difficult to coordinate. Perhaps the most significant outcome of this misadventure was that it established a precedent for a multilateral embargo to be used as a means of coercion.

Sino-Japanese and Italo-Ethiopian Embargoes. In both conflicts, the aggressor was a great power, able either to circumvent restrictions or to bring other political interests into play that weakened the resolve of arms exporters to implement an embargo. In the Sino-Japanese conflict (1931), an arms embargo was among the many solutions repeatedly discussed to halt or signal disapproval with the Japanese aggression in Manchuria. Britain imposed a temporary embargo in 1933, but few other states followed suit. None of the initiatives taken ameliorated the conflict.

During the Italo-Ethiopian War (1934–1936), some 50 members of the League sought to prohibit the export of arms and ammunition to Italy. Most active member states participated in the sanctions, but it had little impact since Italy produced sufficient arms itself. President Franklin D. Roosevelt's embargo proclamation (1935) failed to discriminate between aggressors and victims, thus the result was beneficial to Italy and damaging to Ethiopia. While Ethiopia received a small amount of arms and ammunition from France and Sweden, it was not sufficient to influence the outcome. More damaging to Italy would have been an oil embargo and closing of the Suez canal to belligerents; however, mounting British and French concerns over the intentions of Nazi Germany, and their hope to gain Italy as an ally, rendered such considerations moot.[14]

Spanish Civil War, 1936–1939. Switzerland and the United States initially imposed arms embargoes together with most Latin American countries, except Mexico. In September 1936 signatories of the Nonintervention Convention created a nine-member working group (the Committee) comprising the three countries bordering Spain—France, Portugal, and Britain (at Gibraltar)—and six European arms-producing nations, Belgium, Czechoslovakia, Germany, Italy, Sweden, and the Soviet Union.

The Committee was to investigate reports of arms smuggling and other violations, and devise the means to prevent further foreign intervention. From the beginning, the Committee confronted a dilemma. Information concerning arms shipments abounded, but the Committee sidestepped the issue by barring almost everyone in Spain from presenting evidence of violations. To present evidence of German and Italian activities to the Committee dominated by Britain and France, according to Gerald Howson, "would lead to a head-on collision with the dictators and ruin any chance of reaching the understanding hoped for. If the Committee did its work honestly, therefore, it would not lower tension but heighten it. On the other hand, unless it investigated violations it could not propose measures to prevent their recurrence."

Thus, Germany and Italy delivered men and material for General Francisco Franco's forces directly to Nationalist ports that according to Committee rules could not be reported. The Republicans obtained their arms and men from either the Soviet Union via the Baltic or Black Sea, or by crossing the Spanish frontier from France. These were reported; however, Soviet aid never came close to balancing the equation. Both of these routes "could be easily watched and reported to the Committee under the same rules."

Because "unidentified" (Italian) submarines sunk merchant ships carrying supplies to Republican Spain, the agreement also restricted the deployment of these vessels in the Mediterranean to a specific area. Britain and France had the right to patrol the area and attack any submarines discovered in the prohibited zone. Again, the agreement proved ineffective since Britain and France, despite frequently locating submarines, refused to exercise their enforcement obligations.

What followed, as Gerald Howson has written, was called "the farce of Non-Intervention" as the conservative British and French governments inhibited or failed to protect arms shipments to the Republicans. Political factors ruled out an even-handed functioning of the convention because the two "enforcers" hoped to gain Italy as an ally. The one-sided application of the Non-Intervention pact substantially influenced the outcome of the conflict in favor of Franco and the fascists.[15]

POST–WORLD WAR II

Measures to restrict or control the international arms trade, with the exception of the nuclear nonproliferation pact, only gradually assumed prominence since for nearly five decades global affairs were largely dominated by the Cold War. While several partial proposals were offered, they found few supporters and did virtually nothing to halt the trade or transfer of arms. "Yet the global arms trade has arguably played as large a role in post-1945 world politics (in terms of wars fought and lives lost)," professor Krause has written, "as the nuclear arms race between the superpower blocs, and the change since 1945 in the 'international military system' has been unprecedented."

Three significant trends caused the arms trade to expand from some $12 billion in 1963 to more than $50 billion annually. First, the rivalry between the United States and the Soviet Union resulted in an enormous transfer of weaponry to their European allies in the 1950s and, after 1955, to clients in developing countries. Second, the rise of nationalism and the decolonization resulted in the newly independent African and Asian states seeking to create modern military forces. Third, the European arms industries, rebuilt to produce advanced weaponry, needed to export large numbers of weapons to maintain themselves.[16]

Since international accords to control the arms trade were difficult to obtain, greater emphasis was placed on national control systems. Also, the UN levied arms embargoes specifically targeting certain states or regions in an attempt to alter their behavior.

Tripartite Declaration, 1950. The first postwar regional arms control system was the 1950 Declaration by Britain, the United States, and France that sought to regulate arms transfers in the eastern Mediterranean. The Near Eastern Arms Coordinating Committee (NEACC) sought to regulate arms deliveries to the new state of Israel and its Arab neighbors. Since these nations were then the basic arms suppliers to the region, they arranged their arms deliveries with a view toward stabilizing the region.

The Tripartite pact had two fatal flaws: it was a Western supplier arrangement deeply resented by the Arab Middle Eastern countries and it excluded potential suppliers from the Communist bloc. Consequently, when the Soviet Union brokered the 1955 Czechoslovakian-Egyptian arms deal, the informal arrangement collapsed. Within a few years, Syria, Iraq, and Egypt were purchasing Soviet arms and a regional arms race was underway with Western nations providing arms to Israel.

Acknowledging that the idea behind the 1950 agreement had merit, between 1956 and 1958 the Soviet Union offered to join with the Tripartite powers in regulating delivery of arms to the Middle East, and later linked this proposal to the withdrawal of foreign troops from the region. The Western powers found the proposals unacceptable. After the 1967 war, the United States suggested that arms shipments to the Middle East be reported to the United Nations, as a prelude to reaching an understanding "that the arms-supplying nations will not themselves be responsible for a major renewal of an arms race in the Middle East." A similar goal was reiterated in 1971, but no progress on limiting arms transfers to the region materialized.

For some analysts, the 1979 Camp David accords constitute a successful case of regulating arms transfers to enhance regional security. This arrangement depended less on the restriction of arms transfers than on Washington's willingness to maintain the balance of forces.[17]

United Nations Arms Embargoes. The UN has levied several "embargoes" against specific states. The arms embargo against South Africa, mandated in 1963 by Security Council Resolution 181, was noteworthy for urging member nations to halt the sale and shipment of all arms, ammunition, and military vehicles to South Africa. British officials supported the embargo, accepting a considerable financial loss for their arms industry, and believed French and Swiss weapons merchants were profiting from their sacrifice. Resolution 182 expanded the embargo to include equipment and materials for the manufacture and maintenance of arms. In 1966, a similar embargo was instituted against Rhodesia. The South African embargo was made mandatory in 1977 (Resolution 418), and renewed in 1984 (Resolution 558). South Africa's military continued to strengthen during the initial phase of the embargo due, in part, to an accelerated local arms industry and the licensing for internal manufacturing of specific weaponry. Thus, its effectiveness was, at best, mixed.

Since the end of the Cold War, the United Nations has been actively involved in additional arms embargoes. During the Iraq-Kuwait conflict (1990–1991), several Resolutions (661, 687, and 700) imposed an arms embargo against Iraq. Transfers of weapons to Yugoslavia were prohibited under Resolution 713 (September 25, 1991), in the hope it would lead to a ceasefire ending the civil war. The UN ban supported the European Community's self-imposed arms embargo. To end the Cambodian civil war, the Paris Conference on Cambodia (October 23, 1991) called for "an immediate cessation of all outside military assistance to all Cambodian parties" (Article 10). The UN Transitional

Authority in Cambodia (UNTAC) would supervise the ban. United Nations Resolution 733 (January 23, 1992) that called for a suspension of arms deliveries was an attempt to find an end to the civil war in Somalia. Finally, Security Council Resolution 748 (March 31, 1992) prohibited the exportation of arms and military equipment to Libya. This measure sought to persuade Libya to hand over two accused terrorists accused of destroying a Pan American airliner over Lockerbie, Scotland, in December 1988.

United Nations Resolution 1718, drafted by the United States and Japan in 2006, prohibited "the transfer to and from North Korea of nuclear, chemical or biological weapons; their means of delivery (ballistic missiles); and related materials."[18]

UN Arms Transfer Register. On December 9, 1991, the UN General Assembly by a vote of 150–0 formally established a Register of Conventional Arms. The UN resolution declared that the objective of the register was "to prevent the excessive and destabilizing accumulation of arms, including conventional weapons." In April 1993, the UN opened the register for nations to voluntarily report their arms exports and imports in seven major weapons categories.[19]

Inter-American Convention, 1999. This unprecedented regional convention grew out of a 1997 Organization of American States (OAS) resolution seeking the formal advance notification of arms acquisitions. Nineteen countries, including the United States, signed the Inter-American Convention on Transparency in Conventional Weapons Acquisitions at the 29th Regular Session of the Organization of American States General Assembly. By 2007, there were 12 parties to the convention that entered into force November 21, 2002; however, 8 others had signed but not ratified, including the United States. The convention, unlike the UN arms register, required mandatory annual reports to the OAS from the signatories regarding their imports and exports of battle tanks, armored combat vehicles, large-caliber artillery, combat aircraft, attack helicopters, warships, and missiles and missile systems. Additionally, reporting nations were to provide notification of acquisitions "no later than 90 days after incorporation of imported conventional weapons into the inventory of the armed forces."

Earlier, in 1997, the OAS formulated the Inter-American Convention Against the Illicit Manufacturing of and Trafficking in Firearms, Ammunition, Explosives, and Other Related Materials aimed primarily at improving domestic security by preventing these materials from reaching the drug rings, terrorists and transnational organized criminals. The motivation for the convention was "due to the harmful effects of these activities on the security of each state and the region as a whole, endangering the well-being of peoples, their social and economic development, and their right to live in peace." The focus was on the promotion of "cooperation and exchange of information and experience" among the signatories.

UN Small Arms Program, 2001. In May 2001, the UN General Assembly adopted the "UN Protocol against the Illicit Manufacturing of and Trafficking in Firearms, their Parts and Components and Ammunition," also known as the Firearms Protocol. This legally binding action exempted certain small arms or state-to-state transfers should a state determine its national security was at stake. In July, more than 140 states attempted to expand the Protocol by renaming it the "UN Program of Action to Prevent, Combat and Eradicate the Illicit Trade in Small Arms and Light Weapons in All Its Aspects." It would have biannual follow-up meetings. While the program has not defined what was meant by "illicit" arms trade, "most understand it to refer to trade that is contrary to the law of states and/or international law."

At a meeting in December 2005, the UN General Assembly adopted the "UN Instrument on Tracing Illicit Small Arms" that encouraged all nations to identify legally produced small arms with a unique serial number and country identification. The United States and certain Asian and African countries prevented it from becoming a legally binding document and excluded coverage of ammunition. The next year, the UN again sought to devise more precise recommendations and common standards, but the conference ended in a deadlock. China, Cuba, India, Iran, Israel, Pakistan, Russia, and the United States opposed such efforts. In addition to blocking a debate on the basic issues in 2006, the United States consistently opposed any restrictions on civilian possession of small arms. It opposed this, because it might interfere with its citizens' constitutional rights to bear arms and with "the rights of the oppressed to defend themselves against tyrannical and genocidal regimes."

Convention on Small Arms and Light Weapons, 2006. The leaders of the fifteen member states of the Economic Community of West African States (ECOWAS) meeting in Abuja, Nigeria, signed this legally binding convention. Building on the 1998 ECOWAS Moratorium on Importation, Exportation and Manufacture of Light Weapons in West Africa, the 2006 convention aimed to "prevent and combat the excessive and destabilizing accumulation of small arms and light weapons" currently existing in West Africa.

The convention obligates the parties to create national databases detailing transactions and holdings of small arms and light weapons, and to provide a detailed annual report to the Executive Secretary of the ECOWAS relative to orders and purchases of such weaponry. The 1998 and 2006 actions were designed to provide greater transparency and encourage confidence-building processes in the region where in recent years little reliable information existed regarding arms acquisitions.[20]

NUCLEAR NON-PROLIFERATION REGIME

The prospect of global proliferation of nuclear weaponry, with no measures in place to halt it, was of growing concern during the 1950s and 1960s. "I am haunted," President John F. Kennedy worried in 1963, "by the feeling that by 1970, unless we are successful, there may be 10 nuclear powers instead of four, and by 1975, 15 or 20." In addition to the original four nuclear weapons states—the United States, Britain, Russia, and France—six other states have developed nuclear weapons—China, Israel, India, Pakistan, North Korea, and South Africa; the latter state scrapped its weapons and means of producing them. A number of states that at one time had considered a nuclear weapons program, or had even begun one, have subsequently halted their efforts.

An illicit nuclear trafficking network, allegedly led by Pakistani nuclear official Abdul Qadeer Khan, apparently provided assistance related to the development of nuclear weaponry to Libya, Iran, and North Korea. In 2008, Iran claimed to be interested only in developing civilian-oriented energy capabilities, but is suspected of being interested also in nuclear weapons to offset Israel's arsenal. The status of North Korea's future production of nuclear weapons was unclear as of 2008, but negotiations aimed at halting this production were ongoing. The International Atomic Energy Agency (IAEA) has visited atomic programs in more than 100 countries. Mohamed El Baradei, director general of the IAEA, estimated that as many as 49 nations know how to make nuclear weapons and warned that global tensions could push some over the line. While the non-proliferation regime has not halted the diffusion of nuclear weapons technologies, it has apparently assisted in slowing it down.

The Non-Proliferation Treaty (NPT) was designed to restrict the manufacture and traffic of nuclear weapons and also it has emerged as the main component of a "regime" seeking to prevent the spread of a critical weapon of mass destruction. The non-proliferation regime includes: the activities of the International Atomic Energy Agency (IAEA); efforts to obtain a comprehensive nuclear test ban (see Chapter 6); regional Nuclear Weapons–Free Zones (see Chapter 2); and the restraints of the London Nuclear Suppliers Group. Other measures such as restricting the traffic in missiles and missile technology, listed in the "Multilateral Export Control Regimes" section below, complement nuclear non-proliferation activities.[21]

Additional measures were added by the IAEA in 1980 to provide security for nuclear materials in transit. The subsequent concern over possible sabotage of nuclear facilities or terrorist use of radioactive materials resulted in several efforts to improve security measures. There was also recognition of the dangers posed by an attack on civilian nuclear facilities during military hostilities; see the Pakistan-Indian ban (Chapter 6).

Non-Proliferation Treaty, 1968. Following the People's Republic of China's first nuclear test on October 16, 1964, the United States and Soviets responded to the UN General Assembly's 1965 call to prevent the proliferation of nuclear weapons. Each submitted draft treaties to the Eighteen Nation Disarmament Committee that, after resolving a few differences, emerged identical in 1967. The committee's nonaligned members argued that a non-proliferation pact must not divide the world into nuclear "haves" and "have-nots," but rather balance obligations.

Non-nuclear weapons states would pledge not to acquire these weapons in exchange for access to peaceful nuclear technology and a pledge from the nuclear weapons states to pursue nuclear disarmament. The supervision and safeguarding of nuclear technologies under the IAEA would permit the peaceful use of nuclear energy and the exchange of necessary technology. At the same time, Washington and Moscow reluctantly agreed "to pursue negotiations in good faith on effective measures relating to cessation of the nuclear arms race at an early date and to nuclear disarmament, and on a treaty on general and complete disarmament under strict and effective international control" (Art. VI). Their dilatory or non-execution of this pledge has been a serious point of contention at each of the subsequent five-year review conferences. By 2007, the NPT had 189 member states.

Japan had a small, low-priority nuclear weapons program before the end of WWII; however, its constitution prohibits possessing or manufacturing nuclear weapons. Sweden, considered a top prospect in the 1950s, chose not to pursue nuclear weapons. Indonesia was suspected of pursuing a nuclear weapons program in the 1960s. Egypt apparently began a nuclear weapons program in the 1960s, but gave it up in the 1970s and plans to seek a nuclear power program. Taiwan, which started a plutonium-based nuclear weapons program in the 1960s, also opted out of the nuclear weapons hunt in the 1970s under strong U.S. pressure. South Africa had a fully developed nuclear weapons program— possessing six weapons—before dismantling its facilities in 1990. Brazil and Argentina in 1991 joined in renouncing any designs on nuclear weaponry. Libya abandoned its hopes for a nuclear weapons program under British and American pressure in 2003. The United Nations Special Commission (UNSCOM) dismantled Iraq's nuclear weapons program after the 1991 Gulf War. Belarus, Ukraine, and Kazakhstan returned nuclear weapons inherited at the end of the Cold War to Russia in the late 1990s.

If there were successes, the nuclear nonproliferation also suffered with the addition of China, Israel, India, Pakistan, and North Korea as nuclear weapons states.[22]

International Atomic Energy Agency, 1957. The inspiration for the International Atomic Energy Agency (IAEA) came from the failed 1946 Baruch Plan, but President Eisenhower's 1953 Atoms for Peace program required its establishment. The IAEA was "to accelerate and enlarge the contribution of atomic energy to peace, health and prosperity throughout the world." The Agency was expected to be "a broker in the field of international nuclear cooperation, promoting the peaceful applications of nuclear energy while seeking to ensure that assistance provided by it or under its auspices was not used to further any military purpose."

The IAEA's role significantly expanded when the 1968 Treaty on the Non-Proliferation of Nuclear Weapons (NPT) designated it responsible for monitoring non-proliferation commitments. To carry out its mandate, the IAEA created an elaborate system of procedures and rules. These comprehensive "safeguards" consist of specific procedures designed to assist in verification of compliance of those nations with bilateral and multilateral IAEA agreements. If a precedent had been established, the application of safeguards revealed that they were only partially successful as non-proliferation measures.

An extensive NPT Model Safeguards Agreement (March 10, 1971) was created to ensure non-nuclear states' peaceful nuclear activities. Paragraph 28 of the Safeguards Agreement declared that its technical objective was "the timely detection of diversion of significant quantities of nuclear material from peaceful nuclear activities to the manufacture of nuclear weapons or of other nuclear devices or for purposes unknown, and deterrence of such diversion by the risk of early detection."

In May 1997, the IAEA Board of Governors approved the Model Additional Protocol to Safeguards Agreements that contains provisions giving the Agency the legal authority to strengthen its verification measures. Its principal objective was to provide better tools to give assurance about both declared and possible undeclared activities. Under the Model Additional Protocol, nations are required to provide the Agency with an expanded declaration that contains information covering all aspects of their nuclear and nuclear fuel cycle activities. The nations must also grant the Agency broader rights of access and enable it to use the most advanced surveillance technologies.

Protection of Nuclear Materials and Nuclear Facilities, 1980, 2005. Attempts to improve the security of nuclear facilities formally began with the 1980 Convention on the Physical Protection of Nuclear Material (CPPNM), a name to which was added in 2005, "and Nuclear Facilities." Initial efforts, spearheaded by the IAEA, were aimed at providing safe and secure transport of nuclear materials, but subsequently a concern arose over whether adequate measures were being taken "to deter or defeat hostile actions against nuclear facilities and materials" in transit.

The IAEA, who was instrumental in creating the new guidelines, was concerned "about the possible malicious use of radioactive sources." The Code of Conduct on the Safety and Security of Radioactive Sources (2003) set forth guidelines to meet the new standards to prevent or reduce acts of sabotage. The primary responsibility for carrying out these procedures rested on the various states, including enacting civil penalties for actions that impaired the security of nuclear materials or facilities.[23]

Agreed Framework [United States–North Korea], 1994–. In October 1994, the United States and North Korea signed an agreement—the Agreed Framework—in which Pyongyang would halt construction and operation of nuclear reactors believed to be part of a secret nuclear weapons program. In return, the North Koreans would be provided two proliferation-resistant nuclear power reactors; meanwhile, the United States would supply Pyongyang with fuel oil until the new nuclear facilities were built. The Framework followed a year and a half of negotiations during which North Korea indicated it intended to withdraw from the NPT (which it had signed in 1985). The Clinton administration succeeded in meeting some aspects of the Framework when it eased the country's longtime sanctions against North Korea in order to make possible an increase in trade, financial transactions, and investments.

Subsequently the new administration sent mixed signals to Pyongyang, beginning with President George W. Bush's naming North Korea as a member of an "axis of evil" in January 2002. Washington reported in October that a North

Korean official had admitted that that his nation possessed a uranium-enrichment program that would violate the Framework. The North Korean government denied the charge and in January announced it was withdrawing from the NPT. Thus began a protracted series of multilateral negotiations, interrupted on October 9, 2006, when North Korea conducted its first nuclear test, seeking to have Pyongyang to halt its nuclear weapons program. A major point of contention was North Korea rejection of a verification program, while Washington has insisted upon an inclusive one. It was believed that the North Koreans possessed enough plutonium for 12 nuclear warheads.[24]

MULTILATERAL EXPORT CONTROL REGIMES

Although these regimes often seem to operate as "gentlemen's agreements," they function as an international pact with "politically binding" or "legally binding" effects on the participating nations. Their activities are usually conducted quietly, often secretly; however, sometimes they lack a transparent mechanism for monitoring compliance or sanctions should a member state be acting in bad faith.[25]

Coordinating Committee, 1949–1994. The Coordinating Committee for Multilateral Export Controls' (CoCom) origin was veiled in secrecy, as was much of its operation. CoCom coordinated policies restricting exports of potential strategic value to the Soviet Union, its Eastern bloc satellites, and the People's Republic of China. Between 1949 and 1994, the United States created the agency through bilateral accords with more than 50 nations. CoCom consisted of delegates from all NATO countries (except Iceland) and maintained a small permanent staff in Paris where member nations coordinated policies regarding trade involving arms, industrial equipment, and "atomic" technologies.

The committee not only reviewed military technology transfers for potential embargo, but also tried to anticipate the end use of products manufactured for civilian purposes, such as computers and transistors. Approval of an export license needed unanimous consent of committee members, which extended the United States a "veto." The veto was unpopular with America's allies, who by the end of the Cold War believed that the United States used the committee to promote its own commercial and foreign policy objectives. The disintegration of the Soviet Union and the desire to assist economic and political reform in Russia and the Newly Independent States resulted in the termination of CoCom effective March 31, 1994.[26] (See the Wassenaar Arrangement below.)

The Nuclear Suppliers Group. Between 1971 and 1974, delegates from 15 nations met informally at Vienna, headed by Professor Claude Zangger of Switzerland (hence, also known as the Zangger Committee), to control exports of nuclear materials. In August 1974, the committee established guidelines, adopted by consensus, that were implemented through national export control systems. The guidelines included a *trigger list*—so-called because their proposed export triggered the Group's concern. The list consisted of material, equipment, and facilities that, if diverted from peaceful uses, could contribute to a nuclear weapons program.

Following the 1974 Indian nuclear test, the United States, the Soviet Union, the United Kingdom, France, West Germany, Canada, and Japan formally established the Nuclear Suppliers Group (NSG) that began meeting in London in April 1975. In September 1977, the group adopted an expanded version of the Zangger list, *Guidelines on Nuclear Transfers,* which was sent to the IAEA in January 1978. A 1992 meeting of the group resulted in a reexamination of thousands of items on the dual-list and a tightening of export restrictions. By 2006, the NSG consisted of 45 members and, according to a U.S. authority, had become "a clearinghouse for nuclear-related exports and is still one of the most effective international anti-proliferation tools."[27]

The Australia Group, 1985–. A 1984 UN investigation of Iraq's use of chemical weapons (CW) during its war with Iran found that the Iraqi CW program used chemicals and materials purchased through legitimate trade channels. Subsequently, a number of nations placed export controls on specific chemicals that could be used in manufacturing CW weapons. The Australia Group, as they became known, first met in June 1985 and annually since then to address new threats. Suspected diversion of dual-use materials to biological weapons programs in the early 1990s led to export controls on specific biological agents. The Group developed control lists that included technologies and equipment used in the manufacturing or disposal of chemical and biological weapons.

Participants understood that export-licensing measures were not a substitute for observance of the 1925 Geneva Protocol, the 1972 Biological and Toxin Weapons Convention (BWC), and the 1997 Chemical Weapons Convention (CWC). Thus, members of the Australia Group also are parties to, and staunch supporters of, the BWC and CWC. Individual nations' export licensing measures assist in implementing key obligations under the CWC (Article I, 1 (a) and (d)) and the BWC (Articles I and III) and ensure compliance with UN Security Resolution 1540.[28] (See chapter 3 "Outlawing Weapons and War" above.)

Missile Technology Control Regime, 1987–. The Missile Technology Control Regime (MTCR)—an informal and voluntary association—was established in 1987 by the United States, Britain, Canada, France, Japan, Italy, and West Germany. It developed measures to deny missile, space, and aerospace technologies to potentially hostile states. According to Janne Nolan, there are "four components ... vital to the success of a ballistic missile development program. In descending order of complexity, they are the guidance system, the reentry vehicle, the propulsion system, and the warhead."[29]

The MTCR has attempted to control two categories of items. Category 1 includes complete systems and subsystems capable of carrying a payload of 500 kilograms for a distance of some 300 kilometers and production facilities for such systems. Category 2 includes related components used for the production of Category 1 systems. The technical specifications on the restricted systems attempt to distinguish between military and civilian systems. While the initial concern was with missiles that could deliver nuclear warheads, in 1993 the regime was extended—at the request of non-member states—to include missiles capable of carrying chemical and biological weapons.

Opinions on the success of the MTCR have been mixed. China, North Korea, Israel, and India, for example, are not members. It has no enforcement mechanisms and, despite its detailed restrictions, it does not cover all systems that could contribute to a ballistic missile capability. In 2006, the MTCR had 34 voluntary members.[30]

Wassenaar Arrangement, 1996. The Wassenaar Arrangement on Export Controls for Conventional Arms and Dual-Use Goods and Technologies replaced the Coordinating Committee for Multilateral Export Controls (1949) established to halt technology transfers to the Soviet Union and its allies (see above). Headquartered in Vienna, Austria, it began operations in September 1996 and seeks to enhance transparency and restraints on exporting conventional weapons and sophisticated technologies to countries whose behavior has raised serious concern and to regions of potential instability.

The new system was initially controversial because Washington sought to continue restricting other nations' sensitive exports, while the agreement provided no influence over U.S. transfers. Washington argued that its unique global responsibilities trumped other nation's concerns about U.S. arms transfers, while European countries sought a formula much like that of the Missile Technology Control Regime that provided for greater flexibility. The result has been a weak organization.

The informal association of 40 states created two restricted lists:

1. A munitions list which includes conventional weapons, such as tanks and fighter aircraft, as well as military explosives, biocatalysts, and other military agents; and
2. A dual-use technology list that is broken into two tiers: Tier 1, a basic list made up of sensitive items and technologies; and Tier 2, a list of very sensitive items subject to stringent monitoring.

There is no central coordinating mechanism, allowing each nation to decide if specific transfers are in accordance with the restricted lists.[31]

Proliferation Security Initiative, 2003. The United States organized a group of like-minded nations in May 2003 to seek out and interdict of shipments of unconventional weapons. The Proliferation Security Initiative (PSI) lacks formal structure, indeed, it as been described as "an activity, not an organization." Beginning with 11 nations, by 2008 the membership increased to nearly 90 volunteer states prepared to intercept (at sea, on land, and in the air) suspected international shipments of biological, chemical, or nuclear weaponry together with related materials and missiles before they reach their final destination.

The objectives and undertakings of PSI were not new; indeed, one U.S. official noted, "We have been doing interdictions for a long time, [PSI] is a better way of doing it." The legality of PSI's operations has caused concern. China has challenged not only the legality of armed boarding vessels on the high seas, but also the effectiveness of the program. The UN's watered-down Resolution 1540 has not improved the implementation of the PSI. Even former Secretary of Defense Donald Rumsfeld had to acknowledge that the PSI has "a lot of holes in it."

The secrecy surrounding the operation has made it difficult to evaluate its effectiveness or its legitimacy. However, at a May 2008 conference of participants, the U.S. State Department announced five examples of PSI successes. They involved the impeding of shipments of items to Iran, North Korea, and Syria facilitating the possible production of ballistic missiles and plutonium.[32]

For the various forms of negotiations employed, the several types of verification adopted and the compliance or noncompliance records of many of these agreements, see Part II.

Customs and the Law of War

Although most arms control measures aim at preventing hostilities, others seek to reduce or minimize military violence once a conflict begins. It is at the onset of hostilities that arms control and international law—more specifically, customs and the law of war—intersect to discipline the conduct of the armed conflict. These customs and the law of war seek to protect combatants and noncombatants from unnecessary suffering; safeguard the rights of individuals, especially prisoners of war, the sick, wounded, and shipwrecked, while in the hands of an enemy; prevent any unnecessary interruption of the civilian food chain, including destruction of crops, fruit trees, water supply, and so on; spare historic treasures including art, literary works, buildings, and other objects from destruction; and assist in the termination of hostilities.

The customs and law of war that gradually emerged over centuries are grouped here in three historic stages. The initial phase, the *warrior culture,* found various societies developing a ritualized approach to hostilities. Many tribal societies and ancient peoples sought to limit or reduce the impact of warfare through asylum, limiting casualties (ritualized combat), dueling, defining noncombatants, and providing for prisoners of war. In medieval Europe, clerics emphasized the ethical and moral teachings of Christianity in attempts to restrain combative nobles, although these restrictions might not apply when fighting "infidels," "pagans," or "heretics."

The second phase involved the efforts of European states when *formalizing the law of war*. From the Peace of Westphalia in 1648 to The Hague Conferences of 1898 and 1907—known as the "Grotian period"—was the golden age of formal, positive constraints on the conduct of war. "The law of nations is naturally founded on this principle." As one spokesperson of the era, French jurist Montesquieu, wrote, "that different nations ought in time of peace to do one another all the good they can, and in time of war as little injury as possible without prejudicing their real interests."[1]

The major issue became combatant behavior during hostilities, rather than determining whether the conflict was just. Extensive codification of reasonably precise laws elaborated and expanded the earlier customs of war with an emphasis on what was, and what was not, permitted during hostilities. The formal assembling of the code of conduct for warfare was virtually completed between 1899 and 1907.

The third phase, the *modernizing of the law of war*, saw the convergence of The Hague and Geneva Conventions during the twentieth century which, taken together, came to emphasize International Humanitarian Law. While concern continued for the protections provided to combatants under the law of war, since 1945 more emphasis has been placed upon the protection of civilians or noncombatants. Traditionally, these groups were, as British historian Geoffrey Best has observed,

> of more value to all parties if they were allowed to carry on with their own business as peasants, traders, merchants, etc. They were of more value to armies because you could get more out of a civilian populace by regulated requisitioning than by wasteful looting and vengeful destruction.... Furthermore, there might not be much point in a victor's acquisition of territory which had been devastated and depopulated.[2]

During the twentieth century, the nature of warfare and the protections afforded noncombatants, changed greatly due to mass ideological movements and technological advances with indiscriminate collateral effects. During the eighteenth and nineteenth centuries, mixed opinions arose concerning the issue of civilians suffering under bombardment. While in certain instances civilians might suffer from the bombardment of legitimate military targets, some authorities held that it was unlawful to bombard civilians within a defended location for the purpose of making them suffer, complain, and thus encourage surrender, or for punitive and vindictive motives.

With the onset of World War I, a new version of the "just war" reemerged in the form of ideological absolutes—fed by mass participation and propaganda—that greatly expanded the concept of *total war*. During World War II, the aerial devastation of cities to destroy the morale of the enemy's workers and reduce the production of its arms factories became a publicly accepted strategic objective. During the Cold War, strategists of both superpowers developed plans for obliterating the other's cities. Many observers again questioned the logic of total war. Roman historian Livy had challenged this notion more than 2,000 years ago: "What sort of policy is it, to destroy the things the possession of which is at stake, and to leave for himself nothing except the war?"

Obviously, vastly destructive, indiscriminate weaponry have shaken many of the earlier distinctions. This led one scholar to conclude, "The laws of war belong to a past age, and except for a few minor matters of no consequence, it is futile to attempt to revive them.... War has got beyond the control of law."[3] Rejecting such pessimism, University of Oxford professor Michael Howard has insisted: "To control and limit the conduct of war is ... not inherently impossible" for "without controls and limitations war cannot be conducted at all." The problem with initiating and sustaining controls and limits, he argues, requires understanding that "there are the prudential considerations which demand that, to put it at its lowest, the costs of war do not in the long run outweigh its benefits."[4] This, of course, would require an astute, realistic assessment of political objectives and military requirements.

Military Necessity versus Unnecessary Suffering. The Lieber Code (1863) defined military necessity for the Union Army as "those measures which are indispensable for securing the ends of war, and which are lawful according to the modern law and usages of war." Nearly a century later, the U.S. Army similarly saw military necessity "as that principle which justifies those measures not forbidden by international law which are indispensable for securing the complete submission of the enemy as soon as possible." The balancing of these two basic principles of law and war may appear uncomplicated in theory; however, in practice they often have been difficult to reconcile.[5]

Defining legitimate targets for aerial bombardment was more difficult than directing the fire of army artillery or naval guns. With new military technologies—especially aircraft and ballistic missiles—industrial centers became potential targets because they supplied the complex equipment used by hostile military forces at the front. The 1907 Hague Convention on Bombardment by Naval Forces expanded legitimate military targets to include various naval port support services. During World War I, aerial bombardment introduced new targets such as factories producing aircraft engines, planes, ammunition, and other military equipment. World War II strategists extended targets to urban areas where arms plants, transportation centers, and civilian housing were usually near each other. Imprecise ordnance targeted on a factory could easily destroy nearby homes, a hospital, or a school. Subsequent bombing strategies that targeted urban residences—"dehousing"—posed new questions.

The principle of unnecessary suffering except in actions that violate specific legal prohibitions, is vague. "It may be characterized," according to W. Hays Parks of the U.S. Army Judge Advocate General's office,

> as a violation of either of two general law of war concepts: (1) that of noncombatant immunity from intentional acts of violence, and (2) that of discrimination in the use of violence. Violation of either concept would constitute unnecessary suffering, as neither the direct attack of noncombatants (military wounded, sick, or shipwrecked; medical personnel; and civilians not taking part in hostilities) nor the indiscriminate use of force can be justified by the principle of military necessity.

"The test is whether the action in question genuinely furthers the aim and main strategic concept of the war," Sir Robert Saundby has written. "It goes without saying, however, that all practical steps, short of prejudicing the success of the operation, should be taken to minimize the risk to civilians."[6] Maintenance of the law of war, then, depends upon the ability of leaders to make distinctions, and to forego certain options in an attempt to reduce collateral damage.

Noncompliance Issues. There is no shortage of examples of noncompliance with the law of war. Any thorough examination will find ample evidence of violations of the law of war, due largely to lack of knowledge, individual disdain, and unilateral government decisions. An example of either lack of knowledge or contempt for international conventions may be found in Winston S. Churchill's autobiography that recalls, rather blithely, his carrying illegal soft-nosed bullets while being an illegally armed war correspondent during the Boer War. Among other violations, this action ignored the St. Petersburg Declaration of 1868 that outlawed "dum-dum" or soft-nosed bullets, because they spread on impact and caused horrible wounds. Charges of American violations of this Declaration were levied during the Philippine Insurrection (1901); but United States Army officers claimed this ammunition was essential to halt suicide charges by fanatical bolo-wielding Moros.

Although there are other features to the law of war, compliance issues have focused most prominently on two fundamental aspects: treatment of prisoners of war (POWs) and noncombatants. The fate of prisoners of war prior to the twentieth century was usually not a happy one, W. Hays Parks notes. "Prisoners of war routinely were put to the sword, sold into slavery, held for ransom or permitted to die through malnourishment, inadequate medical care, or other neglect or brutality by a captor." In an effort to remedy this situation, The Hague Convention II (1899), IV (1907) and the Convention on Treatment of Prisoners of War (1929) were established. World War II saw acceptance and denial of the POW rules leading to the Geneva Convention III (1949).

Protections for noncombatants can be found beginning with warrior cultures and then becoming formalized during Europe's medieval era. Yet technological advances in the twentieth century led to weaponry that often showed little regard for civilian noncombatants.[7]

What follows is a representative, chronological sampling, together with a brief narrative description, of the treaties and agreements that demonstrated the historical lineage of the customs and the law of war.

"WARRIOR" CULTURE AND CUSTOMS

Early tribal societies frequently engaged in bloody battles, but often devised techniques to restrict the impact of the combat on their communities. They might set a limit on the number of persons that could become casualties during the course of a battle before hostilities were curtailed, establish ritualized warfare, protect individuals they defined as noncombatants, and outlaw the use of specific weapons. Some of the limits or prohibitions that began as customs or taboos would eventually be codified into international law.

Asylum. Major temples and festival sites were often designated as asylums, safe havens from hostilities or reprisals in the ancient world. Proclaiming sacred truces at a time of major festivals, such as the Olympic and other Pan-Hellenic games, provided a temporary cessation of hostilities and introduced the notion of noncombatancy. These truces also served to ensure that conflicts remained local by preventing them from spreading to uninvolved cities through accidental assaults on their citizens passing through combatant's territories on their way to a festival or during their stay at a sanctuary or festival site.

Ritualized Warfare. Ceremonial battles or ritualized warfare, governed by local customs, were not uncommon among tribal or clan societies. This was the case throughout Oceania. "Although the rules regulating the type of war varied from one people to another," Camilla Wedgwood notes, "they generally included a formal declaration of hostilities, the use of a prearranged fighting ground, restrictions as to weapons and the manner of their use, and a formal peacemaking ceremony to conclude the fighting." Consequently, the casualties were usually minimal and the exclusion of noncombatants was well defined. In this type of contest, the show of force rather than its effective utilization, was the major factor in determining the victors.[8]

Special rules also applied to hostilities between villages on the Small Islands adjacent to Malekula in the New Hebrides. When the cause for conflict was that of avenging insults rather than murder, usually neither party desired a fierce encounter. It was thus agreed that spears would not be used, only clubs and stones. "They not only had a special fighting ground on the beach at the junction of their regular territories," according to John Layard, "but the beach was furnished with a stone fort where it was the custom of the defenders to await attack.... When the two sides met at the stone fort, the fighting consisted of hurling insults and recitations of present and past grievances interspersed with occasional volleys of stones." However, when fighting with other islands or with villages on Malekula, there was no designated fighting area and no restrictions on weapons.[9]

The Willigiman and Wallalua of New Guinea were traditional foes that maintained a designated no-man's-land between them that was scrutinized daily by warriors stationed on 25-foot-high watchtowers. They would arrange for a fight every week or two at one of their traditional battlefields. "Each battle, which was actually more like a dangerous field sport than a war, would last a single day. Although several hundred warriors would come out to fight, only a score would engage in battle at any one time. The battle always stopped before nightfall because of the danger of ghosts, and it was also terminated if it rained because no one wanted get his hair or ornaments wet." The warriors were quite accurate with their weapons since they had trained since childhood, but fortunately they were also quite agile and, consequently, rarely wounded or killed.[10]

In western New Guinea, the Kapauku Papuans had a rather elaborate form of ceremonial battles that began with the attackers "chanting the reasons for the attack and the defenders performing a counter-clockwise dance and then rushing to meet the enemy on open grassland. They fought exclusively with bows and arrows, using no hand weapons such as clubs." Fighting individually, the warriors sought cover in the tall grass and exhausted their supply of arrows.

Their wives, who were considered noncombatants, would move through enemy lines to collect the stray arrows and, frequently, taunt the enemy and even point out their locations. Exploiting their immunity, the women also would shield their mates by walking ahead, on the flanks and behind them to protect the men from ambush.[11]

Prior to the emergence of the Zulu empire, the several African tribes would arrange for a day and place to resolve their disputes by combat. On the appointed day, tribesmen would line up in several ranks approximately 100 yards apart and the selected warriors in the front row would advance to within some 50 yards of each other, taunt their foe, and throw their spears. Each warrior had a 5-foot-long oval shield and two or three light javelins that were unlikely to penetrate their opponents toughened rawhide shield. As the hostilities continued, more and more warriors were drawn into the fray until one side quit fighting and fled or simply dropped their spears. Few wounds were fatal and the number of casualties was low.

When Shaka became chief of the Zulus in 1818 and employed a new fighting technique that involved a close-quarter assault with a broad-bladed stabbing spear, the empire expanded greatly, but so did the number of casualties on both sides. It is estimated that they grew from 3 percent in 1810 to 80 percent of the combatants in 1819, although later they declined to around 42 percent.[12]

Polybius wrote that "the ancients" who preceded the Roman Empire regarded "no success as brilliant or secure unless they crushed the spirit of their adversaries in open battle." These foes would agree among themselves neither to use "secret missiles nor those discharged from a distance," believing that only hand-to-hand combat would be honorable and decisive. Consequently, they "preceded war by a declaration, and when they intended to do battle, gave notice of the fact and of the spot to which they would proceed and array their army." He found few traces of these "ancient principles" of warfare later among the Romans.[13]

The early German tribes, to whom Polybius may have been referring, would frequently select the time and place for an impending confrontation. Or sometimes they would do the opposite: designate neutral zones but allow the rest of the countryside to become a potential battleground. The Pacific Northwest Indians often set aside a day for combat to resolve their differences. After both sides arrived and engaged in battle, the issue was decided when one or two prominent tribesmen fell. The Arapesh, who often engaged in women stealing, would scout out a tribe that had taken one of their women, and then each tribe would drum its insults and challenge to combat. Cleared grounds on the borders were the traditional battlefields; however, the intimate associations between the groups usually restrained the violence. The loss of a man or two was sufficient to cause one side to flee. The same restraints were found among the Bagehu, a Bantu tribe in Uganda, who halted their fighting when one or two warriors had been killed and several injured. The inland Indian tribes of British Columbia also managed to conduct battles without much loss of life.[14]

Dueling. Regulated combat between selected individuals or small groups was another ritualized means of resolving disputes used by tribal groups and ancient societies. The Tasmanians and other Australian aborigines frequently used duels between individual warriors to reconcile differences. Few lives were lost because with the first wound, the combat terminated. The Siberia and Alaska Eskimos frequently would wrestle to settle disagreements or engage in "song duels." The Botocudo of Brazil resolved quarrels, often over hunting grounds, by a duel between tribal champions. The pair would strike away at one another with staves until one gave up. If, however, the losing tribe took up their bows and arrows, a genuine battle would ensue.

Among the Tannese of the New Hebrides, fighting usually was a matter of single combat; indeed, in some instances the general skirmishes appeared to be a series of individual duels. Casualties in their battles were generally limited. When the first warrior was killed, the "man who killed him became the hero of the hour and fighting was generally stopped for the day so that a special demonstration could be given [for the] successful warrior by his tribe and its allies." Occasionally, the Maori of New Zealand would employ a duel when "a valiant warrior might step forth and challenge someone on the other side to single combat." The contest began between the champions, accompanied by one or two associates who might join the fighting if their man was losing, and usually ended with the killing of one man, especially if the victim was a leader.[15]

In seventh century BCE, Argos and Sparta hoped to resolve a dispute by a contest between 300 selected warriors on each side. Unfortunately, all but three warriors were killed and it did not prevent a subsequent bloodier battle. Also, Greek disputes over land often were "settled by struggles between small landholders who by mutual consent sought to limit warfare [hence killing] to a single, brief, nightmarish occasion."

The Old Testament tells of several battlefield duels between individual contestants. Yigael Yadin has referred "to the striking similarity between the duel of Sinuhe the Egyptian" with the "mighty man of Retenu [Syria and Palestine]" and the contest between David and Goliath. The parallel is close, right down to the prior negotiation, the combat, and the result." When David slew Goliath, however, the Philistines fled and the Israelites pursued, inflicting heavy casualties on them and thus negating the goal of using a duel between two champions to limit bloodshed.

Yadin suggests that the use of duels to resolve disputes was common in Canaan long before the Philistines arrived, but was gradually discontinued only to be subsequently reintroduced. "Apparently the stimulus of the duel was not primarily boastfulness or conceit on the part of individual warriors," he suggests, "but the desire of commanders to secure a military decision without the heavy bloodshed of a full-scale battle."[16]

Noncombatants. Some tribal groups recognized specific individuals, most frequently women, as noncombatants and therefore they were immune from martial violence. Many groups, such as the early Samoans, apparently considered it cowardly to kill women during combat. The Kapauku Papuans of western New Guinea, as noted earlier, exempted married women as targets during combat even though they frequently went behind enemy lines or between the combatants to retrieve stray arrows. They also might scout for their males engaged in battle pointing out enemy positions. Occasionally, the women exploited their immunity by using their walking sticks to strike enemy warriors and these warriors might push or strike these women with fists or bows, but to shoot at a female was taboo. If a man did so, he would be taunted by his companions: "If all you can do is shoot a woman, stay home." Although married women had noncombatant immunity on the battlefield, it did not applied to single girls who were considered eligible prizes. Some girls would wander about the field of combat and resulting sexual activity could be either rape or seduction.

Other groups were occasionally given noncombatant immunity. The Lushais, who carried out their campaigns by raiding the villages of their enemies, regarded the practice of waylaying farmers who were cultivating crops as an uncalled for and thoughtless act. As a chief explained: "How can people live if cultivation is impossible?"

Prisoners of War. The ancient practice of torturing and killing prisoners of war gradually ended, according to Maurice Davies, "with the development of agriculture" and the end of nomadic life when it was found more useful to enslave prisoners as laborers. "It was thus the advances of agriculture," according this view, "which laid the foundations for one of the greatest alleviations of the cruelties of war." The Laws of Manu (Sec. 93) provided for taking prisoners. No additional harm should befall "one whose weapons are broken, nor one afflicted [with sorrow], nor one who has been grievously wounded, nor one who is in fear, nor one who has turned to flight; [but in all these cases let him] remember the duty [of honorable warriors]."[17]

Greek diplomacy provided for the ransom of captives, sometimes even agreeing in advance the ransom to be charged for prisoners of war. In the Middle Ages, the taking of prisoners and holding them ransom was commonplace; indeed, in Italy it became so business-oriented that a soldier took care to avoid killing an nobleman in combat because of the loss of ransom. In 1673, France and the States General of the United Provinces—the Netherlands—agreed on the ransom of prisoners in advance of combat, ranging up to 50,000 livres for a general.[18]

Warfare had become diluted by the desire for profit. Even the victorious Zulus would seize as many male and female prisoners as possible, with the prisoners later being ransomed for cattle.

FORMALIZING THE LAW OF WAR

During the chaotic Middle Ages, a series of campaigns in Western Europe were launched by clerics, and later princes, to control the availability and permissibility of arms and suppress crime, feud, and local warfare. These campaigns—

often misunderstood—evolved from the tenth into the sixteenth centuries through three distinct, yet interrelated phases known as the *Peace of God (Pax Dei)*, the *Truce of God (Treuga Dei)*, and the *Peace of the Prince (Landfriede* or "Peace of the Realm"). Perhaps of limited impact over the short run, the campaigns turned into the longest and most comprehensive law and order movement known to western civilization. Among other contributions, they formalized the idea of noncombatant immunity that eventually found its way into international law.

The medieval Peace and Truce of God's efforts to establish a legal structure for local hostilities were not always successful or appreciated then or later. There were formidable enforcement weapons available during the eleventh century—the anathema, excommunication, and interdict. The Church employment of these "moral weapons" could determine, for example, whether a nobleman's family inherited his estate, whether it became Church property, or whether it was assigned to someone else. Later secular laws would provide severe penalties for violations.

If the rules were flaunted it did not mean they were meaningless, any more than modern society's laws against murder and mayhem that are daily violated. They did, however, generate public support and "advance a series of initiatives to ban violence against unarmed persons or places.... Imperceptibly, the focus of the struggle moved away from the moral question of non-combatant rights of protection and security to the jurisdictional question of the right to bear and use arms."[19]

Peace of God, 989. The Peace of God movement began in Aquitaine, Burgundy, and Languedoc, where central authority was virtually nonexistent and the local nobles were constantly engaged in hostilities and lawless behavior. Concerned about public safety, the local clergy undertook to distinguish between lawful combatants and noncombatants and, especially, to prevent attacks upon themselves and the seizure of Church lands. The prohibitions sought to provide immunity from violence to those who could not defend themselves. The Benedictine abbey at Charroux promulgated three cannons threatening the excommunication of anyone who (1) "breaks into a sacred church, or violently removes anything thence;" (2) "robs peasants or other poor of a sheep, ox, ass, cow, goat, or pigs ... and neglects to make full reparation;" and (3) "who attacks, captures or assaults a priest or deacon or any clergyman, who is not carrying arms [that is, shield, sword, coat of mail and helmet]...." A proclamation issued by Guy of Anjou, Bishop of Puy (990), added to the earlier prohibitions that no one shall "seize a peasant, man or woman, for the purpose of making him purchase his freedom," "seize ecclesiastical lands," or "seize or rob merchants."

In the next century, church bodies in other parts of France, Spain, and Germany endorsed and expanded the protection of noncombatants. At the Council of Clermont (1095), Pope Urban II extended papal recognition and approval of the movement, and the Peace of God proclamations survived into the thirteenth century. (He also called for warriors to join a crusade to free the Holy Land and apparently succeeded in removing many of the restless ones from pillaging the European countryside.)

Truce of God, 1027. Where the Peace of God focused on banning violence against the church and the poor, the Truce of God included many of the Peace of God's prohibitions and, additionally, banned fighting on specific days. The Truce sought to restrain violence among Christians, specifically between knights and nobles. The initial bans on fighting from sundown on Saturday until sunrise on Monday and holy days was gradually extended to include all of Lent, and even the Friday of every week.

The initial Truce of God, proclaimed in the Diocese of Elne (1027), declared the "no one should attack his enemy from the ninth hour on Saturday until the first hour on Monday, so that everyone may perform his religious duties on Sunday." A subsequent decree by the Archbishopric of Arles (1035–1041) extended the truce by calling for "all Christians, friends and enemies, neighbors and strangers" to keep the "peace one with another from vespers on Wednesday to sunrise on Monday."

Peace of the Realm, 1103. Over succeeding centuries, these earlier restraints were gradually incorporated into secular law, when the various authorities undertook to define and manage "peace" in political terms. Emperor Henry IV established the Peace of the Realm at Mainz in 1103 when he, the clergy, and nobles "swore to keep peace with churches, clergy, monks, merchants, women and Jews." Their oath essentially criminalized local wars, ransom, feuds, and looting. By 1492, private wars were forbidden throughout the Holy Roman Empire where courts, sheriffs, and legislatures had been established to monopolize the use of force and provide for a system of justice. The Peace of the Realm was the culmination of an extended process.[20]

Saracens and the Code of War. In another part of the world, another of the first systematic codes or law of war was being developed by the Saracens based on the Koran, and was expanded by decisions rendered by Mohammed and his followers. Kindness and chivalry form part of the code's basic precepts that forbade employing incendiary projectiles, the cutting down of trees, intercepting water supplies, and the poisoning of wells or streams.[21]

Hugo Grotius and the Law of War, 1625–1631. During the religious conflicts of the Thirty Years' War, the medieval restraints on war seemed to be forgotten. So chaotic was this situation, that a few commanders felt it necessary to issue short manuals on military ethics dealing with such matters as whether it was permitted to burn a building into which one's enemy had fled, poison wells, and so on. A renowned philosopher, Hugo Grotius, in *De jure belli ac pacis* (*On the Laws of War and Peace*) and subsequent revised editions, recounted the "findings" of Greek, Roman, and other historical figures in his classic work. He argued that:

[T]here is a common law among nations, which is valid alike for war and in war.... Throughout the Christian world I observed a lack of restraint in relation to war, such as even barbarous races should be ashamed of; I observed that men rush to arms for slight causes, or no cause at all, and that when arms have once been taken up there is no longer any respect for law, divine or human; it is as if, in accordance with a general decree, frenzy had openly been let loose for the committing of all crimes.

Grotius's three-part treatise used natural law and the law of nations to offer principles that he believed were binding on all people and nations regardless of local customs. Book 1 (on just war), found that in certain circumstances war was justifiable. Book 2 (on the resort to war) offered self-defense, reparation of injury, and punishment as "just causes" for war. In Book 3 (on the conduct of war), Grotius reviewed the laws that governed the conduct of combat and argued that all warring parties, whether their cause was just or not, were obligated to follow the rules related to, among others, noncombatants and treatment of POWs. His works on war had a profound influence on those concerned with military affairs and later on the formulation of international law generally.

U.S.-Prussian Treaty, 1785. This treaty of amity and commerce expanded many of the prohibitions from the Peace of God and Grotius that were related to noncombatants and POWs. Article 23 stated that should war occur between the two parties, merchants would be able to conduct business for nine months without "molestation or hindrance." Also unmolested should be "women and children, scholars of every faculty, cultivators of the earth, artisans, manufacturers and fisherman unarmed and inhabiting unfortified towns, villages or places."

Prisoners of war were not to be sent to "distant and inclement countries" or crowded into "close and noxious places" but kept in "wholesome situations." They were not to "be confined in dungeons, prison-ships, nor prisons, not be put into irons, not bound, nor otherwise restrained in the use of their limbs." Officers should have "comfortable quarters" and the soldiers "lodged in barracks as roomy and good as for their own troops."

U.S. Army's Rules of War, 1863. During the Civil War, Columbia University professor Francis Lieber submitted his *Instructions for the Government of Armies of the United States in the Field* to the War Department. The Lieber Code, as it became known, was drawn from medieval jurists and incorporated into the Union Army as General Orders No. 100 (1863). It was one of the first field manuals in the modern era detailing what military actions were permitted and what were not. Among other things, the Code recognized the status of noncombatants, regulated treatment of prisoners of war, prohibited the use of poison, forbade the seizure of private property without compensation, and insisted that cultural treasures not be willfully destroyed. Lieber's basic philosophy begins at the end of Article 15: "Men who take up arms against one another in public war do not cease on this account to be moral beings, responsible to one another and to God." Article 16 continues: "Military necessity does not admit of cruelty—that is, the infliction of suffering for the sake of suffering or for revenge, nor of maiming or wounding except in fight, nor of torture to extort confessions. It does not admit of the use of poison in any way, nor of the wanton devastation of a district. It admits of deception, but disclaims acts of perfidy; and, in general, military necessity does not include any act of hostility which makes the return to peace unnecessarily difficult." Finally, Article 29 warns that military leaders must keep in mind that "war is not its own end, but the means to obtain great ends of State."

Lieber's contribution later influenced the Declaration of Brussels (1874) on the rules and customs of war.[22]

Geneva Convention of 1864. This convention, subsequently modified, provided the foundation for "humanitarian law." This pact, according to G. J. Adler, was a "landmark international attempt to reduce the horrors of war." The convention and humanitarian law were closely linked with the International Red Cross and Red Crescent movements. Open to all states, the multilateral treaty focused on three objectives: (1) the universal protection of victims of hostilities; (2) the obligation to extend assistance without discrimination to wounded and sick military personnel; (3) the respect for and marking of medical personnel, transports, and equipment during hostilities with the use of a red cross/crescent emblem.

This unsatisfactory convention recognized the role of the Red Cross as a neutral element among combatants and sought to provide protections for victims of hostilities. In an early test, the Franco-Prussian War, the Germans acknowledged the convention and "observed it quite creditably." The same cannot be said for the French, who initially knew little about it and, when they awakened to its existence, misinterpreted it. French troops were found firing at Red Cross–marked German ambulances and attendants, according to British historian Geoffry Best. "French civilians, hearing rumours of this miraculously effective symbol, in some places festooned their houses along the German lines of advance with Red Crosses, imagining that they would thus gain immunity from billeting, requisitions, and so on." There were also examples of individuals wearing a Red Cross emblem combing the battlefield after the fighting was over, killing the wounded and robbing the dead.

If the Geneva Convention was tarnished by these episodes, the Red Cross gradually became "a force to be reckoned with." During the Serbia-Bulgarian conflict in late 1885, for example, King Milan of Serbia allowed the Red Cross to ship its supplies safely through his territory to the Bulgarian lines.[23]

St. Petersburg Declaration, 1868. Seventeen European nations signed the Declaration which was the first formal, modern agreement prohibiting the use of certain weapons in war. It confirmed the customary rule according to which the use of arms, projectiles, and material of a nature to cause unnecessary suffering is prohibited. The Declaration also banned the use of fragmenting, explosive, or incendiary small arms ammunition ("dum-dum" bullets) under 400 grams because it was claimed that these bullets "unnecessarily aggravate the suffering of disabled men, or rendered their death inevitable." The ban did not prohibit the employment of explosive or incendiary materials in artillery rounds.

This rule was later endorsed in Article 23 (e) of the Hague Regulations on land warfare of 1899 and 1907.[24]

Brussels Declaration, 1874. Representatives of several nations met at Brussels in 1874 upon the invitation of Russian Czar Alexander II, to review the "laws and customs of war." At the so-called Brussels Conference distinguished jurists and authorities on international law undertook an extensive codification of the laws of war. The resulting International Declaration Concerning the Laws and Customs of War of August 27, 1874, was never ratified, but greatly influenced the Hague Conventions.

The Hague Conventions, 1899/1907. A major accomplishment of the Hague conferences was revising and codifying the laws or rules of war, especially those that had been agreed to in 1874 by the conference at Brussels. Ambassador Andrew White, a senior United States delegate in 1899, wrote that a major objective of the conference was "to take measures for diminishing cruelty and suffering in war."

Two conventions updating the law of war were concluded on July 29, 1899—the Convention with Respect to the Laws and Customs of War on Land and the Convention for the Adaptation to Marine Warfare. The conventions defined combatant status, provided norms for treatment of prisoners of war, the sick and wounded, and recognized the status of the International Red Cross. The 1907 Hague conference, influenced by the Russo-Japanese War, amplified and expanded 13 declarations from the first Hague conference. Agreements during this era rarely dealt with the problems and protections of noncombatants, and when they did so the provisions were vague.

These conventions revised the rules of war to restrict armies from using excessive force, especially at the expense of noncombatants and prisoners of war. The Hague rules were acknowledged and reasonably well followed during the Russo-Japanese War (1904). This was in marked contrast to the Balkan Wars (1912–1913) that were "marked by horror upon horror, by atrocious disregard for human suffering. All armies indulged in unbridled cruelties." During the Serbian invasion of Albania, the British attaché in Belgrade reported, "villages were wiped out, old men, women and children were either slaughtered in their homes or driven forth to die of cold and famine, the countryside was wasted in a orgy of wanton destruction." This, it seems, was encouraged by Serbian commanders.[25]

MODERNIZING OF THE LAW OF WAR

During World War I, the law of war was repeatedly and reciprocally violated. German General von Hindenberg argued: "One cannot make war in a sentimental fashion. The more pitiless the conduct of war, the more humane it is in reality for it will run its course all the sooner." Nonetheless, the Paris peace treaties of 1919, Sheldon Glueck observed, took the view that the moral duty of states was overriding and "to the extent that [the Hague rules] are merely declarative of existing customary international law, they were and are binding on all belligerents."[26]

Following WWI, there were attempts to put the genie back into the bottle: to restore and to strengthen the rule against the use of certain weapons, and to abolish or control new weapons that violated customs and law of war. After World War II, the focus was on incorporating a more humanitarian approach to the law of war.

Interwar Years

Hague Commission of Jurists: Rules of Air War, 1923. The initial prohibition of aerial bombing lasted only from 1899 to 1907; subsequently, World War I witnessed the initial use of "strategic bombing" of urban targets. While arms control advocates during the interwar years continued to seek restrictions or abolition of aerial bombing (see also Chapter 3), military strategists were developing plans to bomb the enemy's support infrastructure—inevitably in urban industrial cities. The military also were developing airplanes that could fly greater distances and carry heavier bomb loads in order to conduct "strategic bombing."

The Hague Commission, comprised of legal, diplomatic, and military experts from the Netherlands and France, Great Britain, Italy, Japan, and the United States, met from December 11, 1922, to February 18, 1923. After prolonged discussions, the commission approved a number of rules designed to govern aerial warfare. Article 22 of their General Report banned aerial attacks designed to terrorize civilian populations or injure non-combatants. Article 23 declared bombing to be legitimate only when directed at a military target defined as one whose destruction would constitute a distinct military advantage. Furthermore, Section 3 stated that if military targets "cannot be bombarded without the indiscriminate bombardment of the civilian population, the aircraft must abstain from bombardment." When the U.S. State Department asked the five conferees to agree on a treaty, Japan endorsed the idea but the four European countries rejected the treaty: Italy claimed that technical advances in aviation required further examination, France and the Netherlands offered several proposals for changes, and Great Britain demanded additional negotiations on the nature of aerial bombing. Consequently, The Hague rules failed to gain formal approval.[27]

Red Cross Conventions, 1929. Battlefield experiences of World War I resulted in two conventions signed in Geneva on July 27, 1929: one dealing with the treatment of wounded and sick combatants; and the other related to the treatment of prisoners of war. The Convention for the Amelioration of the Condition of the Wounded and Sick in Armies in the Field sought "to perfect and complete the provisions" of the previous Geneva pacts "for the amelioration of the condition of the wounded and sick." Its main features included provisions that combatants would be "treated with humanity and cared for medically, without distinction of nationality, by the belligerent in whose power they may be.... [T]he belligerent who is compelled to abandon wounded or sick to the enemy, shall, as far as military exigencies permit, leave with them a portion of his medical personnel and material to help with their treatment." Treatment of the sick and disabled was an important point, because during the twentieth century, thousands of combatants had died from disease. Additionally, belligerents must inform each other of "the names of the wounded, sick and dead, collected or discovered" and at the "cessation of hostilities they shall exchange the list of graves and of dead interred in their cemeteries and elsewhere."

The Convention on Treatment of Prisoners of War (1929) expanded The Hague rules (1907), and stressed that POWs "must at all times be humanely treated and protected, particularly against acts of violence, insults and public curiosity. Measures of reprisal against them are prohibited." Among other obligations was that "Difference in treatment among prisoners is lawful only when it is based on the military rank, state of physical or mental health, professional qualifications or sex of those who profit thereby." Also belligerents were charged with notifying each other of their POWs "within the shortest period possible" via various intermediaries. A POW was required "to give, if he is questioned on the subject, his true name and rank, or else his regimental number."

The second of these two conventions set forth conditions for treatment of POWs. Japan was not a party to the 1929 POW Convention, but was to the earlier Hague rules, which may have led the Japanese Army vice chief of staff in 1937 to declare: "... in order to wage total war in China, the empire will neither apply, nor act in accordance with, all the concrete articles of the Treaty Concerning the Law and Customs of Land Warfare and Other Treaties Concerning the Law and Regulations of Belligerency." The same directive ordered the "staff officers in China to stop using the term 'prisoner of war'" in an effort to avoid international reprimands. The Soviet Union was not a party to the 1929 POW convention, resulting in instances of egregious abuse and mixed treatment.

British and American personnel captured by German forces generally received treatment consistent with the 1929 Convention, while Russian prisoners of war in German hands, and vice-versa, suffered a variety of abuses, including summary executions. In the summer of 1944, Adolf Hitler attempted to create a systematic program of executing downed Allied "terror fliers." Senior German military authorities, including Field Marshal Wilhelm J. G. Keitel, General Alfred Jodl, and Commander-in-Chief of the Airforce Hermann Göring, apparently stifled the plan.

American treatment of German and Italian POWs generally adhered to the 1929 rules; however, abuses appear to have occurred in the Pacific. One account claims a colonel protested his superior's order to execute Japanese POWs: "But sir, they are wounded and want to surrender," the colonel complained. "You heard me, Colonel," the general replied, "I want no prisoners. Shoot them all." A young seaman wrote in his diary late in 1943 that "a few Japs parachuted when they were hit.... But a few sailors and Marines on the

20mm opened up on the ones in the chutes and when they hit the water they were nothing but a piece of meat cut to ribbons."[28]

The many Japanese violations of the law of war may be traced back to the Russo-Japanese War. After their victory, Japanese officers looked upon the surrender of their soldiers during the campaign, as contrary to the spirit of Bushido, and therefore, in future conflicts, no Japanese soldier was to be taken alive and he was encouraged to be contemptuous of POWs and noncombatants. This was reflected in their treatment of Australian POWs captured in Malaya and Americans and Filipino soldiers forced to make the Bataan Death March. For Japan's and others' violations of the Geneva Protocol of 1925, see Chapter 3.

Roerich Pact, 1935. Nicholas Roerich, a Russian-born artist, with the assistance of international legal experts, developed a treaty for protection of cultural sites during both war and peace. The Roerich Pact and Banner of Peace movement grew rapidly during the early 1930s, with centers in a number of countries. This treaty, the Protection of Artistic and Scientific Institutions and Historic Monuments, was often known as the Red Cross of Culture. It declared that "unfortified historic monuments, museums, scientific, artistic, educational and cultural institutions shall be considered as neutral and as such respected and protected by belligerents." To identify these facilities "use may be made of a distinctive flag (red circle with a triple red sphere in the circle on a white background)."[29]

Although the Roerich Pact was largely superseded by The Hague Convention for the Protection of Cultural Property in 1954, it is still in force today.

League Resolutions on Bombing, 1938. During Japan's invasion of China in 1937, Japanese aircraft destroyed large areas of such cities as Canton, Hangkow, Nanking, and Shanghai; although in Shanghai, Tokyo agreed to establish a designated sanctuary for refugees. Responding to Japan's bombing of Nanking, the U.S. State Department declared: "This Government holds the view, that any general bombing of an extensive area wherein there resides a large populace engaged in peaceful pursuits is unwarranted and contrary to principles of law and of humanity." For most Europeans and Americans, however, the destruction of Guernica—immortalized by Pablo Picasso's mural—by German bombers during the Spanish Civil War became the most recognizable example of indiscriminate aerial attack.

Inspired by the destructive bombing of Spanish cities during its civil war, Britain's Prime Minister Neville Chamberlain in June 1938 offered three basic principles to restrict aviation warfare. These principles were incorporated into a League of Nations resolution and approved by the League Assembly at Geneva, without dissent, on September 28, 1938. The three principles were: (1) the intentional bombing of civilians was illegal; (2) aerial bombing targets must be identifiable military objectives; and (3) aerial attacks on military targets must be "carried out in such a way that civilian populations in the neighborhood are not bombed through negligence."

These principles, however, failed to distinguish between "civilians" who were noncombatants and those who were not. Many functions behind the front lines, such as those involved in manufacturing, transporting and in other ways handling military items, could be legitimate military targets.

When Germany invaded Poland on September 1, 1939, President Franklin D. Roosevelt publicly appealed to each warring nation "to affirm its determination that its armed forces shall in no event and under no circumstances undertake bombardment from the air of civilian populations or unfortified cities." Within 24 hours, the leaders of Germany, France, England, and Poland replied, in varied fashions, that they would bomb only "military objectives." During the first nine months of WWII, England, France, and Germany abided unilaterally by this prohibition. Poland, especially Warsaw, was exempt from this restraint and later, Rotterdam. By the time the United States entered the war in December 1941, all such restraints had disappeared and bombers of both sides regularly targeted urban areas.

Civilian casualties resulting from post–WW II military operations were labeled "collateral damage." The military's strategic criteria, as the commanders see it, does "not necessarily coincide with the dictates of humanity." As British historian Michael Howard has pointed out:

> The military case against area bombing would be, not that it was inhumane, but that it was ineffective in achieving its objective of demoralizing the civilian populations and reducing war production; that it was psychologically 'counter-productive' and materially wasteful.... The military principle of 'economy of force' may sometimes conveniently coincide with the dictates of transcendent moral values, but there is little historical justification for assuming that this will always be the case.[30]

Post–World War II

The tens of millions of deaths and widespread destruction of World War II greatly overshadowed the toll of its predecessor, and indicated the necessity for further enhancement and expansion of previous treaties defining the law of war. The most significant of these activities were the four 1949 Geneva Conventions which became among the most widely endorsed agreements currently in force. Each of the four begins with "an obligation on the part of the parties 'to respect and to ensure respect' for each of the conventions 'in all circumstances.'" Implied here is a partial rejection of the just war concept. The 1949 conventions are neutral and provide protections for all legitimate combatants regardless of the "just" nature of their wars—whether declared or undeclared. In addition, they "prohibit the persons or objects that are the subject of the treaty from being the object of medical experimentation, torture, reprisal, or collective punishment. Each convention sets forth specific offenses that are regarded as "grave breaches" or major violations. Some 170 states have become party to these conventions—but implementation has been uneven.

Geneva Conventions (I & II), 1949. These two pacts consist of the Convention for the Amelioration of the Condition of the Wounded and Sick in Armed

Forces in the Field and the Convention for the Amelioration of the Condition of Wounded, Sick and Shipwrecked Members of Armed Forces at Sea. The essential aspects of the first convention were defined in the 1864 and 1929 Geneva Conventions (see above). The 1949 change sought protection for wounded or sick combatants ("out of action") from intentional attack. The extensive naval battles of WWII prompted the second convention that provides protection for sick, wounded, and shipwrecked naval personnel.

The initial two conventions also extend protection to regular medical personnel including military chaplains, administrative, and logistical personnel during the period they are carrying out medical-related duties. The Additional Protocol I (1977) provided similar protection to "civilian medical and religious personnel and civilian medical installations and equipment." Unarmed hospital ships and medical aircraft were granted certain assurances of safety.

Geneva Convention (III), 1949. The third 1949 pact, the Convention Relative to the Treatment of Prisoners of War, was grounded on the Annex to the 1907 Hague Convention IV, and the first Geneva Convention Relative to the Treatment of Prisoners of War (1929). POW status is unique in that a former combatant now must be sustained and protected by his captor, provided he does not attempt to escape or injure his captors. Until their repatriation, the captor must provide food, clothing, shelter, and medical care to POWs commensurate to that afforded his own forces. Military medical personnel and civilians captured while accompanying or working with combatants in the field during wartime were to be granted regular POW status. Article XIII holds that "Prisoners of war must at all times be humanely treated."

Additionally, the Third Convention insisted that captors gather information about the POWs in hand and create an information agency that can relay this data to the prisoner's national authorities. The transmission of the collected data may be sent via a Central Prisoners of War Information Agency.

Geneva Convention (IV), 1949. The Convention Relative to the Protection of Civilian Persons in Time of War promulgated in 1949 has a long, checkered history. The modern concept of noncombatants—that civilians should be protected from military violence so long as they were not involved in hostilities—is rooted in medieval Europe's Peace of God pledges although glimpses of it may be found even earlier. According to Article III, individuals with no active role in the hostilities are to be protected from "violence to life and person, in particular murder of all kinds, mutilation, cruel treatment and torture.... outrages upon personal dignity, in particular humiliating and degrading treatment."

Abuses by Germany and Japan arising during World War II prompted the obligation that an occupying power has a special responsibility toward the civilian population. Article XXVII declares that persons in occupied territories "are entitled, in all circumstances, to respect for their persons, their honour, their family rights, their manners and customs. They shall at all times be humanely treated, and shall be protected especially against all acts of violence or threats thereof and against insults and public curiosity."

The principle that civilian population and civilian objects not engaged in the nation's defense or military activities are exempt from intentional military actions rests on solid law. Military officers, who desire to avoid spending resources on individuals or objects that do not threaten their mission, generally support this principle. Yet, as Hays points out, "Application of this simple principle is complicated by the degree to which some civilians in industrialized societies engage in activities that are essential to a nation's defense or military force's mission or, at the lower end of the conflict spectrum, the degree to which a guerrilla force uses the civilian population to conceal its identity or accomplish its mission." This is clearly a dilemma that has been confronted during the beginning of the twenty-first century.[31]

Compliance with the 1949 Geneva Conventions. While the results have been mixed, the existence of these conventions has provided the benchmarks against which a nation's military behavior may be judged. When, for example, Israeli forces withdrew from Lebanon in 1985, they took with them 1,100 Lebanese POWs. A few weeks later, after the United States and other nations protested this action as a violation of the Third Convention, Israel arranged a 2 for 1,100 POW exchange. The 1991 Gulf War provided an opportunity for the new automated Prisoner of War Information System, developed by the U.S. Army, to ensure adherence with the accountability provisions of the Third Convention. An unprecedented 99.99 percent accuracy was achieved in accounting for the 69,820 Iraqi POWs captured by French, British, and American forces.

Since September 11, 2001, the U.S. Central Intelligence Agency (CIA) has operated as though it had the authority to seize, move, interrogate, and secretly detain suspected terrorists at undisclosed locations around the world. This included transferring suspected terrorists, taken in one country, to the security forces of other countries guilty of human rights abuses. Suspected Al Qaeda warriors, taken during the Afghanistan war, were not classified by American authorities as "protected persons" under convention rules and many were shipped to the U.S. base at Guantanamo Bay, Cuba, and elsewhere, for interrogation.

During the occupation of Iraq, some believe that United States officials may have violated the War Crimes Act of 1996, Geneva Conventions, and Uniform Code of Military Justice. U.S. authorities undertook unilaterally and secretly to reinterpret Article 49 of the 1949 Fourth Geneva Convention that protects civilians during occupation, including insurgents, from "individual or mass forcible transfers." A Department of Justice's March 19, 2004, memorandum authorized the CIA to transfer Iraqis out of their country for a "brief ... not indefinite period" and permanently remove "illegal aliens." Questions also have been raised about failure to provide adequate care for noncombatant and possible insurgent detainees at various prisons within Iraq and about possible illegal methods employed during interrogation there and elsewhere.[32]

If twentieth-century treatment of POWs has occasionally matched the brutality of earlier times, optimists believe that overall respect for the law of war regarding their treatment has steadily improved. It is difficult to say the same for the treatment of noncombatants and suspected insurgents.

Hague Convention for the Protection of Cultural Property, 1954, 1999. Following the massive destruction of the world's cultural heritage during World War II, this pact focused exclusively on the protection of cultural sites and activities. Adopted at The Hague, the Convention for the Protection of Cultural Property in the Event of Armed Conflict covered "immovables and movables, including monuments of architecture, art or history, archaeological sites, works of art, manuscripts, books and other objects of artistic, historical or archaeological interest, as well as scientific collections of all kinds."

The states party to the convention, 118 as of 2007, pledged to protect and respect cultural property during armed conflict, establish mechanisms to provide this protection and identify specific buildings and monuments with a designated symbol—a new blue shield that replaced the Roerich Banner of Peace (see above). The International Register of Cultural Property's "special protection" list identifies sites, monuments, or refuges of movable cultural objects under the direction of the Commissioners-General for Cultural Property.

Following a review of the convention in 1991, a Second Protocol to The Hague Convention was adopted at The Hague in March 1999 to remedy certain deficiencies in the original pact. The Second Protocol established a new category of enhanced protection for cultural heritage and enhanced important national legal protection. It also detailed sanctions for serious violations of cultural property and defined situations in which individual criminal responsibility should apply. Finally, it created a 12-member Intergovernmental Committee to supervise the convention and the Second Protocol.[33]

Convention against Torture, 1984. The Convention against Torture and Other Cruel, Inhuman or Degrading Treatment or Punishment obligated each state party to the agreement to "take effective legislative, administrative, judicial or other measures to prevent acts of torture in any territory under its jurisdiction." Torture was defined as "any act by which severe pain or suffering, whether physical or mental, is intentionally inflicted on a person for such purposes as obtaining from him or a third person information or confession." Orders from superior officers or "a public authority" could not be invoked as a justification for torture. Nor could "any statement which is established to have been made as a result of torture" be used "as evidence in any proceedings, except against a person accused of torture." A Committee against Torture, consisting of 10 recognized experts of "high moral standing," would receive reports from convention parties, via the Secretary-General of the United Nations, regarding the measures they had taken to prevent such acts. The Committee would bring to the attention of any state allegations of any violations of the convention, expecting to receive within six months written explanations clarifying the matter and any remedy undertaken.[34]

For the various forms of negotiations employed, the several types of verification adopted and problems of compliance or noncompliance, see Part II.

Stabilizing the International Environment

Modern weaponry has created new challenges—and the need for new arms control techniques—for those nations seeking to sustain a healthy, stable ecological and political environment. The result has been an array of agreements that may be grouped into three general categories: (1) treaties that protect the ecological environment; (2) measures aimed at preventing unintended conflicts; and (3) agreements that focus on confidence-building among nations.

With expanded atmospheric testing of nuclear devices in the mid-1950s that spewed radioactive particles worldwide and that returned to the earth as "fallout," there was concern about its detrimental impact upon human health. Fear of the consequences of radioactive fallout aroused increasing public protest. When a 1957 Gallup Poll revealed that 63 percent of the American people favored banning tests, compared to 20 percent three years earlier, government officials took notice. Albert Schweitzer, Linus Pauling, and a host of "peace" groups led a worldwide protest aimed at halting all testing. Others engaged in the debate included Soviet scientist Andrei Sakharov, who gradually became a staunch advocate of a nuclear test ban. Analyzing available data to calculate the dangers of radioactive fallout, he argued that the radioactive carbon from the detonation of a one-megaton "clean" H-bomb could have long-lasting global effects. This finding directly contradicted the assertions of his Soviet colleagues, as well as American physicist Edward Teller, all of whom insisted that the fallout caused little harm.

The limited nuclear test ban (LNTB) signed in 1963 by the two superpowers, and joined by many states throughout the world, was a partial measure but it greatly lessened testing of nuclear devices in the atmosphere. Unfortunately, once the fear of radioactive fallout was eliminated, nuclear testing no longer was a public issue. Thus, the LNTB gave "the continuation of uninhibited weapons development political respectability" and "the pace of nuclear testing, albeit underground, actually quickened." From 1964 to 1992, the United States conducted 683 announced underground tests, compared with 494 for the Soviet

Union. It was an example of an arms control measure that increased the exploitation of permitted activities.

The superpowers continued to build huge nuclear arsenals despite the fact their use could very likely cause a "nuclear winter" that would wreak havoc throughout the world by greatly disrupting climatic conditions. A group of American and Soviet scientists concluded in 1983 that a nuclear war would sufficiently alter the climate of the Northern Hemisphere to cause months of darkness and freezing weather, substantially reducing food supplies. The U.S. Defense Department admitted that a climatic disaster was possible, but called the American scientists the "tools" of Soviet propaganda and insisted that the solution would be found in technology—perhaps, a ballistic missile defense.[1] In the late 1990s, negotiations for a comprehensive nuclear test ban (CTB) resulted in a treaty that has remained in limbo because a few key nations, including the United States, have refused to ratify it.

A chaotic political and economic situation followed the demise of the Soviet Union; its nuclear and chemical weapons were frequently left in unsecured conditions that risked their theft and subsequent transfer to undesirable groups or states. This unsatisfactory situation prompted the United States to aid in consolidating and securing the former Soviet nuclear arsenal. Initiated by two U.S. Senators, the Cooperative Threat Reduction program (1992) provided financial and technical assistance to ensure the custodial safety of sensitive weapons depots. Belatedly, the United States also provided assistance to dispose of chemical weapons and fissile material extracted from nuclear warheads.

History has demonstrated that warfare's violence can wreck havoc on local environments, some with short-term effects and others having a long-term impact. A select list of such ecologically disruptive activities, ranging from the Persian-Scythian War of 512 BCE to the Kampuchean Insurrection of 1975–1977, may be found in SIPRI's useful study, *Warfare in a Fragile World: Military Impact on the Human Environment*. There is a biblical injunction condemning the chopping down of fruit trees during military operations: "When you besiege a city for a long time, making war against it in order to take it, you shall not destroy its trees by wielding an axe against them.... Only the trees which you know are not for food you may destroy." Later efforts to minimize the impact of hostilities upon the environment were emphasized in the tenth-century Peace of God pacts (see Chapter 5) and continued in various rules governing warfare. French farmers, for example, more than 80 years later still plough up unexploded high-detonation shells dating from 1914–1918. After World War II, German officials were charged with a "war crime" at Nuremberg for the pillaging of Polish forests. The United States' abuse of the natural environment during the Vietnam conflict, together with the use of various chemical agents and physical abuse of the land, led to a new term—ecocide. Concern that such activities posed an unacceptable immediate, as well as a long-term danger to the environment and humans, prompted the Environmental Modification Convention (1977).[2]

To reduce the danger that an accident, miscalculation, or unintentional act might trigger a nuclear attack, quick and reliable communications—hotlines—were established between the heads of government of several nuclear weapons states. The initial hotline (1963), linking Washington and Moscow, was established to reduce the possibility that an isolated incident might spark a much wider unanticipated, especially nuclear, conflict. Later, other states created similar communication links with their adversaries.

Accords aimed at preventing unintended conflicts or seeking to build confidence and trust between hostile states, were frequently ridiculed as "arms control junk food" by skeptics. Yet in a time of high tensions, these bilateral superpower measures could quickly dispatch information to heads of state preventing a serious miscalculation of an opponent's intent. With the end of the Cold War and the advent of terrorist activity, the nature of the threats to a nation's security has changed. It is possible, nevertheless, that some of these arms control measures may find new usages, such as the transfer of information regarding suspicious individuals and/or activities.

These Cold War agreements and others also served as confidence-building measures that without fanfare, allowed civilian and military commanders often near to nuclear triggers, to discuss their apprehensions and concerns about possible miscalculations. To that end, the Conference on Security and Cooperation in Europe (CSCE) brought together three basic groups: NATO, the Warsaw Treaty Organization, and the loosely organized neutral and unaligned states. The superpowers also attended. The decisions emanating from the various discussions—the Helsinki Final Act (1975), the Stockholm Document (1985), and the Vienna Documents (1990, 1992)—played a major arms-control-like role in creating an atmosphere that reduced tensions, established a treaty limiting Europe's conventional weaponry and, probably, pointed the way to the end of the Cold War.

What follows is a representative, chronological sampling, together with a brief narrative description, of the treaties and agreements that demonstrated the historical lineage of stabilizing the international environment.

PROTECTING THE ENVIRONMENT

As modern technology revealed more sophisticated weapons, especially chemical and nuclear ones, a general concern arose regarding their impact upon human beings and the general environment. After a Limited Nuclear Test Ban was signed, the search for a global comprehensive nuclear test ban (CTB) was stalled by the United States' insistence upon continued underground testing in order to "safeguard" its arsenal of nuclear weapons—that is, to maintain their safety and reliability. If Washington's emphasis on the "safeguard" has been used to avoid a complete prohibition of all types of nuclear testing, the United States nonetheless has observed a moratorium on testing since 1992.

During the Indochina conflict (1960s–1970s), a global concern arose over the United States' widespread assault upon Vietnam's environment. The use of some 75 million liters of herbicides to defoliate forest areas suspected of shielding enemy forces left about one-tenth of that nation and some neighboring border areas devoid of greenery. Additional actions severely damaging the environment included excessive "cratering" resulting from aerial and ground bombardments, the use of giant earth-scrapping plows that buried the top soil, the deliberate creation of firestorms to level forested areas, and attempts at weather modification. Such activities raised global concerns and resulted in a treaty that focused on the employment of modern technologies that were likely to cause long-lasting harm to the environment.[3]

Limited Nuclear Test Ban, 1963. Despite serious global concerns about the fallout from nuclear testing in the mid-1950s, a prolonged eight-year diplomatic and scientific debate finally succeeded in overcoming mistrust and national security apprehensions in Washington and Moscow. After seismologists developed acceptable techniques to distinguish between earthquakes and small underground nuclear explosions, the opponents of limits on testing demanded more refinements to reduce the already small error rate. Those American politicians and military analysts arguing against a test ban claimed that with current verification techniques one could not be *absolutely* certain no cheating was going on. In this atmosphere, the Eisenhower administration unsuccessfully pursued a comprehensive nuclear ban with a robust on-site inspection system.

Following the October 1962 Cuban Missile Crisis, diplomats from the United States and the Soviet Union finally agreed to a Limited (or Partial) Nuclear Test Ban. The August 5, 1963, treaty—the Treaty Banning Nuclear Weapon Tests In the Atmosphere, In Outer Space and Under Water (LTBT)—has been often labeled the Partial Test Ban Treaty (PTBT). As its title indicates, the treaty prohibited nuclear weapon test explosions and any other nuclear explosions in three environments: the atmosphere, outer space, and underwater. It did not prohibit or restrict underground nuclear explosions.

The phrase "or any other nuclear explosion" was introduced during the LTBT deliberations specifically to prohibit any so-called peaceful explosions of nuclear devices (PNEs) for civil engineering applications. Since any nuclear explosion could provide militarily useful information, a signatory state could conduct nuclear explosions providing valuable military data while insisting that they were solely for peaceful purposes. Shortly after the signing at Moscow, the treaty was open to other nations for signature and 124 states had acceded to it by 2003. "No other accomplishment in the White House," presidential assistant Theodore Sorensen has written, "ever gave Kennedy greater satisfaction." Yet the pact failed to slow down the nuclear arms race, as many individuals had hoped; indeed, as arms controller Spurgeon Keeny concluded, the limited test ban was largely "an environmental measure."[4]

The Soviet Union's venting of radioactive particles into the atmosphere beyond its borders led to the Reagan administration's complaint of several treaty violations; Moscow reciprocated by pointing out occasions of U.S. venting. It is possible to view such episodes as an unintended violation (see Chapter 9).

Threshold Test Ban Treaty, 1974. When the United States ruled out a comprehensive test ban at their Moscow summit meeting in July 1974, Premier Leonid Brezhnev and President Richard Nixon resurrected an earlier proposal for a bilateral Threshold Test Ban (TTBT). In the agreement, the two nations agreed to restrict underground tests to less than 150 kilotons, to hold the number of tests to a minimum, to not interfere with the other's efforts at verification, and to exchange detailed data on all tests and test sites. Concerned that an occasional test explosion might accidentally exceed the prescribed limit of 150 kilotons, a separate agreement granted both parties a "one or two slight unintended breaches per year." The effective date of the pact was postponed until March 31, 1976, because military chiefs on both sides wanted to complete some high-yield tests.

Possible treaty violations resulted, in part, from cumulative, inflated American seismic readings of Soviet underground testing caused by differences in local geology in their two test sites. Thus, the Carter and Reagan administrations came to different verdicts from the same data. The former held that the evidence suggesting that Soviet tests exceeding the 150 kiloton limit was too ambiguous to charge them with violations. The Reagan administration concluded that "while the available evidence is ambiguous, in view of the ambiguities in the pattern of Soviet testing and in view of verification uncertainties, and we have been unable to reach a definitive conclusion," the Soviets may have violated the treaty. "Taking into account the statistical uncertainty in measuring underground test yields," the Stanford study on compliance concluded in 1988 that "there is no persuasive evidence that the Soviet Union is in violation of the TTBT."[5]

Peaceful Nuclear Explosions Treaty, 1976. This agreement, signed by Brezhnev and President Gerald Ford in May 1976, followed more than two years of discussions to find a way to authorize peaceful nuclear explosions of more than 150 kilotons. The Soviets apparently desired to use such explosions for earth-moving projects, but it was concluded that the larger blasts could yield military benefits. Therefore, the 1976 accord returned to authorizing peaceful nuclear explosives under 150 kilotons for such purposes as creating canals.

The peaceful explosions pact provided, for the first time, on-site inspections under specific circumstances. When the first Non-Proliferation Treaty review conference met in 1976, the non-nuclear nations focused on the lack of progress for a comprehensive test ban. Washington and Moscow agreed to honor the two previously signed agreements, but delayed public discussion on the ratification of both the threshold and peaceful explosions treaties. The United States insisted that verification details be worked out before submitting the treaty for ratification—eventually they were.[6]

Environmental Modification Convention, 1977. Major conflicts, according to Arthur H. Westing, inevitably lead to three levels of environment damage:

1. *Unintentional damage*—refers to such battle related actions as extensive air and ground bombardment and operating heavy off-road vehicles that destroy farms, natural resources, and pollute the local water and air;
2. *Intentional damage*—involves intentionally destroying "fields or forest as a specific means of denying to the enemy ... access to water, food, feed and construction materials, as well as access to cover or sanctuary;" and
3. *Intentionally amplified environmental damage*—means manipulating "one component or another of the environment for hostile military purposes in a way that is intended to result in the release of dangerous pent-up forces."

Examples of damaging the environment prompted by U.S. actions during the Vietnam conflict greatly stimulated interest in providing new protections.

It was, then, prevention of "intentionally amplified environmental damage" that guided the formulation of the Environmental Modification Convention (EnMod). It prohibited the use of techniques that have "widespread, long-lasting or severe effects," in other words, that commit ecocide. "Ecocide means any of the following acts," Richard Falk has written,

committed with intent to disrupt or destroy, in whole or in part, a human ecosystem: (a) the use of weapons of mass destruction, whether ... chemical, or others; (b) the use of chemical herbicides to defoliate and deforest natural forests for military purposes; (c) the use of bombs and artillery in such quantity, density, or size as to impair the quality of soil (or enhance possibility of disease); (d) the use of bulldozing equipment ...; [and] (e) the use of techniques designed to modify rate of rainfall or modify weather.

The 1977 Protocol I Additional to the 1949 Geneva Convention prohibited military actions "intended to or may be expected to cause widespread, long-term and severe damage to the natural environment, which would prejudice the health or survival of the population." If the terms of the two treaties are not synonymous, both treaties do accept the inevitability of conventional battlefield damage.[7]

Comprehensive Test Ban Treaty, 1996. The non-nuclear states' search for a Comprehensive Test Ban (CTB) was closely linked to that of the powers who desired to restrict the spread of nuclear weapons via the Non-Proliferation regime (see Chapter 4). The inability to gain substantial traction during CTB negotiations was a source of considerable diplomatic friction for five decades, especially at the periodic Non-proliferation Treaty review conferences. On two occasions, in 1977 and 1985, the Soviet Union sought to break the deadlock only to have critics in the United States—Senate Cold War hawks, heads of nuclear weapons laboratories, and the military chiefs—kill the efforts. In January 1990, Washington reiterated that it had "not identified any further limitations on nuclear testing ... that would be in the United States' national security interest," despite the United States' increasingly isolated position.[8] In 1992, however, Congress banned all U.S. nuclear testing and the ban has continued.

Finally, the UN General Assembly overwhelmingly adopted a Comprehensive Nuclear Test Ban Treaty on September 10, 1996, and President William Clinton was the first world leader to sign the agreement. Unfortunately, the Senate Foreign Relations Committee's Republican chairman, Jesse Helms, a long-time opponent of the test ban, blocked its consideration until late in 1999, when the Senate unexpectedly scheduled a quick ratification vote. After a short but bitter partisan debate, the Senate failed to ratify the treaty in October 1999 by a vote of 51–48, falling far short of the 67 votes needed.

Cooperative Threat Reduction Program, 1992. The demise of the Soviet Union and the chaos that followed led to the U.S. Cooperative Threat Reduction (CTR) program, usually called the Nunn-Lugar program after its sponsors Senators Sam Nunn (D-GA) and Richard Lugar (R-IN). The Nunn-Lugar legislative act of November 12, 1992, provided U.S. financial assistance to the Commonwealth of Independent States, especially Russia, to consolidate the former Soviet nuclear arsenal and ensure their custodial safety. Later, assistance in the destruction of former Soviet chemical arms was added to the program. The 10-year, $4 billion program was designed to:

1. "destroy nuclear weapons, chemical weapons, and other weapons";
2. "transport, store, disable, and safeguard weapons in connection with their destruction," and
3. "establish verifiable safeguards against the proliferation of such weapons."

The United States also sought to assist in defense conversion and increased military to military exchanges. The cost of the program, some $400 million per year, has been less than half of what Americans spend on cat food annually.

Retired Maj. Gen. William Burns, who had presided over a truly landmark agreement that enabled the United States to purchase 500 metric tons of highly enriched uranium from dismantled warheads, negotiated the umbrella agreement and a few implementing arrangements with the Russian Federation. Subsequently, the Clinton administration selected Ambassador James Goodby (1993–1994) to work out the details of the Nunn-Lugar agreements with the countries that had departed the Soviet Union and arrange the financial commitments made to the recipient countries.

In more than 15 years of CTR efforts, much has been accomplished: 6,954 nuclear warheads deactivated; 644 ICBMs and 606 SLBMs eliminated; 155 strategic bombers destroyed; 12 security upgrades implemented at nuclear weapon storage sites; and 328 train shipments of nuclear weapons were moved to more secure, centralized storage sites. The Global Partnership, including CTR programs, reported in 2008 that they upgraded security at 75 percent of nuclear weapons material sites "of concern," including all 50 Russian navy nuclear sites, 11 Russian Strategic Rocket Forces sites, and 175 individual buildings containing weapons-grade materials. Russia has decommissioned some 18 nuclear-powered submarines each year with the assistance of donor states.

Additionally, the program purchased the large quantity of highly enriched uranium from dismantled warheads and prompted the dismantlement of nuclear weapons installations in Belarus, Kazakhstan, and the Ukraine.

While the program had made significant progress in many areas, there were nonetheless several complaints voiced about the management and implementation of America aid. Among major concerns, as cited by William Potter, were: (1) "the slow pace of implementation, both at the top decision-making levels and between [the Department of Defense] and contractor on the ground;" (2) the United States' "lack of management flexibility" and the insistence of imposing American accounting systems, work plans, and schedules on Russian participants; (3) the redundant senior "level of bureaucracy" and the great "number of 'consultants' who consumed CTR resources but contributed little to specific projects;" and (4) the employment of mostly American contractors at higher cost and with greater delays than using qualified in-country personnel and suppliers.[9]

These "bumps in the road" were minor compared to the possible loss of interest on the part of the American and Russian governments to ensure that the program's goals were met.

PREVENTING UNINTENDED CONFLICTS

Although history may hold few examples of accidental or unintended conflicts—World War I's "accidental" origin has been frequently cited—the advent of nuclear weapons, and the premium placed on striking first, gave rise to fears that miscalculation, misperception, or hasty decisions might bring about an "unintended" nuclear conflict. The desire to provide each side with the opportunity to consider fully a potential "crisis situation" before undertaking irreversible, cataclysmic action led to diplomatic, usually bilateral, negotiations designed to improve rapid, direct communication between heads of state or military chiefs in times of high tension. These measures, including accidents, measures agreements, hotlines, risk reduction centers, and so on, have been called "quiet" arms control techniques, because they have had "the least intense and divisive expectations."

Some of the tension-reducing and confidence-building measures mentioned below, indicate where they relate to other arms control agreements. Examples include the confidence-building measures in Europe that provided prior notification of military maneuvers, in order to reduce fears that a surprise attack was underway. Also discussed below are bilateral activities between the United States and the USSR—and later between other states—that provided for the so-called hotlines and other measures designed to prevent untoward incidents.

"Hot Line" Accords, 1963. The 1963 "Hot Line" agreement was the first bilateral agreement during the Cold War that recognized the perils implicit in modern nuclear-weapons systems that combined incredible destructive power

with short flight times. Informally known as Molink, the first hotline was established after the 1962 Cuban Missile Crisis, which painfully emphasized the lack of facilities for leaders in Washington and Moscow to communicate directly. On June 20, 1963, at Geneva, American and Soviet representatives signed the "Memorandum of Understanding Between the United States of America and the Union of Soviet Socialist Republics Regarding the Establishment of a Direct Communications Link." The agreement provided that each government would be responsible for arranging the link on its own territory, including the continuous functioning of the link, and the prompt delivery of received messages to its head of government.

An annex set forth the routing and components of the link and provided for allocation of costs, exchange of equipment, and other technical matters. The direct communications link would comprise:

1. two terminal points with teletype equipment;
2. a full-time duplex wire telegraph circuit (Washington-London-Copenhagen-Stockholm-Helsinki-Moscow); and
3. a full-time duplex radiotelegraph circuit (Washington-Tangier-Moscow).

If the wire circuit should be interrupted, messages were to be transmitted by the radio circuit. The Direct Communications Link in Washington consisted of a group of machines—IBM terminals, encryption machines, and teleprinters, among others—manned locked in a room between the National Military Intelligence Center and the National Military Command Center.

During the 1971 SALT talks, it was agreed that two other links be added to the original cable by using an American commercial satellite (INTELSAT) and a Soviet government satellite (MOLNIYA). In 1984, hotline technology was further modernized when the system added high-speed facsimile transmission so that maps, charts, texts, and photographs could be quickly sent and received. An urgent message from a Russian leader to the president's ear took less than five minutes, including translation. The 1971 accident measures agreement contains provisions for a parallel, but lower level, direct communications system.

Other nations adopted the concept of a direct communication system. The British and French established their own direct links with Moscow; while Israel and Egypt created a direct line, North and South Korea became linked, and India and Pakistan have been connected since the 1971 war.[10]

Accidents Measures Agreement, 1971. The Soviet Union first proposed specific safeguards against surprise attack in 1954, while it also expressed concerns about the danger of an accidental or unintended conflict. The Conference of Experts on Surprise Attack was held in Geneva during 1958, but recessed without achieving conclusive results. However, the meeting did stimulate technical research regarding the basic issues that subsequently led to the United States' offer of measures to reduce the risks of war in its General and Complete

Disarmament proposal of September 25, 1961. These included advance notification of military movements and maneuvers, observation posts at major transportation centers and air bases, and additional inspection arrangements. An international commission would be established to study possible further measures to reduce risks, including "failure of communication." No action was taken at that time.

The 1971 Accidents Measures Agreement urged both sides to undertake measures to improve the safety and security of their nuclear activities, and to notify each other immediately of unauthorized or accidental nuclear weapons detonations. The agreement provided for certain mutual constraints on military activities and for advance notice of missile test launches in the direction of the other party.

Overriding the objections of the Joint Chiefs of Staff, Washington unilaterally released general information concerning its procedures for safeguarding against an accidental launch of a nuclear weapon. Although this action did not elicit a corresponding response, the Americans hoped it might prompt the adoption by the Soviet Union of similar safeguard measures. Washington ignored several suggestions by Moscow to include other nations in the pact because of suspicions that the Soviets might be trying to weaken the Western alliance. France (1976) and Great Britain (1977), however, did negotiate similar separate bilateral arrangements with the Soviet Union.[11]

Because of the secrecy surrounding the agreement during the Cold War years, and the subsequent lack of interest by analysts, it is difficult to discern acts of compliance or noncompliance. Indeed, the public record suggests that the main provisions of the Accidents Measures Agreement were never invoked. This may have been because of the wide latitude extended to the parties to define what the provisions involved. Examining the months from early 1979 to the end of June 1980, the American early warning system reported 147 low-level alerts indicating a potential threat to the United States, including four instances of reaching the second-highest alert level. Yet there is no readily available public evidence to indicate that the American officials requested clarification from the Soviets via the 1971 agreement. Conversely, when high Soviet intelligence officials became alarmed about a NATO nuclear exercise (Able Archer 83) in early November 1983, there is no indication that they quizzed Washington concerning its duration or purpose.

If it is unclear whether the AMA's provisions were ever employed, it "has enjoyed at least one unambiguous success. Since 1971 both sides have refrained from testing missiles on flight paths in the direction of the other (Article 4)." Additionally, America instituted or upgraded several changes to provide safeguards to prevent accidents in its command and control system for nuclear weapons. While some of the measures pre-date 1971, they included "computer-constructed key codes, coding devices and interlocks, a sealed authenticator system, permissive action links, overlapping communication systems, a personnel reliability program, emergency destruction devices and a two-man rule." The Soviets/Russians have not revealed implementation of any similar measures.

In another minor achievement, representatives of the Standing Consultative Committee agreed in 1976 on a code that provided prompt transmission of the nature of any accident involving nuclear weaponry. They did not, however, define the nature of accidents that required notification—an indication of the low regard with which this agreement was held. From the available evidence, Moscow held this and similar agreements in much higher regard than did Washington.[12]

High Seas Accord, 1972. During the 1960s and early 1970s, Soviet and American naval commanders engaged in various forms of harassment on and above the high seas. These actions were intended to obtain additional intelligence regarding the nature of their opponent's equipment and tactics. This behavior included an occasional game of "chicken" where two rival warships would threaten to ram each other until one or the other turned away; buzzing an enemy ship with an aircraft; aiming one's large guns at an opponent's ship; and nudging or "shouldering" opponent's ships. Eventually both sides recognized the need to modify the aggressive behavior of both fleets and expand the traditional naval "rules of the road" to prevent an unintended military engagement.

The resulting document regulated dangerous maneuvers and required ships to maintain a certain distance from each other during aircraft takeoffs and landings. Simulated attacks were strictly forbidden, as was excessive use of searchlights and "buzzings" by aircraft. The accord resulted in the development of unique military signals to augment existing international ones so that ship captains could contact each other. The pact also established a navy-to-navy communications channel to be used by naval attachés to report or discuss violations, and annual review meetings to discuss problems and solutions.[13]

Prevention of Nuclear War Accord, 1973. This agreement came only after complex negotiations, beginning with Moscow's desire to gain a mutual pledge not to use nuclear weapons against each other. Basing its position on the possible need to employ nuclear weapons in support of NATO to repel a conventional Soviet attack in Europe, the United States refused to issue a "nonuse of nuclear weapons" pledge or to renounce the option of "first use" of nuclear weapons.

Additionally, the Soviets sought American assistance in preventing provocations by other nuclear weapons powers. Not wanting to give the impression of joint superpower dominion, Washington "redirected the negotiations toward provisions to avoid nuclear war, such as renouncing the use of force in diplomacy and pledging to consult in situations that contain the risk of nuclear war." The Prevention of Nuclear War pact, much like the Accident Measures Agreement, provided few "rules of behavior" as guidelines, and little effort was expended in establishing the pact as an operational reality.[14]

USSR/Russia "No-first-use" of Nuclear Weapons, 1982–1993. Moscow's 1982 pledge not to use nuclear weapons first during a crisis was not reciprocated by the United States, as noted above. A decade later, after the collapse of the Soviet Union and with the reductions required by the CFE treaty, the Russian Federation's Security Council in November 1993 reversed the 1982 policy.

Since Russia's conventional forces had become inferior to both the NATO and Chinese conventional forces, Moscow adopted the earlier U.S./NATO strategy that it would consider the first use of nuclear weapons to deter or repel any invasion from the East or West.

Russia's new doctrine stated it would employ nuclear weapons "in the case of an immediate threat to the sovereignty and territorial integrity of Russia that had emerged as a result of external aggression." The Russian Security Council's statement exempted non-nuclear states as targets under the first-use doctrine, to comply with assurances connected to the nuclear non-proliferation treaty. This position was later adopted by the Russian Federation, Belarus, Ukraine, and Kazakhstan in 1993. Prior to India and Pakistan's display of nuclear weapons in May 1998, Russia's first use doctrine applied to the four major nuclear powers: the United States, Britain, France, and China. China announced its no-first-use nuclear policy in October 1964.

Nuclear Risk Reduction Centers Agreement, 1987. American and Soviet negotiations held in Geneva on January 13 and May 3–4, 1987, resulted in the accord signed in Washington on September 15, 1987. The Agreement, of unlimited duration, called for each party to create a Center in its capital and establish a dedicated facsimile communications link between them. The Centers became operational on April 1, 1988. The American Center was established in Washington in the Department of State and the Soviet Center, later the Russian Center, was established in Moscow in the Ministry of Defense. The Nuclear Risk Reduction Centers (NRRC) supplemented existing communication systems and provided direct, reliable, high-speed transmission systems by direct satellite links that could rapidly send full texts and graphics.

In this respect, the Centers possess a communications capability similar to—but separate from—the modernized hotline reserved for heads of government. The Centers were not intended to replace normal diplomatic channels or the hotline, nor were they intended to have a crisis management role. The principal function of the Centers was to exchange information and notifications as required under various arms control treaties and other confidence-building agreements.

There were two protocols to the NRRC Agreement. Protocol I identified the notifications the parties agreed to exchange. These included ballistic missile launches required under Article 4 of the 1971 "Agreement on Measures to Reduce the Risk of Outbreak of Nuclear War," and under Paragraph 1 of Article VI of the 1972 "Agreement on the Prevention of Incidents on and over the High Seas." The protocol allowed the list of notifications transmitted through the Centers to be altered by agreement between the signatories, as relevant to other agreements. Thus after the signing, the involved parties agreed to exchange inspection and compliance notifications, as well as other information, through the Centers as required under the INF Treaty, and called for under the "Ballistic Missile Launch Notification Agreement."

Protocol II established the technical specifications of the communications and facsimile links, the operating procedures to be employed, and the terms for transfer of, and payment for, equipment required by the system. To help ensure the smooth operation of the Centers, the agreement called for regular meetings at least once a year between representatives of the two national Centers to discuss operations.

Under separate accords with Belarus, Kazakhstan, and the Ukraine, the U.S. NRRC provides similar communications links with those countries in support of the START and INF Treaties.[15]

Ballistic Missile Launch Notification Agreement, 1988. This agreement grew out of the START talks, but traced its lineage to the SALT II negotiations. The SALT II Treaty had obligated each superpower to notify the other prior to launching any intercontinental ballistic missile (ICBM), except for single launches intended to remain within its national territory. It did not mention notification of submarine-launched ballistic missiles (SLBMs), since it was believed that international law obligated the announcement of such events.

The bilateral Ballistic Missile Launch Notification Agreement (BMLN) called for the United States and the USSR to notify each other—via the Nuclear Risk Reduction Centers—"no less than 24 hours in advance, of the planned date, launch area, and area of impact for any launch of an ICBM or SLBM." As such, it expanded the Accident Measures Agreement and placed additional responsibilities upon the Nuclear Risk Reduction Centers (see also two sections below, *Joint Data Exchange Center, 1998, 2000*; and *Hague Code of Conduct, 2002*).

The Prevention of Dangerous Military Activities, 1989. Several incidents in the early 1980s caused the superpowers to reassess various military activities and seek to prevent them from getting out of control. During 1983–1984, the Soviets inadvertently outraged American officials and public opinion with the downing of Korean Airlines Flight 007, and the shooting of a U.S. Army officer in East Germany. President Ronald Reagan's provocative rhetoric and his administration's greatly expanded military buildup, together with NATO's military exercises in the fall of 1983, unintentionally provoked Moscow into issuing a military alert fearing a possible United States preemptive nuclear attack.

Strained relationships eased in the mid-1980s as meetings between Reagan and Mikhail Gorbachev gradually established a new rapprochement. In December 1987, the first meeting between highest-ranking military officers of both nations took place. The Soviet desire for additional such contacts led to the 1989 pact designed to improve military-to-military communication in times of crisis. It also created areas of "special caution" where forces of the United States and Soviet Union were operating in close proximity, outlawed the dangerous use of lasers, and prohibited jamming command and control communication networks. They agreed to treat minor territorial incursions as accidental or unintentional rather than as automatically threatening greater consequences.[16]

"Open Skies" Treaty, 1992. The "Open Skies" accord was signed at the Conference on Security and Cooperation in Europe ministerial meeting in Helsinki on March 24, 1992. The initial concept was proposed in July 1955 by President Dwight Eisenhower ostensibly to provide aerial reconnaissance to

eliminate "the possibility of great surprise attack, thus lessening danger and relaxing tensions," and to "make more easily attainable a comprehensive and effective system of inspection and disarmament." At the time, the Soviets rejected the American idea as essentially an espionage plot.

After itlay dormant for three decades, President George H. W. Bush gave the Open Skies concept new life in 1989, as an alternative means of verifying the Conventional Forces in Europe Treaty then being negotiated. Bush advanced his proposal because he needed a new arms control proposal, and because the operation of aircraft provided a cheap, more flexible means of verification for those members of the accord without satellite capabilities. The use of aircraft for reconnaissance provided NATO nations with the means of directly observing former Soviet-bloc nations without relying on U.S. satellites.[17]

Joint Data Exchange Center, 1998, 2000. At a summit meeting in September 1998, Presidents Boris Yeltsin and William Clinton signed a loosely worded agreement designed to share data on the launch of ballistic missiles and space launch vehicles and to reduce the possibility of raising a false alarm. This pact expanded pledges contained in the Ballistic Missile Launch Notification Agreement (1988). Although both sides had declared the Cold War to be over by 1998, the United States and Russia still maintained "thousands of nuclear weapons in an operational state poised to initiate a massive attack within a few minutes." Thus, John Steinbruner noted, "as a result of that practice, each country constantly presents to the other the greatest physical threat that it encounters from any source." A functioning Joint Data Exchange Center could strengthen the deterrent effect, and introduce another element of stability by reducing the prospects of an unintended warning system failure.

Despite the Kosovo crisis, eighteen Russian military officers and their American counterparts established an operational temporary missile monitoring facility at Peterson Air Force Base in Colorado from December 21, 1999, to January 16, 2000. The project was advanced in June 2000 when President Clinton and President Vladimir Putin signed a Memorandum of Agreement to establish a Joint Data Exchange Center in Moscow. Its task was "to ensure the uninterrupted exchange of information on the launches of ballistic missiles and space launch vehicles." In December 2000, American and Russian officials signed an additional Memorandum of Understanding, stipulating in considerable detail on how the Center would conduct the exchange of notifications related to missile launches.

The inauguration of George W. Bush brought the project to a halt. His administration focused on abrogating the ABM Treaty (1972) and, later, deploying an antiballistic missile system in Central Europe. Moscow objected to these decisions and its Joint Data Exchange Center project ceased and remained dormant in 2008.[18]

Hague Code of Conduct, 2002. The Hague Code (HCOC) asked its more than 120 participating nations to "exercise maximum possible restraint" with regard to ballistic missiles capable of delivering biological, chemical or nuclear warheads. Participating states were expected to share annual inventories of their missiles and provide advance notices of ballistic missile and space launches to HCOC member states.

From the few reports available, compliance appeared to be mixed. Several participating states, including the United States, have not carried out all of their commitments. Russia stopped providing HCOC members with pre-launch notices of its ballistic missile launches effective January 1, 2008, a cessation that supposedly will last one year. Russia is expected to continue submitting its annual report. Apparently, there were two reasons for the Kremlin's actions. First, Russian officials' desire to gain support for their proposal to make annual reports and pre-launch notices optional rather than politically binding in the hope of gaining more information from nonmembers. This was in recognition of the growing missile and space activity by nonmembers such as Brazil, China, India, Iran, North Korea, and Pakistan. Secondly, Russia's action was in response to the fact that some member states were not providing pre-launch notice, especially the United States, although Washington has filed annual reports.

Since all HCOC activities are confidential, there was no public announcement of the Kremlin's decision.[19] (See also *Ballistic Missile Launch Notification Agreement, 1988,* above.)

South Asia Agreements

The UN General Assembly, at Pakistan's request, considered a South Asian nuclear weapons–free zone (NWFZ) in 1974, shortly after India tested a nuclear device. Repeated General Assembly resolutions urged the creation of such a zone, and belatedly gained the support of the United States. While initially both states endorsed the idea, there were significant differences in their approach. Until it tested its own devices in 1998, Pakistan consistently held that the conditions existed for the creation of such a zone. India argued that a South Asia NWFZ was unrealistic given that nuclear weapons states moved and deployed such weapons in various areas of the world, including the Indian Ocean. In 1982, India's foreign minister insisted that his nation could not, according to a UN account, "subscribe to the legitimization of the possession of nuclear weapons by a few Powers, by agreeing to live under their professedly benign protection in the guise of a nuclear weapons–free zone."[20]

Consequently, at the dawn of the twenty-first century, a cold war dominated South Asia as, ideologically and militarily, India and Pakistan were engaged in a bitter dispute over the control of Kashmir. The hostile attitudes took on a similarity to the earlier cold war between the United States and the Soviet Union, as the two South Asian states had armed themselves with nuclear weaponry and ballistic missiles. But then, too, mutual fears concerning the possible unintended use of these weapons led to a series of similar bilateral arms control arrangements.

Nuclear Facilities Agreement, 1988. Fearing that an attack on each other's nuclear facilities might have disastrous long-term consequences, India and Pakistan agreed not to target these installations. The December 31, 1988, pact, calling for exchanging lists of nuclear power plants and research facilities annually on January 1, entered into force on January 27, 1991. In January 2004—the 13th exchange—India listed details of their 10 nuclear installations, while Pakistan provided information of its 6 similar installations.

Advance Notification Pact, 1991. On April 6, 1991, India and Pakistan signed agreements designed to provide advance notification of military exercises, and to acknowledge military violations of each other's airspace.

India-Pakistan "Hot Lines," 1997. Amidst the continuing Kashmir crisis, where Indian and Pakistan military forces confront each other, prime ministers of the two nations agreed in 1997 to direct communications between their army headquarters. Amid the continuing hostilities, however, the initial communications link was largely ignored, but was revived in 2000. Four years later, the improvement of the military hotline and the prospect of establishing another one between their foreign secretaries were still being discussed.

Missile Notification Pact, 2005. After two rounds of confidence-building discussions in 2004, India and Pakistan agreed to notify each other in advance of missile test flights. The pact, signed on October 5, 2005, called for at least 72 hours before a ballistic missile flight test. The countries pledged to prevent missiles from flying on a trajectory approaching, or land close to their accepted borders, or the Line of Control running through the disputed province of Kashmir. Test missiles were not to fly closer than 40 kilometers to these borders or land closer than 70 kilometers away from them. According to the provisions of the pact, the Indian government notified Pakistan of an impending test of a ballistic missile on February 26, 2008.

Reducing the Risk of Nuclear Accidents, 2007. In the midst of terrorist attacks in both countries, the foreign ministers of India and Pakistan on February 21, 2007, agreed to reduce the risk of an accident, miscalculation, or any other unintended event which could result in the use of nuclear weapons. Details were scarce, but apparently the Joint Commission, established in 1983 (only to be ignored) and rejuvenated in 2005, was to be the principal mechanism for implementing the agreement.[21]

CONFIDENCE-BUILDING MEASURES

The formulation of realistic confidence-building measures, often known as the Helsinki Process, stemmed from specific activities in Europe from the early 1970s to the 1990s. This process, according to James Macintosh, has been "a much more contextually-bound concept and arms control approach than is frequently appreciated." Accordingly, "most analysts would agree that confidence building is an arms control-like approach employing purposely designed, cooperative measures" called CBMs or CSBMs—confidence- and security-building measures representing second-generation CBMs. The two terms, however, often have been used interchangeably.

The objective of CBMs has been "to help clarify states' military intentions, to reduce uncertainties about their potentially threatening military activities, and to constrain their opportunities for surprise attack or the coercive use of military forces." However, CBMs never sought to deal directly to force limitations or reductions. While few diplomats expected that CBMs would head off premeditated or preemptive attacks, they did argue that such accords could "minimize accidental conflicts" and, perhaps most importantly, enhance a sense of security "among suspicious, but not belligerent, neighbors." Any additional transparency of military infrastructures was a positive step in itself.

The various "documents" or "acts" that emerged from the process, according to John Fry, "pioneered an innovative confidence- and security-building regime that added a new dimension to European security, and offered a model for other areas of European affairs."[22]

Conference on Security and Cooperation in Europe, 1972–1975. Preliminary talks began at Helsinki, Finland, in November 1972 to identify the topics to be discussed during formal negotiations opening in July 1973 and that continued until August 1975. Thirty-three European nations, the United States, and Canada were among the participants in the Conference on Security and Cooperation in Europe (CSCE). Essentially these nations formed three basic groups: NATO, the Warsaw Treaty Organization, and the loosely organized neutral and unaligned states. The two superpowers at various occasions also sought to exercise their influence during the talks.

Despite his claims in his *Years of Renewal*, it is evident that National Security Adviser Henry Kissinger was, at least at the beginning, disinterested in the CSCE negotiations. He apparently saw it as a "loser for the West" and summed up his opinion in a quip at a December 1974 staff meeting: "They can write it in Swahili for all I care." Despite Kissinger's dismissive attitude, the Helsinki Final Act would play a major role in opening the closed Soviet satellites that awakened their sense of nationalism and their desire to free themselves from Moscow's domination.

Helsinki Final Act, 1975. The comprehensive concluding document emerging from the CSCE has been labeled the Helsinki Final Act—less formal than a treaty or agreement, the Final Act was a political, not legally binding, document. Three basic elements (or "baskets") were included in the document dealing with: (1) "Security in Europe;" (2) "Cooperation in the Fields of Economics, Science and Technology, and the Environment;" and (3) "Cooperation in Humanitarian and Other Fields."

The Document on Confidence-Building Measures and Certain Aspects of Security and Disarmament in the first "basket," contained several preliminary confidence-building measures. The most significant of these from an arms control standpoint, was the suggestion that CSCE countries notify each other of military maneuvers involving more than 25,000 personnel, at least 21 days in advance, unless that they had been arranged on short notice. The notification should also include basic information about the maneuvers. "This combination of advance activity notification and information," Macintosh has noted, was "perhaps the archetypical CBM and it has operated at the heart of each succeeding confidence building agreement." Also suggested in this document were the voluntary extending of invitations to foreign military observers, and an expanded "discretionary military movement notification."

Basket 1's formal acknowledgment of the Warsaw Pact by the West constituted a virtual recognition of the Soviets' Eastern European empire. However, Basket 2 permitted commercial relations between East and West, while Basket 3 provided for a free flow of information, visitations, and so on. Several commentators have held that Moscow's reluctant relaxation of restrictions on freedom of information and movement spurred the rise of nationalism in Eastern Europe and contributed to the end of the Cold War.

The document also contained an agreement to meet at Belgrade, Yugoslavia, in 1977 to decide on the means of implementing the Final Act. Also, there was a commitment to hold follow-up conferences that would seek more fully developed measures.

Stockholm Document, 1986. The modest confidence-building measures in the Helsinki Final Act were more important for what they led to, than what they initially offered. It was the beginning of a lengthy process that, over some 15 years, gradually led to a significant transformation in the manner with which European nations came to view each other. During an era of contentious East–West political relationships, the Belgrade (1977–1978) and Madrid (1980–1983) follow-up meetings faltered; nevertheless, the so-called Madrid Mandate committed the membership to meet again at what would become the truly successful Stockholm conference.

The Document of the Stockholm Conference on Confidence- and Security-Building Measures and Disarmament in Europe, was formally completed on September 19, 1986. This Document included: a declaration on "Refraining from the Threat or Use of Force"; providing a 42-day prior notification and information of military activities involving specified numbers of personnel and/or equipment; inviting observers to "any exercise or transfer" of specified numbers personnel; providing specific information of a nation's activities one year in advance; and requiring two years' advance notice involving the movement of 40,000 or more troops. An additional measure called for an aerial or ground on-site inspection by four inspectors within 36 hours of a request by a CSCE member to examine suspicious or untoward activity. No state had to accept more than three inspections per year. These steps took place after Mikhail Gorbachev assumed power in Moscow and befitted from his new policies.

The true impact of the Stockholm Document is difficult to evaluate. Even viewed in narrow terms, however, it has played a constructive role in helping to reduce suspicion and improve confidence in Europe. In general, its specific measures maintained a solid record of compliance.

Vienna Confidence- and Security-Building Measure Negotiations, 1986– 1992. After the successful Stockholm conference, twin negotiations opened in Vienna. One, the Conventional Armed Forces in Europe (CFE) negotiations, continued the discussions to reduce the armed forces of the NATO and Warsaw Treaty Organization states. The second brought all 35 CSCE states together to enhance the Stockholm Document's CSBMs. Of the two separate but parallel negotiations, the CSBM discussions proved less difficult but was held back because the two negotiating processes were to end with agreements at the same time. Given the complexities and importance of the CFE talks, the Vienna CSBM negotiations periodically languished.

Vienna Document, 1990. This comprehensive agreement, based on the Stockholm Document's military information exchanges, was completed by November 17, 1990. The Vienna Document included a new, more complex Compliance and Verification Measure that called for two types of activities—inspection and evaluation. The former was similar to the Stockholm formula, while the evaluation measure permitted verification of the accuracy of officially supplied military information. The procedure worked "on the basis of a quota system for each state that obliges one mandatory evaluation visit each year per 60 reporting units (a unit being a brigade/regiment or its equivalent) deployed by that state. However, no state is obliged to accept more than 15 visits a year."

Linked to the evaluation element was an "information" measure that required participating states to annually submit a detailed report of their military organization, manpower, and major weapons and equipment systems. It would also include command organizations; subordinate units; peacetime location; personnel strength; and major combat systems. Additionally, the participating states had to exchange information each year itemizing their defense expenditures.

The final measures included a requirement to consult and cooperate in the event of unusual military activities or hazardous military incidents; an invitation to participating states to visit an air base at least once every five years; the establishment of a direct communications network linking CSCE capitals; and an Annual Implementation Assessment.[23]

Subsequent follow-up meetings further strengthened the verification and notification requirement of participating members.

For the various forms of negotiations employed, the several types of verification adopted and problems of compliance or non-compliance, see Part II.

PART II

Comments on Arms Control Processes
Negotiations, Verification, and Compliance

When evaluating past arms control and disarmament experiences, the first question usually asked is, "Was the agreement successful?" Although this is a quite reasonable enquiry, it ought to be preceded by others, such as "What was the political/military environment during negotiations? What was the agreement attempting to accomplish? Were verification procedures employed? Did the political/military environment change over time? Did continuing negotiations explore accommodating adjustments?" Then one may realistically proceed to discuss issues regarding compliance or noncompliance and the general applicability of arms control measures.

The arms control process, to expand on the description of Allan Krass who has examined it both as an academic and an official of the U.S. Arms Control Agency, may be seen as unfolding in five sequential stages. "It begins with *negotiation*," he states, "in which states attempt to find an agreement that is consistent with their interests in both national security and international stability."[1] The diplomat's negotiation strategy, of course, emanates from senior officials, usually a head of state—monarch, dictator, or president—who established or endorsed the basic arms control objectives sought. Only a few, highly trusted envoys ever have had the independence to "freelance" during the negotiations without the guidance and approval of the chief executive.

Tribal chiefs and early monarchs never had to contend, as have twentieth-century leaders, with government bureaucracies, legislative bodies, and influential domestic media all influencing policymaking. Ranking among most senior officials' arms control priorities have been efforts to enhance national security, reduce international tensions, meet public expectations, enhance a leader's image, gain propaganda points in the international arena, and occasionally, limit military expenditures. Thus, if basic arms control objectives have not changed greatly over the past decades, the intensity, complexity, and impetus have substantially increased as a result of the dangers posed by weapons of mass destruction.

Should a realistic modern proposal emerge aimed at limiting or reducing weaponry, it would find two competing strategies: *a political-based approach*, such as that employed at the 1922 Washington naval conference, and *a technical-based approach* that dominated later interwar naval discussions and post-1945 strategic weapons negotiations. Professor Emily Goldman suggests politically oriented strategies, merging both technical and political factors, were more sensitive to "security concerns that could not be deduced from the state of technology or the military balance." Technical-based strategies that elected "to treat political dialogues as purely technical issues, exacerbated insecurities and threat perceptions," were unlikely in the long term to accomplish their objectives.[2]

Experienced policymakers and diplomats understood that all states involved will usually seek to gain or keep an advantage, whether major or minor, and that compromise would usually be required. Indeed, many agreements have been "a combination of asymmetries" and the "marginal advantages on one side or the other do not undermine stability." Negotiations should not be avoided because they may involve asymmetries or risks, since a failure to negotiate may lead to even greater risks.[3]

Once a treaty has been signed, the second stage begins. It now "must go through a process of *ratification* in which it is incorporated into the laws and practices of each of the parties." In an authoritarian state this process may be uncomplicated. In a democratic, parliamentary nation, however, the principals need to keep in mind during the negotiations that ultimate success comes only with achieving ratification. Individuals and opposition parties often may challenge an arms control treaty seeking to gain an advantage in domestic politics. Democratic Party leaders, in a partisan response, found fault with the Washington naval treaties during the biannual congressional elections. Later, the opposition to arms control pacts by many strident Cold Warriors and neo-conservatives was based on their ideological convictions and, sometimes, to enhance their political opportunities. Thus, those leaders who sponsor arms control treaties must develop strategies to deal with the challenges that may arise from political opponents.

After ratification, the third stage should be to *implement* the treaty. "Obligations incurred in the treaty must be carried out by all parties," Krass insists, "usually according to procedures and schedules agreed on in the treaty text or protocols." These commitments may be involved and continuous or they may be quite passive with few requirements. This may involve scrapping battleships or dismantling ballistic missiles; it may require prior notification of the intent to transfer any large number of armed forces. It may demand that military planners and technical staff follow certain qualitative restrictions in the development of future armaments. The Cold War arms control agreements often involved an extensive number of complicated provisions.

The process of implementation is typically subject to some method of *verification*—the fourth stage. Since the middle of the twentieth century, there usually has been a serious attempt to provide each arms limitation treaty with an effective verification regime. These measures, some more complicated than others, seek continually to reassure the various parties to an agreement that its terms are being complied with, or that there are additional issues that require resolution. The latter situation frequently arises testifying to the fact that negotiations do not end with the signing of an agreement.

For centuries, the basic method of verifying arms control pacts has involved each party's use of its own intelligence-gathering process known as "national means." Later, during the Cold War, the employment of such devices as satellites and sophisticated electronics provided an added feature—the use of "national *technical* means." In Chapter 8, five methods of verification that have been employed are briefly reviewed—(1) mutual self-monitoring, (2) notification procedures, (3) reporting commissions, (4) enquiry commissions, and (5) on-site supervisory commissions.

The fifth stage is the long-term *compliance* period that involves "nurturing" the arms control treaty. "Almost from the very day they enter into force," Krass aptly puts it, "most treaty regimes are confronted with unexpected political developments, new technological possibilities, and unforeseen financial difficulties by one or more of the parties."[4] The classic example of arms control nurturing is world's oldest, still functioning, arms control accord—the bilateral Rush-Bagot Pact of 1817 where the British and Americans (and later Canadians) agreed essentially to demilitarize the Great Lakes. Despite several technical evasions and occasional political unrest generated on both sides of the Lakes, the entire border between the United States and Canada gradually became demilitarized. For this to take place, the United States, Britain, and Canada had to employ diplomats over the decades who were willing to acknowledge that mutual long-term economic and political interests were far more advantageous than the various transitory issues. During negotiation of complex treaty regimes in the Cold War era, most agreements recognized the likelihood of unforeseen issues arising and, consequently, created consultative groups or other mechanisms to deal with the problems arising from implementation and compliance.

Issues questioning compliance on the part of a state, arising from verification procedures, may be considered and dealt with in various formal and informal interactions. This is because the nature and origin of actual evasions may differ widely. The response of the aggrieved state may take several forms, varying from ignoring the evasions because they caused no actual military threat, to formal protests that may include threatening to abrogate the treaty. Or, as in the case of the Reagan administration, domestically driven, politically inspired protests may stem from hard-edged ideological commitments.

Consequently, the ideology or anxiety that drives political behavior can play a significant role in how treaty compliance is evaluated. If the majority of officials are satisfied that an arms control agreement has reduced tensions and stabilized the international scene, they are most likely to not to be upset with minor evasions, should these to be shown to be non-threatening. In a hostile political environment, however, anxieties aroused by an ideological framework may well magnify discrepancies that result from different interpretations of treaty terms. Perhaps at times, as H. A. L. Fisher wrote during the interwar years, "in reality, security is a state of mind; so is insecurity."

Arms control verification arrangements can aid, and have aided, in enhancing a nation's sense of security, especially when these procedures were adequate to the task of ensuring compliance or at least moderating treaty evasions. This was especially the case when consultative processes were available to assist in ensuring compliance and improving public understanding about the nurturing of arms control agreements. But diplomats and political leaders must be prepared to confront issues of ambiguity that will surely arise whether the terms are closely or broadly drawn. Thus, negotiations or "nurturing" should be seen as an ongoing process.

In sum, the arms control process, certainly that involving those treaties calling for extensive arms restrictions and reductions, require that policymakers and the public be comfortable with the risks involved. The maintaining of large nuclear arsenals involves the risk of their purposeful or unintentional use; while arms control treaties placing extensive restrictions and reductions on these arsenals incurs the risk of treaty evasions and noncompliance. It is true that reaching an agreement with a potential adversary is an unusual way to seek enhancement of national security. Or, as Paul Warnke once put it, "an unnatural act." Often, however, it is preferable to the alternative.

The chapters that follow provide a glimpse of the various issues and dilemmas confronting the process of developing and sustaining arms control measures—the formulation of objectives, negotiations, and politics, various verification mechanisms, and questions related to compliance. Since space prevents a more detailed discussion, the notes related to each chapter provide sources for those who wish to delve deeper into these matters.

Arms Control Negotiations

When arms control issues have arisen, negotiations and politics always have been intimately connected. Diplomatic objectives are shaped often by short-term domestic and international political considerations that can be varied and unpredictable. Arms control proposals thus must be designed to meet domestic expectations and national security needs. Yet to be successful, these proposals and negotiations must also meet the test of "mutuality"—that is, satisfy many of the basic perceived needs of other involved parties. Mutual interests may mean that states will have identical interests in reaching an agreement, as was, for example, the situation in the Hotline pacts (1963). Or states may have divergent interests yet see advantages in agreeing to a treaty, such as in the Helsinki Accord (1975), where Washington focused on the technical dimensions and Moscow on the political aspects. Then, too, treaties have been arranged where there are both shared and complimentary interests as was the case in the Austrian State Treaty (1955) and the Incidents On and Over the High Sea agreement (1972). "Without common interest there is nothing to negotiate for," one-time arms control chief Fred Iklé has aptly noted, "without conflict there is nothing to negotiate about."[1]

Finding a mutuality of interests in the twentieth-century arms control negotiations was complicated by having to weigh public concerns stemming from fears and suspicions usually stimulated by individual ideological commitments, domestic political ambitions, and state-sponsored propaganda. This is so especially in democratic nations that had to take into consideration the public mood. During the Cold War, creating a sense of insecurity in their publics' mind became a political staple of Moscow and Washington. Soviet officials stressed the capitalist military encirclement as their greatest threat, while American leaders constantly posed the specter of communist world domination.

Thus, both superpowers were too frequently blinded by a combination of self-righteousness and exaggerated fears that resulted in a misinformed assessment of an opponent's strengths, weaknesses, or intentions that influenced negotiations. For much of this era, Strobe Talbott concluded, "Western policy has been based on a grotesque exaggeration of what the U.S.S.R. could do if it wanted, therefore what it might do, therefore what the West must be prepared to do in response." Gerald C. Smith, a prominent American arms control negotiator who headed the United States delegation to the initial SALT-ABM talks, concurred. He found Washington's policies toward the Soviet Union often influenced by "myth, misconception and plain ignorance." Soviet leader Mikhail Gorbachev came to believe that the superpowers had become "mesmerized by ideological myths" which ruled out any meaningful discussions of a political accommodation for more than four decades.[2]

ESTABLISHING THE ARMS CONTROL AGENDA

Developing arms control objectives in anticipation of negotiations, which at one time had been uncomplicated for tribal chiefs, emperors, and kings, had become compartmentalized and quite complex by the twentieth century. Now the decision-making process had to consider the demands of military professionals, the advice of technical experts, and the concerns of bureaucracies with differing agendas. Then, too, diplomats in past centuries had a considerably freer hand in the conduct of negotiations because of irregular, greatly delayed communications with their superiors. In the modern era, however, negotiators were in instant contact with their superiors and usually found themselves held closely to their instructions.[3]

Virtually all studies of arms control enterprises have emphasized that a strong, committed chief executive was vital for success. The general formulation of arms control objectives may be the work of subordinates, but to merge them successfully into realistic negotiable proposals often required bringing to bear the full authority of the chief executive's office. Only this office, according to two former arms control negotiators, "can insist on the prompt formulation of positions that are not merely the least common denominator between government agencies." Another study by arms control practitioners similarly concluded that the highest-ranking officials "must provide strong leadership, particularly if there is bureaucratic opposition to their objectives."[4]

The chief executive also must decide the bargaining strategy to employ. An ancient negotiating approach, according to George Bunn, is that of "bargaining from strength" which involves manipulating "the other side's perception of one's negotiating strength by threatening to worsen their position unless they agree; that is, to persuade them by increasing their costs without agreement."[5] This strategy has, however, a mixed record. An early-twentieth-century example took place at the 1922 Washington naval conference where the British and American battle fleets were substantially greater than those of Japan, France, and Italy. Consequently, the big two were able to press their positions because the other states were unwilling to meet the costs of competitive building.

During the early years of the Cold War, the United States obviously held the upper hand during discussions of international control of atomic weaponry as outlined in the 1946 Baruch Plan. Choosing to emphasize this fact, Bernard Baruch replied to critics of his hard-line approach: "America can get what she wants if she insists on it. After all, we've got it and they haven't, and won't for a long time to come."[6] The strategy did not work: the Soviets' rejected his plan and soon were producing nuclear weaponry, albeit at a heavy cost. Baruch's failed effort did not prevent Paul Nitze from arguing in 1952 that a U.S. H-bomb monopoly could be used "as a lever for accomplishing our objectives"—that is, to create conditions for disarmament. The idea of "negotiating from strength" continued to be the justification for more and more sophisticated strategic weaponry, especially nuclear warheads and delivery systems. Unfortunately, when the negotiations occurred, they rarely sought to define the Cold War's fundamental political differences; instead they came to focus on stabilizing the environment created by the strategic weaponry (see Chapter 10).

During the 1980s, the Reagan administration reintroduced the bargaining from strength strategy, by persuading Congress to increase the defense budget substantially before opening negotiations with the Soviets. It is by no means clear that this strategy worked for when the new Soviet leader Mikhail Gorbachev assumed power, he had already decided to end the arms race. He was determined to reduce Soviet armaments sharply, either by treaty or by unilateral actions, because he was convinced "nobody is going to attack us even if we disarm completely." For Gorbachev, continuing the arms race would lead to greater insecurities than the risks assumed in ending it.[7]

Other modern arms control bargaining strategies have included such concepts as "linkage" and "bargaining chips." With these strategies, depending upon one's definition of the terms, there also were mixed results. President Richard Nixon and National Security Advisor Henry Kissinger initially planned to "link" their desire for Soviet assistance in resolving the Vietnam War and Middle Eastern differences with negotiation of strategic arms limits. Moscow, for its part, wanted formal recognition of a détente between the superpowers, with economic benefits, to coincide with arms limitation measures. Each party gained some linkage, but was it more than the normal concessions that take place during ongoing negotiations? The so-called bargaining chips—weapons built to discard when concessions were extracted from antagonists—are equally difficult to evaluate. Did Nixon-Kissinger's use of the nascent U.S. anti-ballistic missile system actually persuade the Soviets to agree to the 1972 ABM Treaty? How much credit should go to Moscow's realization that technology was not equal to the task of defending against a foe's ballistic missiles?

As weapons systems became more complicated, greater emphasis was placed upon technical and military experts in the shaping of arms control initiatives and in the negotiation process. That the advice of experts is vital to the proper shaping of negotiating positions cannot be seriously questioned. Yet, America's faith in technology, according to Stanley Hoffman, had by the mid-twentieth century given rise to an "engineering approach" toward resolving foreign policy—and, we might add, arms control—issues.[8] To be successful, the negotiation of an arms control and disarmament agreement shouldn't be viewed as an engineering exercise or war game by technicians or military officials. Interpreting the many facets of a nation's basic interests, such as domestic opinion, allied positions, and immediate and long-range security risks, is—after taking the experts advice—essentially a political undertaking.

The Military Professional's Role. Since many arms control measures placed restrictions on the activities, strategies, and tactics of the armed forces, military professionals seldom favored them. By training and experience, these officers always desire numerically superior forces and the most technologically advanced weaponry to enable them to carry out future missions. Consequently, they disliked such concepts as parity, equality of forces, strategic stability, reasonable sufficiency, or mutual deterrence that were usually put forward in support of arms limitation measures.

Not surprisingly, the first negotiated multilateral arms limitation pact—the Washington Naval Treaty (1922)—drew mixed reviews from most naval officers. Japan's Naval Minister Kato Tomosaburo bypassed the naval bureaucracy, obtained the Supreme Military Council's approval, and won the endorsement of the much-admired Fleet-Admiral Togo Heihachiro to gain Tokyo's approval. Many younger officers, however, expressed strong opposition to the pact, especially Admiral Kato Kanji, who never accepted the treaty's inferior ratio. Viewing the ratio as "imposed," he declared, "As far as I am concerned, war with America starts now. We will take revenge on her. We will!" Kato Kanji's leadership and outspoken condemnation of the naval agreements stoked the disapproval of both naval and civilian ultra-nationalists and would later prompt Japan to terminate its participation in the Washington treaty system.

If most British naval professionals disliked granting parity to the United States, many American naval officers were equally hostile to the Washington naval pact because they saw America surrendering an opportunity to gain naval superiority. Captain Dudley W. Knox wrote, "Of the five nations affected by the naval treaty the United States is the only one that has lost any substantial naval advantage, and she has gained the least so far." He believed that the Harding administration had given up an opportunity to build a "navy second to none."[9]

Yet not all American or British admirals were opposed to the various naval limitation agreements. Strong endorsements for the London Naval Treaty of 1930 came from U.S. Admirals William V. Pratt, Harry E. Yarnell, and A. J. Hepburn during the negotiations and later during the ratification process. Pratt predicted that the treaty provided "for the first time in our history ... a definite program" that would provide for a consistent "naval building program." Unfortunately, he had incorrectly assessed the mood of Congress regarding naval expenditures. Following the mixed reception given the Anglo-German naval pact (1935), British Fleet Admiral Sir A. E. M. Chatfield complained the agreement had not gained full recognition of its value. "I think the Anglo-German

Treaty," he wrote, "is of the greatest benefit not only from a military stand-point but from a political and international one."[10]

Cold War military chiefs in both Washington and Moscow rarely considered the political dimensions of global affairs, because they viewed contentious issues in essentially military terms. President Dwight Eisenhower encountered this situation at a November 1954 meeting with the Joint Chiefs of Staff. They feared that once the Soviets achieved parity with the United States, Moscow might launch a general war. Consequently, the Joint Chiefs argued that the administration "must realize it will be not only fruitless, but perhaps even haz-ardous, to continue its efforts to arrive at solutions to world problems through the normal processes of negotiations with the U.S.S.R." They urged the presi-dent to take a more aggressive posture and accept greater risks in confronting the Soviets, but they failed to specify what "risks" he should assume.

If Eisenhower never achieved a major arms control pact with Moscow, he did understand that to pursue his military chiefs' "get tough" policy could lead to an increasingly hostile political environment. Four years later in 1958, CIA analyst and historian Raymond Garthoff drewup an initial estimate of the Soviet Union's disarmament policies for the administration. His conclusion, that Mos-cow "would consider arms control and reduction agreements that would curb its pursuit of military superiority," met with "military opposition and a strong Air Force" rebuttal.[11]

This is not to suggest that American military professionals opposed every arms control measure or proposal. In February 1981, for example, President Reagan met with six advisers: Secretary of Defense Caspar Weinberger, Direc-tor of Central Intelligence William Casey, National Security Advisor Richard Allen, Secretary of State (general) Alexander Haig, Chairman of the Joint Chiefs General David Jones, and National Security Agency Director (admiral) Bobby Inman. They discussed withdrawing the SALT II Treaty from the Sen-ate, where it lay dormant. "The three civilians advised the president to with-draw it," according to arms controller Thomas Graham, "while the military officers (Haig, Inman and Jones) opposed withdrawal." During April and May 1986, the issue of whether the United States should exceed the SALT II limits arose among members of the Reagan administration. Admiral William Crowe argued against such action for there was no operational reason to do so; how-ever, shortly afterwards Reagan endorsed withdrawing from SALT II.[12]

On one occasion, Soviet military chiefs outsmarted themselves. As the new Soviet leader was preparing to address the United Nations in January 1986, the chiefs "advanced the idea of complete disarmament," convinced that Ameri-ca's rejection would put Washington in an uncomfortable position. The military leaders had unwittingly provided Gorbachev with substantial authority "to act in this field" of arms control, not realizing the General Secretary desired to end superpower nuclear competition. As Russian arms controllers put it, the military had been "entrapped by their own gambit" and later were unable to challenge Gorbachev successfully.[13]

In sum, military professionals tended to be more critical than supportive of arms control, but most senior officers understood that it was an issue they had to consider. They therefore sought to design proposals that were often quite unrealistic from a negotiator's standpoint, which would benefit their forces and restrain their adversaries.

Surveying Competing Constituencies. Since the early twentieth century, competing intergovernmental factions such as military establishments, foreign affairs bureaucracies, and frequently legislative leaders, have had a marked impact on shaping the final arms control drafts. The steering of these drafts among interested or threatened agencies, often has been a strenuous affair, which was even quite intense at times. Proposals for military and naval limitation during the interwar years, for example, found the military services and foreign affairs ministries at odds. After being taken by surprise and playing a minor role in developing the proposal for naval reductions at the Washington Conference (1922), the affected naval establishments subsequently developed their arguments, gained media and political support, and demanded a greater role in determining what was negotiable.

During the Cold War, the political establishments in Washington and Moscow played a major role in developing arms control initiatives. Any American chief executive who wished to negotiate and have ratified an arms control agreement, needed to consider the Joint Chiefs of Staff (JCS), civilian defense and state department officials, members of the National Security Council, the intelligence community, and congressional leaders, especially senators with seats on powerful security-related committees. When President Richard Nixon and National Security Advisor Henry Kissinger drew up their proposals for SALT I discussions with the Soviets, the Defense Department, JCS, and powerful conservative Senators insisted before granting their approval, that strategic weapons systems under development—including the Trident submarine, submarine-launched cruise missiles (SLCMs), and multiple independently targeted warheads (MIRVs)—were not negotiable. Moscow found its military complex equally firmly opposed to any ban on the MIRVs. The Americans had rejected a ban on MIRVs because they were ahead, the Soviets because they did not wish to be left behind. After each side had deployed their MIRVs, they realized that this weaponry actually made them less secure. As a troubled observer noted at the time, "Like war, the historic task of setting limits on strategic weapons—of inhibiting man's push toward the outer reaches of the self-destructive process—exceeds the competence of bureaucracy, splintered as always by agency bias. Bureaucracy cannot decide what is negotiable and what is not."[14]

Soviet arms control proposals or negotiating points were often generated by the Big Five—representatives from five agencies—the Central Committee of the Communist Party Soviet Union (CPSU), the Ministry of Foreign Affairs, the Ministry of Defense, the KGB, and the Military Industrial Commission (the VPK)—and sent to the Politburo for approval. "There always existed a hidden competition ... between the agencies ...," according to the Big Five's historians.

"The Defense Ministry and the Ministry of Foreign Affairs ... were often at the heart of these controversies." Since the Defense Ministry maintained a monopoly on all information regarding Soviet strategic forces, initially Soviet negotiators were ill prepared to deal with the basic issues under discussion. In later years, they drew information about their own strategic forces from western sources—especially the publications of the London-based International Institute for Strategic Studies, and the Stockholm International Peace Research Institute.[15]

During Reagan's second administration, when it sought to respond to proposals by Soviet General Secretary Gorbachev, the result was time-consuming, interminable bickering over technicalities between Washington agencies. The resulting confusion prompted a senior member of the National Security Council staff to complain: "Even if the Soviets did not exist, we might not get a START treaty because of disagreements on our side." Responding to the intensity of the political and technical disagreements, another despondent high-ranking American official complained that if the Soviets "came to us and said, 'You write it, we'll sign it,' we still couldn't do it."[16]

Participants in these bureaucratic struggles have suggested that intergovernmental negotiations in Washington and Moscow were often more intense than those between American and Soviet diplomats. A strong, politically sensitive executive and committed staff, consequently, is necessary to cajole, persuade and mediate in order to gain a bureaucratic consensus for their proposal. The compromises resulting from the vigorous debate among various individuals and agencies resulted in written "instructions" as to what was to be negotiated and accompanied by "safeguards"—specific limits on the negotiator's freedom to compromise. While safeguards might delay or deadlock the diplomatic process, their intent, after a treaty has been agreed upon and signed, was to eliminate most internal political obstacles to ratification.

Despite many frustrations, proposals somehow emerged from the bureaucratic jungle. This was due in part to the recognition that new and unpleasant risks may be incurred, should a situation be allowed to drift. The realization or prospect of such a situation can bring squabbling parties to a consensus.

Types of Arms Control Proposals. The factors prompting leaders to determine arms control proposals have varied widely, some more exemplary than others. The more focused proposals seek to reduce international tensions, curb the mounting costs of armaments and/or enhance their nation's security. Ideally, bilateral or multilateral negotiations could accomplish all three objectives, as was the case, for example, of naval limitation at the Washington naval conference (1922) and of demilitarizing the Great Lakes (1817), the Antarctic (1959), and several nuclear weapons–free zones. Many bilateral superpower agreements were able to accomplish only two of the three objectives, for few accords actually reduced costs. In all of these instances, successful proposals focused on specific, limited objectives that registered the interests of the parties involved.

Conversely, several broad-based arms control proposals have been initiated, with little or no expectation of an agreement, in order to achieve propaganda points at home and abroad, to reassure domestic or foreign audiences and/or appease nervous allies. The Soviet Union in March 1928, proposed that all nations join in an immediate, complete, and general disarmament program that within four years would scrap all army and naval weaponry, raze all fortifications, and eliminate military service. Four years later, the United States urged all nations to reduce their armed forces by one-third and abolish tanks, large mobile guns, chemical weaponry, and prohibit aerial bombardment. Again, in 1962, the Soviet Union and the United States each offered new proposals for "General and Complete Disarmament." It is difficult to believe that all of these initiatives were offered with any realistic expectation that they would generate serious responses. It is likely that the primary objectives of such proposals, were to improve the initiating government's negotiating positions and its domestic and international image.

There have been initiatives offered, which if endorsed, would have maintained or led to a nation achieving military superiority. The Baruch Plan, presented to the United Nations atomic energy committee in 1946, was seen by the Soviet Union and other nations as an attempt to prolong America's atomic weapons monopoly. It failed. Washington also launched two arms control initiatives—dealing with intermediate and strategic nuclear weapons—in the early 1980s which critics immediately labeled "non-starters." To placate aroused publics at home and in allied countries, the Reagan administration announced a "zero option" plan to eliminate intermediate nuclear missiles based in Europe. It called for the United States to cancel *scheduled* deployment of its new intermediate missiles if the Soviet Union would dismantle and withdraw its *existing* missiles carrying some 1,100 warheads. Moscow initially refused to discuss the initiative, as its authors expected. Later, it should be noted that Mikhail Gorbachev, recognizing that the Soviets' recently deployed intermediate-range missiles, which initiated a U.S. response, had backfired and Soviet security had been actually diminished. Subsequently, an INF Treaty (1987) resulted in the destruction of all intermediate-range missiles systems—"Thanks almost entirely to continuing concessions from Gorbachev."

President Ronald Reagan outlined a plan for the opening of the START talks in May 1982. It called for the "practical phased reduction" of strategic nuclear weapons in two stages, where warheads would be reduced by one-third, with significant cuts in ballistic missiles, and a ceiling would be placed on ballistic missile throw-weights and other elements. The first phase required the Soviets to scrap most of their best land-based strategic weapons, while the Americans could keep most of its Minutemen intercontinental missiles, deploy one hundred more new land-based MX missiles, place cruise missiles into service, and modernize its submarine and bomber fleets. In the second phase, Washington insisted that the Soviets reduce the aggregate throw-weight of their missiles by almost two-thirds, although the United States would make no cuts at all. The

American public responded enthusiastically to President Reagan's initiative for limiting strategic weaponry but it was obviously so one-sided—as was the "zero option" plan—that it was non-negotiable.[17]

THE NEGOTIATORY PROCESS

The arrival of increasingly destructive modern weaponry in the twentieth century, especially at mid-century, brought a dramatic enhancement of the role of arms control. In previous centuries, the decision to employ one or another type of arms control was often much less complicated because even if it focused on basic security issues, it was likely to play a minor supporting role in the resolution of broader political considerations. Formal deliberations focusing exclusively on specific arms control measures became routine by the early 1920s. Multilateral conferences, often sponsored by the League of Nations, the United Nations, or regional organizations, sought to deal with military expenditures, arms traffic, geographical demilitarization, general disarmament, and various security issues. Consequently, at one time or another, the League of Nations and its subcommittees, together with the UN General Assembly and its subordinate bodies, have discussed practically every aspect of the arms control process.

Some of these deliberations, often protracted, succeeded in arriving at agreements, but many did not. Among the unsuccessful efforts were the World Disarmament Conference's attempt to write a general treaty (1932), debate in the United Nations Atomic Energy Committee on the Baruch Plan for international nuclear controls (1946), and Eighteen Nations Disarmament Conference's (ENDC) lengthy search for a comprehensive nuclear test ban. Yet, there was merit even in the failed attempts. As Arthur H. Dean, who represented the United States at the ENDC, noted, "The discussions—at Geneva, at the United Nations, and in confidential diplomatic conversations—were a necessary means whereby the nations of the world could become educated on disarmament questions and the ground could be broken for concrete agreements."[18]

Superpower negotiations during the Cold War focusing on strategic nuclear weaponry (SALT and START) followed a similar pattern. Months of negotiations soon became years, even decades, as the negotiations to limit and subsequently reduce nuclear weaponry marched on.[19] Apart from the focus on arms control measures, these talks provided a means of easing tensions between Moscow and Washington. (See Chapter 10.)

Types of Arms Control Negotiations. The diplomatic process that transforms arms control objectives into acceptable agreements or understandings may vary dramatically. This process could involve bilateral talks, multilateral conferences, unilateral initiatives, or less formal, ongoing "politically binding" regimes. Bilateral and multilateral negotiations may focus on arms control objectives only, or arms control may play a relatively small part in the overall accord. The

Rush-Bagot agreement (1817), Anglo-French naval pact (1787), the Turko-Greek (1930) and Turko-Soviet naval protocols (1931), the Anglo-German naval pact (1935), and the Cold War strategic arms treaties—SALT and START—all concentrated on arms control procedures. Meanwhile, the various treaties calling for the defortification of the Azov (1605) and Dunkirk (1713–1783), and the Argentine-Chilean naval pact (1902), sought to resolve a considerable number of territorial, political, and economic issues. The bilateral treaty between Argentina and Chile was unusual in that it required the assistance of third-party (British) diplomats to bring the agreement about.

Multilateral conferences that treated arms control as a subsidiary matter include, for example, the Treaty of Westphalia (1688) that demilitarized a few small areas and Treaty of Paris (1856) that neutralized the Black Sea. The treaties following the end of both world wars also included a wide variety of territorial, political, and economic issues, but placed considerable emphasis upon limiting armaments. The Treaty of Versailles (1919) and the agreements with former Central Powers, along with political penalties, severely restricted arms and military personnel and forbade possession of specific weaponry. That same was essentially the case for post–World War II peace accords with Rumania, Bulgaria, Hungary, Italy, and Finland (1946–1947). There were, of course, many multilateral conferences that focused on specific arms control objectives. A few examples might include the major interwar naval conferences—Washington (1922), Geneva (1928), London (1930, 1935–1936)—as well as conferences, eventually successful, which sought to limit conventional weapons during the Cold War (1973–1990). Added to this list were the meetings that created several nuclear weapons–free zones, and the negotiations leading to the prohibition of biological weapons (1972) and chemical weapons (1993). There have been, and are, several ongoing examples of other multilateral projects.

Arms control objectives may be achieved by unilateral actions that seek to gain a similar response from an adversary—that is, it becomes a "negotiating" strategy—or it may be a declaration of national policy. In the first sense, an announced unilateral action by one party may trigger a similar, reciprocal unilateral action by its counterpart, as were Presidents George H. W. Bush and Mikhail Gorbachev's unilateral initiatives (1991–1992) relating to tactical nuclear weaponry. During the 1935 Anglo-German naval discussions, Berlin employed a "take it or leave it" negotiating position to gain an agreement. Unilateral declarations of national intent are frequently appended to formal agreements, when their contents could not be agreed upon for insertion into the treaty texts.

There are also unilateral arms control declarations that may or may not be reciprocated or which may be simply warnings. The United State's unilateral no-first-use policy with regard to toxic chemical agents, in 1943, would be an example of the latter intent. China's unilateral declaration (1964) regarding its policy of no-first-use of nuclear weapons and the Soviet Union's subsequent similar declaration (1982), which had propaganda value, did not elicit a reciprocal response from the United States.

Finally, there are less-formal, ongoing arms control regimes. These are understandings with less transparency that operate more as "gentlemen's agreements" and tend to be largely "politically binding" rather than legally binding. Examples of this type of arms control activities can be found in the multilateral export control regimes initially established during the Cold War but which have continued: the Coordinating Committee (1949–1994), the Nuclear Suppliers Group (1974), and the Missile Technology Control Regime (1987); for more details, see Chapter 4.

At the Conference Table. Experienced diplomats understood that all parties involved in negotiations would seek to gain or keep every possible advantage, even those quite minor ones. They also realized, however, that compromise would be required to reach a satisfactory agreement. Negotiated agreements thus seek to balance the asymmetries in order that the advantages of one party do not result in security risks for the others.[20]

The manner with which one's adversary is viewed may be crucial to the political environment, and hence, the negotiation process. President Ronald Reagan's labeling of the Soviet Union as an "evil empire," and George W. Bush's post–Cold War designation of Iran, Iraq, and North Korea as the "axis of evil" may resonate well at home, but they complicate the diplomatic process. Since negotiations involve a "give and take" approach searching to accommodate common interests, denigrating delegates across the table is unlikely to accomplish the desired objectives. Negotiators would be well advised to follow the advice of a former British army officer, and later military correspondent, Liddell Hart: "[K]eep cool. Have unlimited patience. Never corner your opponent, and always assist him to save face. Put yourself in his shoes—so as to see things through his eyes. Avoid self-righteousness like the devil—nothing is so self-blinding."[21]

What may seem to be a routine matter, the maintaining of a transcript of discussions, can be important not only during negotiations but also occasionally years later. A prominent example of the reexamination of the treaty transcripts occurred when the Reagan administration sought to circumvent the Antiballistic Missile Treaty (1972) in order to test defensive missiles under the president's Strategic Defense Initiative. A prompt rebuff by the Senate, with a revisiting of the records, ended that maneuver. In some quarters, this raised a concern about translators and translations since negotiations are usually conducted in more than one language. A first-class interpreter is also basically a stenographer, former ambassador Ralph Earle has pointed out, and "they write down everything both parties say because they have to read it back. In the Nixon era, we didn't have such notes." Surprisingly, when President Gerald Ford met with Premier Leonid Brezhnev at Vladivostok, Earle reported, "it was the first time in the history of individual summits—with just the president and foreign ministers present—that an American official was present who spoke Russian. In other words, Nixon and Kissinger had been dealing with the Soviet leader though a Soviet interpreter. And in all of those years, the only person taking notes was

Kissinger." Subsequently, senior U.S. officials were provided with their own interpreters.[22]

Disagreement over what role experts should play at the conference table has been a recurring dilemma, whether experienced military professionals or skilled civilian technicians. At The Hague conferences, as well as at several of the interwar League of Nations disarmament and naval limitation conferences, many delegates from various nations were military or naval officers. At the First Hague Conference (1899), the accredited military and naval delegates quickly squelched any notion of serious limitations of armaments, and usually criticized attempts to restrict the use of specific weaponry.

During the preparations for the 1922 Washington naval conference and subsequent negotiations, the Harding administration made it clear that while the advice of naval officers would be accepted, the arms control agreement would be based on political considerations. During the ratification process, Lodge explained to the Senate: "It is not for technical experts to make this treaty, any more than I regard it as a duty of technical experts to make the Tariff Bill. The idea should be dismissed that the naval experts were to formulate the policy to be pursued, or that we should ever have allowed them to do it. The policy, be it good or bad, was the policy of the government represented by the American delegates at the Conference."[23]

A diplomatic episode a few years later emphasized Lodge's point. Shortly after the Washington conference, Admiral William S. Sims argued that delegations at any future naval conference should include senior naval officers "in order to avoid rules and treaties being made by men who do not understand the technical side of warships." At the ill-fated 1927 Geneva naval conference, American and British naval officers served as delegates and bewildered other conferees with elaborate formulas comparing the technical merits of 8-inch versus 6-inch guns and heavy versus light cruisers. After they succeeded in deadlocking the conference, a senior British diplomat returned home bemoaning the lack of political guidance. From now on, he declared, experts should be on tap, but not on top.[24]

Specialists in and out of uniform can, and often do, complicate issues. A case in point: during the early test ban negotiations, seismologists sought a verification system that could distinguish between earthquakes and small underground nuclear explosions. After techniques were developed, acceptable to most scientists and diplomats, technical experts kept searching for more and more refinements to reduce the already low error rate to be *absolutely certain* that no cheating was going on. In the process, diplomats undertaking negotiations and senators holding hearings became quite knowledgeable about the technical features of seismology. As a result, Freeman Dyson argued, "This over-emphasis on technical details made the problem of verifying the test ban seem more and more formidable."

The negotiation of the Partial Test Ban in 1963 reinforced the notion that the successful arms control negotiations are essentially a political endeavor. When

Ambassador Averell Harriman journeyed to Moscow to conduct the negotiations, he took scientific advisers with him but deliberately excluded them from the negotiating team. As he later explained, "The expert is to point out all the difficulties and dangers ... but it is for the political leaders to decide whether the political, psychological and other advantages offset such risks as there may be."[25]

SALT I proved, however, that not having adequate staffing and advice, both technical and diplomatic, would result in "a mess" for which "the blame ... should be placed on [Henry] Kissinger." The specialists from the Arms Control and Disarmament Agency and the SALT delegation, who devised the carefully drawn Anti-Ballistic Missile Treaty, were ignored when drafting the Interim Agreement. The inadequacies of SALT I resulted in "considerable time" being "spent during the SALT II negotiation correcting" the earlier errors.

The SALT II agreement was a mix of an engineering document and a lawyer's brief—the text was not only extraordinarily complex, but also appended extensive definitions and elaborate "counting rules." As a result, opponents could employ the "fine print" to justify their claims that Backfire bombers were not properly counted, or that the allowed "heavy" missiles provided the Soviets with an unacceptable advantage. Part of the reason for this lay with the senior U.S. military delegate General Edward Rowny. His motto was "Peace is too important to leave to diplomats" With his connections to Pentagon official Richard Perle and Senator Henry Jackson, he tried his best to see that a SALT II treaty never emerged. During the 1978 negotiations, Rowny insisted, contrary to earlier and later evidence, that the Backfire be considered and limited as a heavy bomber capable of reaching the United States and landing in Cuba. The chief of the Soviet General Staff Nikolai Ogarkov offered Rowny a Backfire bomber if he would fly it—without refueling—to Cuba. Included in his invitation were assurances of "flowers for the widow Rowny."[26]

More than once during Cold War negotiations, "a reasonable treaty was nibbled to death by people raising small technical objections," complained Ambassador Ralph Earle, the former head of the U.S. Arms Control and Disarmament Agency. "Just as, according to Gresham's law of economics, bad money drives good money out of circulation," Dyson added, "so, in the public perception of arms control agreements, unimportant technical issues drive broader political objectives out of sight."[27]

ARMS CONTROL IN A DEMOCRATIC ENVIRONMENT

Public opinion historically has had a mixed impact on arms control negotiations. An early positive example of public influence on the formulation of arms control policy occurred when opposition arose in British parliament to the pending Act of Brussels in 1890 that sought to limit arms traffic in East Africa. The British public, which firmly linked the arms trade to slavery, demonstrated its support for the Act in meetings and protests. Special interests were finally defeated, and the Act secured Parliament's endorsement.

Public support in the United States for The Hague Conference (1899), however, went for naught. President William McKinley took the position that "it behooves us as a nation to lend countenance and aid to the beneficent project," but held that America's armed forces were so insignificant that discussion of limitations was meaningless.[28] So while Americans collected petitions, memorials, and other demonstrations of support for the limitation of armaments, Captain Alfred T. Mahan, the U.S. delegate, worked closely with Admiral John Fisher, the British naval delegate, at The Hague meetings, to prevent a limitation of naval forces. Captain William Crozier likewise resisted restraints on aerial bombing.

Public sentiment in several countries followed and usually endorsed post–World War I sensationalized investigations of armament manufacturers (the "Merchants of Death") and their arms traffic. Conspiracy theories were spread by the media with "detail upon detail, incident upon incident" cited in congressional hearings purporting to show that armaments makers applied "the two axioms of their business: when there are wars, prolong them; when there is peace, disturb it."[29] In the end, however, this popular disgust failed to produce an international agreement to control the arms traffic.

Public opinion in the United States during the Cold War always reflected a distinct ambiguity regarding arms control negotiations and agreements, especially with the Soviet Union. Polls invariably showed that a majority of Americans favored the bilateral arms control agreements with the Soviets; at the same time, a majority also indicated that they expected the communists to cheat if given an opportunity. Not surprisingly, many politicians sought to follow the polls. If candidates spoke in favor of arms limitations, they never hesitated to insist that they could be depended upon to be "tougher on Communists" than their opponents, and to be stronger supporters of a stout national defense.

As the Cold War lengthened, politicians' desire to be seen as strong on national defense often resulted in critical appraisals of arms limitations. Yet while hawkish politicians might flourish in the legislature, the same image did not fare as well in presidential politics. The American people were reluctant to support ambitious senators who opposed arms control, as Barry Goldwater, Henry M. Jackson, Howard Baker, Robert Dole, John Glenn, and others can attest. Even the "Teflon" president, Ronald Reagan, who was on record opposing every arms control agreement from the Limited Test Ban to SALT II, found it necessary to appear supportive of limiting arms during his reelection campaign. Voters may have been "uneasy about negotiating with the Soviet Union," as Michael Krepon has suggested, "but they are also uncomfortable with national candidates who oppose arms control."[30]

Some Cold War hawks worried that arms control negotiations would weaken the American public's support for the Pentagon's efforts to expand its weaponry. American defense analysts referred to this concern as a "lulling effect."

According to one such analyst, William Van Cleave, "If there is a strategic arms limitation agreement, there will be a tendency to euphoria in the United States, which might well result in a paralysis of strategic force programs well beyond the actual terms of the agreement." Richard Perle, known around Washington as the "Prince of Darkness," was more direct as he endorsed doomsday scenarios as vital to sustain the nation's security. "Democracies will not sacrifice to protect their security in the absence of a sense of danger," he explained in a *Newsweek* article on February 18, 1983, "and every time we create the impression that we and the Soviets are cooperating and moderating the competition, we diminish the sense of apprehension."

When both superpowers were testing nuclear devices in the atmosphere during the 1950s, there were widespread public protests not only in the United States, but also around the world. This public concern was not lost on President John F. Kennedy who succeeded in obtaining the Limited Test Ban Treaty of 1963. Reflecting a remarkable public sense of unease, the nuclear-freeze movement managed to influence Reagan's 1984 reelection campaign. He responded by stressing his desire to seek, after the election, direct contact with Moscow on nuclear issues. To what extent the nuclear-freeze movement influenced the administration's second term dramatic shift in support of arms control negotiations is difficult to assess.

Yet whatever the merits of a specific arms control agreement, a greater question arises. Can it survive the democratic process? Democracies like the United States have diverse groups of people who lack interest in broad complex issues, but are ideologically bound to a specific cause. During the Cold War, strident anticommunists—émigrés, individuals with ethnic ties to communist-controlled states, labor leaders, Catholic Church officials, and so on—frequently objected to any accommodation with Moscow short of taking its surrender. They might accept the basic idea behind an arms control pact, but would argue that the Soviets were likely to cheat, were cheating and/or were trying to build a superior strategic arsenal. Physicist Edward Teller, considered by Gerald Smith to be "a baleful influence" because of his persistent criticism of arms control proposals, strongly objected to the Limited Nuclear Test Ban. "I think through our policy of arms limitations we already lost our superiority.... And I think we might repeat the tragic mistake of the 1930s, where war has not been the consequence of an arms race, but the consequence of a race in disarmament."[31] Past experience indicates that fears aroused by the doomsayers, rather than optimistic aspirations, have had a greater impact on public opinion and, hence, on arms control activities.

Narrowly defined national interests have not always driven arms control policies, as occasionally states have responded to public support for humanitarian objectives. Because of considerable international sympathy, for example, the "humanitarian" approach carried the initial efforts to gain a ban on the use of landmines. The Ottawa Land Mine Convention was designed to reduce the estimated 2,000 people, some 80 percent of who were civilians, who then were killed or maimed each month. The 1997 Nobel Peace Prize was awarded to the International Campaign to Ban Landmines and its coordinator, Jody Williams.

Cold War Ideologies. America's strident Cold Warriors, both military and civilian, dwelled on worst-case assumptions regarding Soviet capabilities for decades and, most of them employed "faith-based" analyses that denied the appropriateness of arms control. Within months after the end of World War II, the American people were told that Stalin was bent on world domination, and that the only way to contain the Soviet Union was to build and maintain a superior military force. In a September 1946 memorandum, presidential counsel Clark Clifford argued: "The United States, with a military potential composed primarily of highly effective technical weapons, should entertain no proposal for disarmament or limitation of armaments as long as the possibility of Soviet aggression exists." Moreover, America "must be prepared to wage atomic and biological warfare."[32]

In turn, the National Security Council (NSC) suggested to President Truman in 1948 that "an essential element in the ideological conflict" consisted of a strong negotiating position that was perceived by the American public opinion to be fair and equitable. After emphasizing the importance of strengthening America's arsenal, NSC-68 went on express its belief that "any offer of, or attempt at, negotiation of a general settlement could be only a [Soviet] tactic. Nevertheless ... it may be desirable to pursue this tactic both to gain public support for the program and to minimize the immediate risks of war. ... Negotiation is not a possible separate course of action but rather a means of gaining support for a program of building [military] strength."

Early in 1960, Chairman of the Atomic Energy Commission John McCone was convinced that the Soviet Union was secretly violating the current nuclear test moratorium. When Pentagon scientist Herbert York insisted that he "had just gone over every shred of intelligence" available and "had found no evidence whatsoever supporting such a claim," the hawkish McCone angrily declared that York's view was "tantamount to treason."[33]

Long-time Soviet ambassador to Washington Anatoly Dobrynin acknowledged in his memoirs that Moscow's Cold War policies too were "unreasonably dominated by ideology, and [that] this produced continued confrontation." "The flaw in Soviet foreign policy," Mikhail Gorbachev has added, "consisted in the fact that all its energy came from an ideological source. A hard core of ideological constructs ultimately determined the behavior of the USSR on decisive questions of international relations, and nourished an atmosphere of confrontation toward the West, which was of course also partly a response to the no less confrontational policy pursued by the West toward the Soviet Union." He concluded: "I have come to the conclusion that the policy pursued by both sides was dictated by mutual fear and was ideologically driven."[34]

Looking back, it is difficult to judge which was more ideologically driven—Moscow or Washington. These ideological constraints, of course, made it difficult to negotiate the compromises necessary to achieve serious arms limitation agreements. It was completely contrary to one of Winston Churchill's favorite axioms: "We arm to parley."

Ratification of treaties in a democracy, consequently, has involved public perceptions and leadership skills. Michael Krepon's study of several such American efforts led him to conclude, not surprisingly, that it was easier for an arms control agreement to be ratified if it was publicly perceived as a substantive accomplishment.[35]

The Verification Process

Arms control agreements, as with other treaties, have always employed some form of "verification" to ensure compliance with their terms.[1] While the process of verification and determination of compliance or noncompliance are, indeed, two sides of the same coin, these two issues have been separated for examination. Verification mechanisms, imposed or negotiated, are designed to assure confidence in an arms control agreement by demonstrating that its terms are being properly implemented. Thusly, verification measures are defined, according to George Bunn and Wolfgang K. H. Panofsky, as having three objectives: "(1) detection of a class of 'suspicious events,' that is, possible violations; (2) identification of these events to determine whether or not they are prohibited; and (3) measurement to verify compliance or noncompliance" with a treaty's qualitative and quantitative limits or prohibitions.

In this process there is considerable and necessary overlap with other, more general, intelligence activities; indeed, the collection of general intelligence assists in arms control verification and vice versa. More involved than simply collecting information and creating a database is the vital and sensitive task of interpreting gathered material. Human analysts are involved in the process and, no matter how well schooled, there is a predisposition "to see what one expects to see." Thus, if one is predisposed to see evasions, one will usually find them; if one favors continuation of an agreement, one may overlook or downgrade significant factors.[2]

Any verification system has various degrees of desirability. For quite some time, various states have viewed extensive intrusiveness to verify treaty compliance as legalized espionage. This was the case with Tokyo during the 1930s and Moscow during much of the Cold War, although the Soviet position shifted during the Gorbachev era. Imposed arms control's intrusive verification regimes have invariably encountered resistance. Then, too, those promoting intrusive measures have occasionally had second thoughts because, due to reciprocity, these measures may conflict with the protection of one's own military and commercial secrets. Thus even though calls for intensive on-site verification had been a hallmark of United States policy since the 1946 Baruch Plan, Washington rejected Moscow's insistence in the mid-1980s on reciprocal rights to inspect highly classified systems within the American submarine fleet and production centers. To modify a proverb: the Reagan administration found out that what is sauce for the goose is not always sauce for the gander.

Another consideration that has placed limits on verification is cost. Substantial funds and manpower may be required to carry out verification procedures and, thus, officials may wish to consider the proper allocation of their resources. Should these resources be expended on verification processes or would national security be better served with them dedicated to other goals? When raised, these considerations are often questionable because armament costs usually exceed greatly those of verification expenses.[3]

METHODS OF VERIFICATION

Arms control agreements have stipulated differing types of verification. Historically, several methods or techniques have been employed to monitor compliance that may be classified as ranging from "cooperative" to "intrusive." The traditional non-intrusive approach to monitoring treaties required each signatory to employ "national means," that is, human observers of various kinds to confirm compliance or noncompliance. After World War I, however, the Versailles treaty—as well as the treaties with other defeated Central Powers—insisted on intrusive on-site inspection and supervision of imposed limits and restrictions upon the armed forces of their vanquished foes. Arguments for and against intrusive methods of verification and control, especially on-site inspections, emerged during discussions at various League of Nations' conferences during the 1920s and 1930s.

The insistence upon intrusive verification of various types figured prominently in the formulation of early U.S. Cold War arms control proposals, and in their negotiations. The 1946 Baruch Plan for international control of nuclear weapons floundered largely on the issue of invasive supervision and control. President Dwight Eisenhower's arms control adviser, Harold Stassen, continued to insist that inspection and supervision were "the first requirement for a sound [disarmament] agreement." When pleading America's case before a United Nations committee in 1955, he argued that "history indicates that agreements without adequate inspection lead to doubts and suspicions and uncertainty and new tensions between signatories.... [I]n fact, agreements without adequate inspection have been counter-productive in earlier periods." Yet, as a close observer subsequently warned, "On-site inspection is not a panacea. Effective national technical means remain at the heart of any verification system. Moreover, there is some concern that on-site inspection has been oversold and may create barriers to the negotiation of future treaties as well as present new sources of tension."[4]

Since not all arms control agreements involve substantial reductions or limitations of weaponry, but have much more modest goals, a wide range of verification methods or techniques have been designed to fit specific objectives. While negotiators expect that all parties intend to fulfill their obligations, they also anticipate that their governments will employ some verification methods to validate their expectations. Historically, the verification methods that have been used include: (1) self-monitoring, (2) notification procedures, (3) reporting commissions, (4) enquiry commissions, and (5) on-site supervisory commissions. Some of the recent, wide-ranging treaties have employed more than one of these various methods of verification. This is particularly true where notification procedures are connected to inspection techniques.

A few examples of each basic verification method are offered below. In those cases that employ multiple methods, each method is treated separately below under its appropriate category.

SELF-MONITORING

The "self-monitoring" of negotiated arms control agreements—which leaned heavily on national self-restraint, integrity, and common interest—was initially verified by *national means* (later, during the Cold War, by national *technical* means as well). Ancient imposed arms control restrictions were surely carefully scrutinized by available national means. National means has historically focused on human observers including diplomats and military attachés, international businessmen and tourists, and clandestine or undercover sources managed by state intelligence agencies. Often these sources were supplemented by other monitoring systems, such as notification, reporting, and enquiry.

Prior to World War II, army and navy attachés played a vital role in the collection of military intelligence and its assessment. They were particularly valuable in verifying arms control agreements because of their expertise and their ability to conduct visits (inspections) of military facilities on the basis of reciprocity. There were considerable differences, nation to nation, on which installations could be observed and what was restricted. A concern with the principle of reciprocity prompted the U.S. Office of Naval Intelligence during the 1920s and 1930s to insist that its attachés, seeking access to another country's "sensitive" facilities, obtain advance permission from Washington. Not surprisingly, U.S. naval attachés' requests to inspect certain foreign facilities were occasionally denied by Washington because officials did not wish to provide foreign attachés similar access to American bases and ships. The U.S. Navy did on occasion prevent visitation of its aircraft carriers because it wished to keep secret certain features; in return, the British and Japanese could, and often did, restrict visits of United States attachés to their carriers.[5]

Desperate to gain information regarding Soviet military capabilities in the early 1950s, Presidents Harry Truman and Eisenhower authorized the U.S. Air Force to fly over Soviet territory. In an attempt to legalize these activities, Eisenhower offered a plan at a 1955 summit meeting for reciprocal aerial reconnaissance—Open Skies—to reduce the possibility of a surprise attack, relax Cold War tensions and achieve a more readily comprehensive system of verification. The Soviets immediately rejected the idea, calling it thinly veiled espionage. Much later, the Open Skies concept gained a new life during the 1990s in conjunction with the Treaty on Conventional Armed Forces in Europe.

Ignoring international law, Washington officials later instituted their own version of "open skies," as its RB-47Es flew 156 missions over Soviet territory from March 21 to May 10, 1956. With the intelligence gathering missions completed, the Eisenhower administration dispatched a diplomatic note to Moscow, expressing regret that navigational errors led to the intrusion into Soviet air space. Subsequently, the United States employed the U-2 airplane to continue ferreting out and photographing Soviet military installations until 1960, when Francis Gary Powers was shot down. Technology finally resolved the issue. An American "spy" satellite began operating on a regular basis in August 1960, and the Soviet Union was employing its own space reconnaissance vehicles by 1962. Both superpowers now embraced the age of national technical verification—the Soviet's perhaps less enthusiastically—that opened the way to arms control agreements on strategic weaponry.[6]

With the advent of modern electronics, photography, space vehicles, and other devices, "national technical means" added to the effectiveness of self-monitoring. Such devices could verify, with reasonable accuracy, both the quantitative and qualitative features of strategic weaponry, particularly the numbers and characteristics of ballistic missiles, providing information vital to negotiations and to the monitoring of actual agreements. In ironic fashion, the sophisticated technologies developed by the superpowers as part of their military competition, had contributed greatly to progress in verification techniques. The "billions of dollars and rubles" that had been invested, according to Allan Krass, "gave each side a remarkably accurate picture of the military capabilities of its adversary."[7]

Twentieth-century diplomats recognized the value of arms control measures that were grounded on common interest and verified by national and national technical means. The multilateral interwar naval treaties and bilateral Cold War agreements by the superpowers have been among the large number of agreements employing these methods of self-monitoring.

The Washington Naval System. While no formal procedures for inspection, verification, or supervision were contained in the naval limitation system, the signatories understood that the 1922 Washington naval treaty terms would be monitored by national means. The U.S. naval attachés in Tokyo during the 1920s and 1930s were able to accumulate reasonably accurate statistics related to the size, tonnage, speed, and armament of Japanese warships, even though

Japanese officials increasingly sought to hamper their activities. While some information was obtained from "agents,"—such as technical data concerning the Type 93 *Long Lance* torpedo and the cruiser *Mogami*'s armament—the analysis of foreign publications, especially commercial and industrial reports, was probably more important. In such documents, sharp-eyed readers detected significant changes taking place in the allocation of resources, and the establishment or conversion of factories.

The attachés monitored the appropriations debates in the Japanese Diet, read the accounts of a well-connected British journalist Hector Bywater, who often learned of new Japanese warships before they did, and tracked the activities of German and British specialists who were hired to assist with Japanese naval construction. Additionally, they monitored Japan's purchase of diesel and steam turbine engines from Germany, Switzerland, and Italy. The U.S. naval attachés in Tokyo, as historian Thomas Mahnken has noted, estimated that "about 95 percent" of the necessary information was available in public sources. When in the 1930s the Imperial Navy undertook extensive modernization of its older battleships for speed, firing range and protection, U.S. attachés reported this information in considerable detail. The Office of Naval Intelligence, however, failed to utilize this data to update its estimates of Japan's battle fleet; instead, it continued to list the battleships at their pre-modernization displacements. It also failed to grasp from the provided data that the *Long Lance* torpedo had a larger warhead, greater speed, and a longer range than American or British models.[8]

Japanese Pacific Mandated Islands. The only mechanism for verifying Japan's non-fortification pledge related to its mandated islands, was contained in the League of Nations' mandate agreements. In 1923, the U.S. secretary of state urged that key strategic areas, including the mandates, be open to mutual inspection by attachés. The proposal floundered when the secretary of the Navy responded: "I think that there should be no question of the good faith of the signatory powers and that ... visits of inspection either to ships or to stations to verify the execution of the terms of a treaty are undesirable and may be provocative of friction." Six years later, the U.S. Navy reversed its position and sought visitation rights to the mandated islands. Japanese officials did not reject the American requests, but either "lost" them or issued such complicated regulations that no inspection took place.[9]

National means did not resolve the U.S. Navy's questions regarding Japanese activities in these Pacific islands, nor were the League's efforts of much value (see League's Mandates Commission, below).

Test Ban Agreements. The spread of radioactive fallout resulting from U.S. and USSR atmospheric nuclear tests aroused worldwide public protests in the 1950s and prompted the search for a way to halt the testing. While seismologists offered a verification system that could distinguish between earthquakes and small underground nuclear explosions that was acceptable to most scientists and diplomats, there was continued pressure to keep searching for more and more refinements to improve detection. Thus it became politically impossible to achieve a comprehensive test ban because critics, most of whom did not want all nuclear testing halted, argued that it was impossible to be *absolutely* certain that there was no cheating going on.

On August 5, 1963, the United States and the USSR signed the limited (or partial), rather than comprehensive, nuclear test ban that prohibited above ground or atmospheric testing, but allowed underground testing. Since the Kennedy administration was unable to provide Congress and its critics guarantees of absolute Soviet compliance, verification was not mentioned in the text of the Limited Nuclear Test Ban Treaty (LNTB).[10] Because they were not signatories to the LNTB, France and the People's Republic of China continued for some time to conduct atmospheric tests.

In July 1974, the two superpowers bilaterally agreed to a Threshold Test Ban Treaty that established a 150-kiloton limit on underground tests, prohibited interference "with national technical means of verification," and provided for an exchange of information on the geology and location of test sites.

ABM, SALT I & II Treaties. By early 1965, satellite cameras could count antiballistic missile systems, land-based strategic ballistic missiles, aircraft on the ground, and submarines in port with reasonable accuracy. Some minor evasions might take place, but a major violation would be detected. There was initially some worry that cloud cover over Russia, as well as camouflage and other methods of concealment, might prove to be a problem. These concerns were discounted, however, because the Central Intelligence Agency proved that it could monitor Soviet missile deployments with a substantial degree of accuracy.[11] In an October 1967 speech, Assistant Secretary of Defense Paul Warnke urged the Soviets to discuss limiting strategic weapons, stipulating that the United States would consider an agreement that would be verified by "our own unilateral capability" rather than on-site inspections.

The protracted strategic arms limitations talks (1969–1972), resulted in the Interim Agreement (SALT I) and the Anti-Ballistic Missile (ABM) Treaty, placing limits on vastly different strategic nuclear arsenals, and terminating ineffective anti-ballistic missile programs. Article V of the SALT I pact declared that: "Each Party shall use national technical means of verification at its disposal in a manner consistent with generally recognized principles of international law;" that "Each Party undertakes not to interfere with the national technical means of verification of the other Party;" and that "Each Party undertakes not to use deliberate concealment measures which impede verification by national technical means." In identical paragraphs, the ABM Treaty endorsed national technical means for verification purposes.[12] Significantly, this was the first mention in any arms control treaty of prohibitions on hindering or limiting verification efforts. Noteworthy as well, was the creation of the Standing Consultative Commission quietly to examine questions regarding the treaty's implementation (see below).

NOTIFICATION PROCEDURES

This method, together with data exchanges, has been employed as an adjunct to national means and, especially, national technical means in verifying an arms control measure. This system has taken several forms, among them: (1) notifying others of intended increases in armaments or military maneuvers; (2) advance notices containing substantial qualitative design data; and (3) exchange of complex technical data, as called for by some U.S.–USSR bilateral accords, to permit monitoring procedures.

Brussels Act or Convention, 1890. While no multinational verification or enforcement clauses were called for in this effort to restrict the sale of arms in Central Africa, the signatories did agree to coordinate their respective national export policies, and to enforce the agreed-upon measures of the Act in their colonial territories. Additionally, the signatories were to *notify* each other of any arms traffic, permits granted, or measures taken to repress the arms trade.

Minor Interwar Naval Agreements. The Turko-Greek pact (1930), which sought to stabilize naval forces in the Aegean Sea, and the Turko-Soviet protocol (1931), which sought the same for the Black Sea, stipulated that any increase in naval armaments would be preceded by a six-month notice of intent. The procedure was expanded in the Anglo-German naval pact (1935), to include the reciprocal exchange of information concerning the construction of warships. The procedure, though not formally stated, consisted of the British and German naval staffs exchanging information on their respective construction plans for 1936 to 1942. Progress in naval construction was to be part of ongoing exchanges that presumably would be verified by naval attachés. The British accepted the pact, convinced that Germany could not violate the agreement without London officials becoming aware of it.[13]

Michael Papp has suggested that the reciprocal exchange was "misleading," arguing that the German Naval Command communicated *quantitative* information to the British Admiralty, but that "the Germans 'forgot' to inform the British of their technical advances in naval construction." Neither Papp nor any other source, however, suggest that the British Admiralty informed the Germans of their development of submarine detection—the forerunner of sonar— or their other technical naval improvements. Apparently, both parties accepted that there would be a certain amount of secrecy regarding *quantitative* improvements.[14]

The London Naval Treaty of 1936 saw the full flowering of notification procedures, by providing for the annual exchange of detailed information by each nation of its building, acquisition, and modernization programs. Appended to this yearly "Advanced Notification and Exchange of Information" was a separate appendix containing the technical particulars of such activity—for example, tonnage, armaments, and speed. In the case of new ship construction, the technical information was to be forwarded no later than four months prior to the laying of its keel.

Among the parties to the 1936 London treaty and its bilateral accessions, an intriguing question developed over which countries would receive copies of the stipulated annual exchange of information. Many observers thought that all signatory powers, no matter how they were interrelated, would receive the data; but Great Britain—the central intermediary—maintained sole possession of the collected information. Particularly jealous of this practice, American officials protested being denied access to the German's naval plans. Germany and France's reluctance to have their plans become the property of the other had thwarted British efforts for widespread distribution.

This issue was discussed during the negotiations leading to the bilateral accession pacts, but without resolution. Finally in November 1938, the British Foreign Office sought authorization for them to act as a clearinghouse for the exchange of naval construction data. Refusal by the Nazi government to open "any fresh direct treaty relations" with Russia derailed the proposal. Until the Germans denounced the accord, their naval staff—unlike the Russian authorities that never fulfilled their obligations—continued to exchange construction data with the British.[15]

The exchange of naval information appeared to function reasonably well and it was verified by naval attachés. While none of these naval agreements contained provisions for enforcement or sanctions, they did, either implicitly or explicitly, provide "compensation" mechanisms. Thus, the addition of naval armaments by one nation could be offset through compensating acquisitions by the other signatories without terminating the basic agreements.

Helsinki Final Act. The Final Act (1975) called for advance notification of military exercises involving more than 25,000 troops, and urged granting invitations to observers to view the activities. It was expected that increased information about military maneuvers would reduce the possibility of a miscalculation by Warsaw Pact or NATO members. These measures were expanded in the Stockholm Document (1986), CFE (1990), Open Skies Treaty (1990), and three Vienna Documents (1990, 1992, and 1994) that eventually reduced the size of military exercises requiring notification to 13,000, required the invitation of observers, and introduced on-site inspections.[16]

SALT II. This agreement required an initial exchange of data on stipulated forces ("agreed data base") and another similar exchange every six months thereafter. This exchange would have constituted an important part of the verification process, but the treaty didn't come into force. The information supplied by one party could be compared to the information collected by the other, thus providing an incentive to supply actual figures and avoiding the risk of being discovered to have withheld information. This was often overlooked but subtle cooperative activity considerably enhanced the prospect of compliance.

All of SALT II's extensive rules for inclusion and definitions of objects and activities were to enhance the significance of an "agreed data base" semiannual review. Adopting SALT I's prohibition against interference with each party's national technical means of verification aided in providing independent information for the periodic reviews. Finally, a Standing Consultative Commission was to be available to resolve differences of interpretation that might arise.

START I & II. Drawing upon the previous arrangements for SALT II, the bilateral U.S.-U.S.S.R. START I accord (1991) created an avalanche of notifications and data exchanges between the superpowers. The same monitoring system was essentially incorporated into the START II pact (1993), except with a modification of stipulated accounting rules. The START programs emphasized cooperative measures such as the exchange of relevant weapons inventories and telemetry tapes after missiles test flights, which would enhance verification via national technical means.[17] The telemetry exchange was a new arrangement.

Joint Data Exchange Center. The September 1998 and December 2000 agreements—expanding pledges contained in the Ballistic Missile Launch Notification Agreement (1988)—were designed to share information on the launch of ballistic missiles and space launch vehicles to avoid the possibility of a false alarm. While the Cold War was over, both the United States and Russia nevertheless maintained, on alert, thousands of nuclear warheads. Thus, arrangements that reduced the chance of a miscalculation regarding a nuclear attack could strengthen the deterrent effect of the two powers' considerable nuclear forces. Unfortunately, George W. Bush's abrogation of the 1972 ABM Treaty and efforts to deploy an unproven antiballistic missile system in Eastern Europe prompted Moscow to halt installing its Joint Data Exchange Center. In 2008, the facility remained empty in Moscow.

India-Pakistan Missile Notification Pact. Seeking to reduce tensions, the two nations signed an agreement on October 5, 2005, to notify each other in advance of missile test flights. Notification was required 72 hours before launching a ballistic missile flight test. Additionally, the pact prohibited test missiles from flying on a trajectory approaching, or that would land close to their accepted borders or the Line of Control, running through the disputed province of Kashmir. In accordance with the agreement, the Indian government notified Pakistan of an impending test of a ballistic missile on February 26, 2008.

REPORTING COMMISSIONS

Essentially a twentieth-century approach, this method was largely an auditing system that could function as part of a larger verification procedure, an ongoing independent project, or an ad hoc measure that terminated upon completion of its task. The more permanent commissions often served as clearinghouses for information, either by an international body or to members of a specific treaty.

The Straits Commission. The Straits Commission, provided for in the Lausanne Convention (1923), was representative of the reporting method but it also carried out demilitarization obligations. The commission was initially charged with defining the precise boundaries of the demilitarized zones and verifying the destruction of fortifications within the zones. Once these conditions were met, the nations affected—Turkey, Greece, and Bulgaria—were responsible for continued execution of the demilitarization terms. After some internal dissention, the commission reported to the League of Nations Council on November 16, 1925, that the initial demilitarization of the Straits had been accomplished.

Located on Turkish territory, the commission's primary duties consisted of monitoring the warships traversing the Straits. It maintained surveillance of the Soviet Union's Black Sea fleet and sought to restrict the passage of foreign warships through the Straits to a comparable ratio. The Soviets initially refused to provide the commission with data about the composition of their Black Sea fleet, but later changed their mind. They decided to cooperate because they feared that the commission might employ imprecise data and set the ratio too high—thus permitting a larger number of foreign naval forces through the Straits than accurate figures would authorize. The commission, which lacked the power to employ sanctions, limited its activities to sending the League of Nations Council annual reports of naval activities in and around the Straits. The commission was disbanded after the Treaty of Montreux (1936).

Biological and Toxin Weapons Convention, 1972. The initial text contained no reference to verification procedures. However, a suspected Soviet violation involving the release of anthrax pathogens, at Sverdlovsk in 1979, prompted the convention's Second Review Conference in 1986 to require nations formally to submit "information on high-safety research facilities," to provide data on "unusual outbreaks of infectious diseases," to publish research related to BW agents, and to include information on activities "which might be of relevance to the Convention." The threat of Iraq's biological arsenal during the First Gulf War prompted the Third Review Conference's (1991) expanded reporting requirements in an effort to build confidence in the convention. States were to report information on national biological defense research and development programs, to report on domestic legislation relevant to the convention, to declare past research on offensive and defensive BW, and to identify their human vaccine production facilities. The United States took the position that the convention was not verifiable, but other nations created a "Group of Verification Experts" that began a protracted, scientific, and technical examination of potential measures, and a review of possible verification techniques.

In 2001, U.S. officials walked away from efforts to craft a verification protocol to the Biological Weapons Convention (BWC), arguing that the protocol's on-site inspection measures might jeopardize American commercial proprietary information, while offering little ability to detect would-be cheaters. While there has been growing support for a monitoring mechanism, Washington chose to emphasize the need for national responsibilities of control.

The UN Office of Disarmament collects the reports and provides that information to signatories of the convention.[18] (See below for "enquiry" dimensions of the pact.)

Armaments Year Book: General and Statistical, 1924–1940. After the League of Nations' unsuccessful efforts to control the export and import of armaments, its Disarmament Section in 1924, with the endorsement of the Temporary Mixed Commission, launched an annual statistical survey of the arms trade. It became the sole international collection agency for arms trade information during the interwar years. Unfortunately, it had little success in gaining the confidence of all nations; therefore, while its intentions were commendable, its data was frequently incomplete.

UN Register of Conventional Arms, 1992. The General Assembly instructed the Secretary General in 1988 to determine ways of "promoting transparency in international transfers of conventional arms on a universal and non-discriminatory basis." The resulting UN register divided data into two categories— "requested" and "invited." No procedure was created for systematic verification of the voluntary data submissions; however, a "request" suggests "a higher level of political obligation" than just the regular "invitation."

Data was requested for the exports and imports of seven classes of heavy conventional weaponry—battle tanks, armored combat vehicles, large-caliber artillery, combat aircraft, attack helicopters, warships, and missiles and their launchers. In addition, nations were "invited" to provide information relating to export and import arms policies and their relevant legislative and administrative procedures. The UN Office for Disarmament Affairs has collected and stored individual submissions in a computer data bank that has been available to all member states and made public in annual reports.[19]

COMMISSIONS OF ENQUIRY

Most of these formal commissions were employed prior to 1945 and drew their assignments and authority from international organizations such as the League of Nations. They served on an ad hoc basis or as permanent bodies. The post-1945 era found several agreements that permitted ad hoc enquiry groups, when particular issues arose that could not be easily resolved by treaty mechanisms. The Standing Consultative Commission, created in the 1972 ABM and SALT I treaties, was established to deal with issues raised by national verification regimes. The START treaties instituted a new standing commission. "Challenge inspections" that appeared in several 1990s pacts might also be considered in this category, but they usually involved on-site inspections.

Aland Island Convention. After World War I, Finland agreed—as the Russians had in an 1856 pact—"not to fortify" the Aland archipelago in the Gulf of Bothnia. If any signatory power or powers believed that the terms of the convention were being evaded, charges could be presented directly to the Council of the League of Nations. If the Council believed the charges were serious enough, it could launch an inquiry into the matter. The League Council was empowered to decide what measures should be taken in case of a violation; however, the demilitarization pledges of the convention were never challenged.

League's Mandate Commission. One of the more serious challenges to the "enquiry" method of arms control supervision, occurred during the interwar years. The League's Permanent Mandates Commission undertook in the 1930s to determine whether the Japanese were honoring their pledge not to fortify their central Pacific island mandates—the Mariana, Caroline and Marshall islands. From 1932 to 1935, the commission, sitting in Geneva, pondered Tokyo's annual reports, and interrogated Japanese representatives regarding the increasing expenditures for harbor improvements and other similar construction programs. Lacking the authority to visit these islands without Japanese permission—which Tokyo ingeniously neither granted nor denied—the skeptical commissioners ended their inquiry without resolving American and British suspicions.[20]

Standing Consultative Commission (SCC). This confidential commission was established by the 1972 ABM Treaty—and endorsed by the SALT I and II pacts—as a means of adjudicating differences that might arise over the interpretation of "ambiguous" features of the treaty, as well as "unintended interference with national technical means of verification." It was believed that quiet technical discussions by appointed delegates could more easily resolve contentious ambiguities than formal, politically charged negotiations. The SCC was also to provide consideration of "possible changes in the strategic situation." The Commission conducted extensive discussions of queries and issued several important clarifications to implementation practices under the ABM Treaty. As a former U.S. commissioner to the SCC Robert Buchheim elaborated:

> The essence of the standing consultative commission implementation task is to head off gross dislocations or irretrievable circumstance by acting early enough and finding mutually acceptable measures to sustain intact the agreements within its field of responsibility. The initial requirement of this task is to raise potential problems for resolution before they get out of hand and become causes for undesired reconsideration of an entire agreement.

SALT II incorporated the two provisions, national technical means and the SCC, and expanded on the clauses related to non-interference and non-concealment, through limits on the encryption of missile test telemetry. The Reagan administration's distrust for the SCC resulted in replacing it in the START I treaty with a Joint Compliance and Inspection Commission (JCIC) for resolution or clarification of compliance issues. The creation of the JCIC appeared at the time to enhance the use of national technical means for verification. However, according to one critic, "it ended up causing more suspicion than reassurances in the 1980s. Accusations of excessive encryption of missile flight test telemetry were among the most important of the many charges leveled by the Reagan administration against the Soviet Union."[21]

Biological & Toxin Weapons Convention, 1972. This convention was not, in its original text, supported by a stipulated means of verification, and efforts to devise an agreed-upon verification protocol have been unsuccessful to date. After the Soviets intervened in Afghanistan, the review conference of the BW convention authorized the United Nations Security Council, in an ad hoc fashion, to investigate allegations of violations as it deemed significant. In 1982, the United States claimed that that the Soviet Union had violated the BW convention when "selected Lao and Vietnam forces, under the direct Soviet supervision, have employed lethal trichothecene toxins and other combinations of chemical agents" (the "yellow rain" charge) against resisting H'Mong people. Moreover, it was claimed that the Soviets were using deadly mycotoxins in Afghanistan. The UN created a Group of Experts to investigate the charges. After it visited Thailand to interview witnesses, the group was only able to report that its findings were inconclusive. Later, the group visited Pakistan to interview Afghans who allegedly had been affected by toxins. The report, however, did not reveal conclusive evidence of illegal activities.[22]

Strategic Offensive Reduction Treaty (SORT). This agreement differs greatly from its predecessors (SALT and START pacts) in its brevity and its absence of verification procedures. It was not clear how SORT would be verified. The treaty's text declared that START would remain in force, and indicated that it would rely upon its intrusive and extensive verification regime to monitor SORT. Article III simply establishes a Bilateral Implementation Commission—a "diplomatic consultative forum which shall meet at least twice a year, to discuss issues related to implementation" of the treaty.

With the 1991 START I's extensive verification and information exchange regime set to expire in December 2009, the supervision of President George W. Bush's loosely framed SORT pact could be threatened unless some type of "bridging" accord is agreed to by the end of 2009. Discussions reported in October 2007 indicated that the American intelligence community had warned the administration that without the START I verification regime, it would not be able to assess Russia's future compliance with any confidence. Administration officials insisted, however, that such intrusive verification measures or agreements to reduce arms limits were "unnecessary" given what they saw as improved relations between Moscow and Washington.[23]

ON-SITE INSPECTION

On-site inspection systems constitute the most intrusive method of verification. Comprehensive inspection and monitoring systems figured prominently in Washington's Cold War arms control proposals—often, one suspects, because it was known to be totally unacceptable to the Soviet Union. However, a close observer pointed out that mutual on-site provisions were open-ended, "since one side's efforts to inspect such [sensitive] installations would invite similar requests by the other side." This prediction came true when the Soviets reversed themselves and began pressing Americans for complex verification arrangements. As Secretary of Defense Frank Carlucci was forced to admit, "verification has proven to be more complex than we thought it would be. The flip side of the coin is its application to us. The more we think about it, the more difficult it becomes."[24]

The Antarctic treaty, the Modified Brussels Treaty (1954), the International Atomic Energy Agency (IAEA), and the Strategic Arms Reduction Treaty (START I), for example, authorize on-site visits with different rules for inspections, and have been carried out in cooperation with various treaty members because of the perceived mutual advantages. The Treaty of Versailles and the Iraqi armistice, on the contrary, charged inspection teams with verifying that imposed disarmament terms were carried out. An on-site inspection system, established to supervise the carrying out of arms control terms, is more likely to be successful if the terms have clearly perceived mutual benefits. Where unilaterally imposed terms were viewed as unfair, often the inspectors received little cooperation.

Versailles Treaty. The victorious Allies established the first elaborate on-site verification system—the Inter-Allied Control Commission (IAAC)—in the Treaty of Versailles (1919). Article 204 of the treaty charged the IAAC with supervising Germany's "complete execution of the delivery, destruction, demolition, and rendering things useless" according to the military terms of the treaty. The IAAC consisted of three separate organizations: the Inter-Allied Military Commission of Control (IAMCC), the Inter-Allied Naval Commission of Control (IANCC), and the Inter-Allied Aeronautical Commission of Control (IAACC). Each commission was divided into units with specific duties, the IAMCC headquartered in Berlin, for example, had six sub-commissions: (1) outside liaison, (2) fortifications, (3) effectives, (4) armaments, (5) translations and press reports, and (6) administration. Initially the Commissions reported to the Supreme Council in Paris, which consisted of Allied chiefs of state or their representatives. After 1921, the IACC dealt with the Council of Ambassadors and the Allied Military Committee, both located in Paris, regarding verification and compliance until 1931.

The under-manned Inter-Allied Commissions, comprising representatives of Britain, France, Italy, Belgium, and Japan, were initially staffed with slightly more than 1,000 men. The IACC conducted thousands of on-site inspections throughout Germany during the course of its existence. The German population, as well as their military and civilian authorities, felt the terms were unfair, and never fully cooperated with the inspection teams. The IACC's efforts to verify the demobilization of German armed forces, the conversion of manufacturing plants and the destruction of massive amounts of arms and munitions, though imperfect, nevertheless constituted a substantial achievement.[25]

Modified Brussels Treaty, 1954. The Agency for the Control of Armaments (ACA) for the Western European Union (WEU) was created as Protocol IV of the modified treaty. The ACA was unusual for its task as it was verifying that the members of the Union were abiding by Protocol III "not to manufacture certain types of armaments" and to "control ... the level of stocks of armaments" of various specified types that were "held by each member." In order to accomplish this mandate, the ACA gathered and examined statistical and budgetary data that was collected from members of the WEU and "appropriate NATO authorities."

The ACA had the authority to conduct on-site inspections, "question those in charge," "take extracts from documents and accounts," and undertake "test checks" to ensure that the collected data was valid. West Germany's membership in NATO had aroused its neighbors' interest in establishing the verification process.

International Atomic Energy Agency, 1957. The Vienna-based International Atomic Energy Agency (IAEA) has been the principal agency to ensure compliance with the nuclear Non-Proliferation Treaty. Established in July 1957 as an autonomous agency under the United Nations, its initial purpose was to coordinate President Dwight Eisenhower's Atoms for Peace project that sought to promote and safeguard peaceful uses of atomic energy. The IAEA was to provide a system of international safeguards aimed at preventing nuclear materials bound for civilian use from being diverted to military programs. To carry out its mandate, the Agency created an elaborate system of procedures and rules. The first step in verification required inventorying all material subject to a safeguard, and the preparation of a vital "initial report" that listed (and limited) items that were subject to ongoing inspections.

The verification process, thereafter, employs three types of inspections that vary in frequency—ad hoc, routine, and special. In brief, ad hoc inspections generally focus on international transfers of nuclear material at areas identified for the Agency. Routine inspections monitor and examine reports and records to verify the location, identity, quantity, and composition of nuclear materials covered by safeguards. Special inspections take place if the IAEA considered that the information gathered by routine inspection was "not adequate for the Agency to fulfill its responsibilities under the Agreement."

The May 1997 Model Additional Protocol to Safeguards Agreements, required a signatory nation to provide access to any part of a nuclear site and to other locations where nuclear material is, or may be, present. The nation also was required to provide access to all locations that are or could be engaged in nuclear activities related to the nuclear fuel cycle and, in cases where such access may not be possible, to make every reasonable effort to satisfy the IAEA requirements promptly through other means. Finally, the Additional Protocol provides for streamlining administrative procedures for designating inspectors, providing them with visas, and improving communications with IAEA Headquarters. "The strengthened system," according to the IAEA, "is based on a political commitment to support an 'intelligent' verification system—one where qualitative assessment takes place alongside quantitative accounting measures."

The Agency, however, does not possess the authority to "roam the country-side of a safeguarded state in search of clandestine activity or evidence of non-compliance" except as provided by special arrangement. The various, often irregular, Iraqi inspections from 1991 to 2003 were one such exception and this was implemented under specific UN resolutions.[26]

Antarctic Treaty, 1959. This treaty completely demilitarized an entire continent by prohibiting all conventional and nuclear weaponry. As Soviet activity increased on the continent during the 1950s, Western governments—led by the United States—decided that international accommodation, with safeguards, was desirable. Initial treaty membership was 12, but gradually expanded to 40. An innovative verification system was established whereby the treaty parties might conduct aerial inspections and, at any time, undertake on-site visitations at all areas and installations. It was the right of each consultative state to conduct unannounced on-site inspections. "All areas of Antarctica, including all stations, installations and equipment within those areas, and all ships and aircraft at points of discharging or embarking cargoes or personnel ... shall be open at all times to inspection by any observers designated."[27]

INF Treaty, 1987. The intermediate-range nuclear force (INF) treaty established a timetable and specific instructions for the removal of the missiles. All in all, it marked a truly significant breakthrough in the evolution of the verification process. On-site inspections verified the removal and destruction of the missiles under the direction of a new U.S. umbrella organization—the On-Site Inspection Agency. The format of on-site inspections conducted under the INF agreement could well serve as a model for future verification regimes.

Anticipating disputes during implementation of the treaty, a Special Verification Commission was created in 1988 to resolve such questions as might arise. In spite of a few controversies, the verification process functioned successfully.

The START Treaties. The complex and lengthy 1991 START I agreement contained an extensive and intrusive verification regime. In addition to the exchange of stipulated data and verification by national means, START I provided for 12 types of on-site inspections. The same monitoring system was incorporated into the START II pact (1993), except where certain accounting rules had been modified. In addition to relying on national technical means, the START programs emphasized cooperative measures, such as the exchange of relevant weapons inventories and telemetry tapes after missile test flights. The START regime also created a Joint Compliance and Inspection Commission to provide a forum for resolving compliance issues, clarifying ambiguities, and facilitating implementation (see Standing Consultative Commission, above).[28]

Conventional Armed Forces in Europe (CFE), 1990. NATO proposed, in December 1985, a verification regime calling for a detailed exchange of data and 30 on-site inspections per year. The following April, Soviet General Secretary Mikhail Gorbachev asked for "substantial reductions" of conventional forces and weaponry to be supervised by "both national technical means and international forms of verification and, if need be, on-site inspections." In drafting the Protocol on Inspection (Article XIV), negotiators drew extensively on past verification methods and experiences; indeed, they often mentioned preventing a recurrence of the Versailles treaty's problems. The final document, comprising of 27 pages, elaborated upon "definitions," "general obligations," and "pre-inspection requirements," as well as other categories.[29]

President George H. W. Bush reintroduced Eisenhower's Open Skies concept in 1989 to supplement the CFE verification regime. The proposal was attractive because cheap and flexible aircraft would allow European nations to conduct aerial inspections without relying on U.S. satellites. The "Open Skies" accord was signed at Helsinki on March 24, 1992, and entered into force on January 1, 2002. Treaty signatories begun trial flights in 1993, and as of 2002, 26 nations were eligible to conduct short-notice, unarmed flights—in certified aircraft carrying up to four different types of sensors—over any treaty member's entire territory. Each nation has been assigned the number of over-flights it must permit each year.[30]

In a decade and a half, the CFE's thousands of on-site inspections, aerial surveillance, and forums such as the Joint Consultative Group, the Extraordinary Conferences, and the Review Conferences greatly increased transparency.

Chemical Weapons Convention. For what was probably the first time in the negotiation of an arms control agreements, "practice" on-site inspections, seen as central to a successful treaty, were carried out. From June 1989 to August 1991, some 60 such inspections were unilaterally conducted at civilian and military facilities in more than 30 nations. This experience played a major role in developing the convention's complex inspection system.

As a result of these exercises, the Chemical Weapons Convention (1993) introduced a controversial verification concept of an "anywhere, any time" challenge inspection that permitted, as in the additional protocol for the IAEA, a signatory's unimpeded access to suspect locations. Initiated by the United States, it provided that whenever a state or group of states detected an activity that might be a violation of the convention, the state on whose territory the activity was taking place would be obliged to permit a prompt, internationally conducted on-site inspection to determine whether a violation had indeed occurred. This agreement permitted chemical experts to visit each nation's chemical production facilities on 48 hours' notice to determine whether chemical weapons were being manufactured.

Additionally, the Organization for the Prevention of Chemical Weapons, likely to be the largest arms control agency ever designed, would oversee the destruction of existing chemical weapon stocks, and consider questions raised regarding treaty compliance.[31]

UN Inspections of Iraq, 1991–2002. Following the U.S.-led coalition's victory over Iraqi forces, the UN Security Council adopted Resolution 687 on April 3, 1991. The resolution mandated the complete elimination of Iraq's biological, chemical, and nuclear weapons projects, as well as its ballistic missiles with a range beyond 150 kilometers. To supervise compliance, the resolution created the UN Special Commission (UNSCOM) to oversee the removal of Iraq's biological, chemical, and restricted missile programs and stipulated that the International Atomic Energy Agency (IAEA) would ensure Iraq's nuclear weapons program was dismantled.

The on-site teams headed by Hans Blix, director-general of the IAEA and Rolf Ekeus, chairman of the UNSCOM, launched inspections in May and June 1991. They met with Iraqi obstructionism consisting of removing prohibited items from inspection sites and the denial of access to facilities and records. This scenario persisted with varying intensities for the next decade. In 1992 the Iraqi government admitted having had more of the proscribed missiles and chemical weapons than it initially acknowledged, but insisted that they had unilaterally destroyed them. Not only did this violate the requirement that the inspectors were to supervise such destruction, it left no formal record of the unilateral destruction. In 1999, a UN review of the inspectors' activities concluded that the bulk of the prohibited weaponry, indeed, had been destroyed.

Two problems arose during the inspections. First, in 1999 the United States acknowledged it had placed intelligence agents on the inspection teams, prompting the Iraqi government to expel the inspectors. Secondly, President George W. Bush refused to believe reports of a successor UN commission—the UN Monitoring, Verification, and Inspection Commission—that no dire threat from Iraqi weapons of mass destruction existed. Nevertheless, the UN on-site inspections had accomplished their objectives, despite Washington's refusal to acknowledge their success.[32]

SHIFTING NATIONAL POSITIONS ON VERIFICATION

National positions on verification, especially on-site inspection and supervision, have shifted considerably since World War I. While the importance given to verification has increased greatly in the nuclear age, since 1919, no nation's policies regarding intrusive methods have vacillated as widely as those of America and Russia.

During the interwar years, several nations adjusted their policies regarding inspection and supervision. Italy opposed such international controls in the 1920s but reluctantly agreed in 1932 to accept them if substantial arms reductions took place. In Germany, the Weimar government, undergoing supervision dictated by the Versailles treaty, was disposed toward an international system of inspection and supervision as long as it was applied equally to all nations. So apparently was Hitler's regime during its first two years. Japan consistently rejected inspection and supervision throughout the 1920s and 1930s on the grounds that such activity impinged on its national sovereignty.

The British governments in the 1920s endorsed the Japanese position. In the early 1930s, however, the British altered their stance once they realized a control system was a prerequisite for any agreement on general disarmament. But British support for on-site inspections waned in 1935, when they feared that a perusal of their production centers could reveal their precarious military condition. Only with German and French reciprocity would the British join any agreement calling for an on-site inspection of its armaments.

France's attitude poses a more complex puzzle. In 1919, it held that inspection and control were vital to sustaining arms limitations, particularly the limits placed on the vanquished Germans. Yet as the other nations came around to this view, but insisted that equality should prevail, Paris sought to avoid such mutual commitments by escalating its demands. The crux of the matter lay in Franco-German relations, for by the 1930s, revisionist-minded Germans claimed equality in armaments, while the fearful French insisted on an international guarantee of "security" which included, ultimately, the application of sanctions in case of treaty violations.

After 1945, the western European nations, as members of NATO and Japan, entertained a flexible attitude toward the control and verification of arms limitation programs. In general, however, they tended to follow Washington's lead while occasionally demonstrating a willingness to entertain less intrusive proposals.

United States, Positions. The United States' policy has gone through at least four phases. From 1919 to 1931, Washington sought arms limitation treaties but opposed the creation of any international system of controls and inspection that might impinge upon its national sovereignty. From 1932 to 1945, American policy advocated a routine, automatic "on-the-spot" inspection system of any general disarmament program to investigate alleged evasions and endorsed supervision by the League of Nations, and later, the United Nations. From 1946 to 1954, Washington's position became much more rigid as on-site inspection, supervision, and control became, as in the Baruch Plan, the *sine qua non* of any arms limitation pact. Indeed, this approach held that any limitation of conventional or nuclear arms must not only involve inspection and supervision, but must have enforceable sanctions.

In 1955, President Eisenhower proposed a system of aerial inspections, the Open Skies program, that might have reduced mutual suspicions and opened the way to more arms control activity. Yet President Johnson's offer of a "nuclear freeze" in August 1964, involving the freezing of nuclear inventories, insisted again on the on-site monitoring of inventories, which turned out to be no more acceptable to the United States bureaucracy than to the Russians. It was only in October 6, 1967, that Assistant Secretary of Defense Paul Warnke stated that in any talks on limiting strategic weapons, Washington would not insist on on-site inspections and, instead, seek an agreement that could be verified by "our own unilateral capability" or national means. American policy makers subsequently recognized that insistence on a comprehensive arms control package, based on "foolproof" controls, was unrealistic. They now sought arms control pacts that were more limited in scope, and undertook to tailor inspection and supervision mechanisms accordingly.

While the demands and expectations of inspection and supervision mechanisms became greater as weaponry evolved, the Reagan administration discovered that there was another untoward, dimension to the issue. The Pentagon had not seriously considered the reciprocal impact of their on-site inspections upon American facilities. Consequently, during the Reagan-Gorbachev discussions, Washington insisted on exempting certain weapons systems from such inspections.

Soviet Union/Russia's Positions. Meanwhile, the Soviet Union and Russia's policies have alternated with those of the United States. In 1928, Moscow endorsed a permanent international system of controls to be established three months after any League-sponsored general disarmament treaty went into effect. A special Commission of Enquiry was to be created for "on-the-spot" inspections of suspected violations. In its June 1946 reply to the Baruch Plan, however, the Soviet Union retreated from its earlier position. Now controls were to be established, after nuclear disarmament took place, under the direction of the United Nations Security Council with each permanent member of that body retaining its veto power over verification activities. To Moscow, on-site inspection without disarmament was essentially espionage.

The Soviet attitude toward inspection and supervision did not remain completely negative. On occasions, from the late 1950s to the 1980s, when serious arms limitation negotiations were underway, the Soviets conceded the necessity for some type of a verification system. During early test ban discussions, for example, Moscow tentatively accepted the idea of a verification system that included national technical means and tamper-proof seismic monitoring sites (black boxes). "Challenge" on-site inspections were discussed, even though their value was questioned, but no agreement materialized because the United States kept increasing its demand for more sites and inspections. In the mid-1980s, Mikhail Gorbachev reversed the Soviet position. At his direction, Moscow agreed to comprehensive verification systems, including intrusive on-site inspections for INF Treaty and other arms control accords.

Taken broadly, these shifting national postures suggest that the issues of inspection, supervision, and control were shaped by several factors. During the nuclear era, technological advances such as satellite and electronic monitoring often influenced diplomacy. Yet, even in the age of weapons of mass destruction, it is the political process—inspired by the immediate demands of various agendas, such as domestic politics, international propaganda, or a guarantee of compliance—that has defined verification measures.[33]

Compliance and Noncompliance

As anyone who has been involved with arms control issues can attest, Allan Krass wrote, "one thing is perfectly clear: like the poor, noncompliance and the suspicion of noncompliance will always be with us. Ambiguities and suspicions are an inevitable part of the process."[1] Controversy regarding compliance with arms control measures is usually prompted by a state's fears regarding their adversaries' intentions and military behavior. When tensions have been high and a possibility of hostilities loomed, officials fretted about continuing to adhere to an arms control treaty that limits their own military options while adversaries may be reaping an advantage by evading the treaty.

If charges of "cheating" have been frequent during the twentieth century, they resulted from a variety of causes. "In an atmosphere of high political tension," Gloria Duffy has noted, "the distinction can be lost between legitimate obligations that are sanctioned by international agreements, and expectations, promises, or verbal statements that do not constitute legally binding commitments." Such a failure may, and has, led to charges of suspected violations that rested on dubious grounds, as often was the case during the 1930s, 1980s, and the early twenty-first century. The result was an unnecessary loss of confidence in the entire arms control process.[2]

Arms control analysts George Bunn and Wolfgang K. H. Panofsky, however, assume "that a world with unconstrained nuclear arms competition is no more tolerable than a domestic society without law." Therefore, they conclude: "The choice cannot be between perfect compliance with arms control and no arms control at all. Such a choice is no more feasible than one between perfect law enforcement and absence of law."[3]

THE COMPLEXITIES OF COMPLIANCE

Every arms control agreement depends, to varying degrees, on each party's confidence in faithful implementation. How much confidence is necessary depends on the type of agreement that, in turn, will dictate the complexity of the verification regime needed to assure compliance. Clearly, the issue of compliance is interwoven throughout the whole arms control process, which begins with drafting the treaty provisions that the verification procedures must observe during implementation. A complex nuclear arms limitation treaty text will undoubtedly require more sophisticated monitoring procedures than will some other accords. Monitoring will provide data, but compliance disputes begin when differing interpretations of the data arise as it relates to various treaty provisions.

Drafting the Treaty. When negotiators formulate the basic treaty provisions, they must deal with the states' asymmetrical demands and values that ultimately will be vital to determining compliance. Bunn and Panofsky have suggested that there are several such basic factors related to compliance that should be considered during negotiation and ratification.[4] First, there is the matter of how narrowly or broadly the terms of the treaty should be drawn. If the military provisions are initially too precise, the probability exists that ambiguities and loopholes will develop as time goes on and situations change. Conversely, should the provisions be drafted too broadly, it is likely that "gray areas" will occur during implementation which negotiators should have anticipated. An example of how terms become outdated may be found in the 1990 Conventional Armed Forces in Europe (CFE) Treaty that aligned quotas to NATO and the Warsaw Pact, which no longer existed at the end of the Cold War. The NATO countries in 2008 refused, over a dispute related to Moldova and Georgia, to ratify the updated 1999 "adapted" CFE Treaty that removed the outdated Warsaw Pact quota. The Russians have indicated they may withdraw for the CFE accord if the West refuses to adopt the 1999 modifications.[5]

Second, there are the instances where delegates patch over their differences on critical issues with "creative ambiguities." Occasions arise during negotiations where delegates find it expedient or even unavoidable to settle on ambiguous provisions in order to gain an agreement. Avoiding the initial resolution of such contentious issues may be an invitation to future differences. The SALT II Treaty provided an example of a deliberate ambiguity regarding encryption. Both the American and Soviet delegations understood the importance of intercepting a missile's telemetry data during its test flight in order to determine that system's basic characteristics. It was also recognized, as Bunn and Panofsky note, that missiles tests employing encrypting, encapsulating, or a data container which is dropped to be later picked up can deny much information needed for verification purposes. Since a total prohibition of this interference could not be reached, the delegations declared that telemetry may not be denied when "such denial impedes verification of compliance with the provisions of the [SALT II] Treaty." The Soviets later expanded their encryption of telemetry and, when the United States challenged this action, the Soviets agreed to open those channels that the Americans insisted were necessary for verification. But Washington did not wish to identify the specific channels, because to do so would compromise the "sources and methods" of their data collection. The later START pact (1991) included a total ban on encryption, but meanwhile the United States chose to adhere to the ambiguous compromise.[6]

Third, where restrictions on specific weapons systems are being considered, delegates need to be concerned with future technologies that are likely to alter the initial intent of treaty provisions. Thus, the treaty text might be designed to anticipate changes in technology, at least to provide a diplomatic avenue to deal with any such innovations. An interesting example of this dilemma occurred during the 1972 Anti-Ballistic Missile (ABM) Treaty negotiations that focused on current and future technology. The ABM Treaty defined an ABM system as "a system to counter strategic missiles or their elements in flight trajectory, currently consisting" of radars and interceptors, including their launchers. Moreover, the accord specifically forbade the development, testing, or deployment of "ABM systems or components which are sea-based, air-based, space-based, or mobile land-based." Paul Nitze convinced the Soviet and American delegations of radar's crucial role in the ABM system, and devised a complicated formula for an index of radar's power-aperture product, which permitted an agreement on limits for the size of radars and prevented future technologists from altering anti-aircraft radars for anti-missile use.

Attached to the ABM pact was a footnote that stated: "the Parties agree that in the event ABM systems based on other physical principles and including components capable of substituting for ABM interceptor missiles ... created in the future, specific limitations on such system and their components would be subject of discussion ... and agreement." As this language sought to prohibit systems that were not available in 1972, it became the basis for a nasty political battle during the 1980s between the Reagan administration and Congress over the types of interceptors that could be tested, and ultimately deployed, under Reagan's Strategic Defense Initiative.[7] Here was a treaty that attempted to lock in existing generic technology and hoped to forestall any future systems using different technologies. That, of course, is the reason President George W. Bush abrogated the ABM Treaty in order to deploy a ground-based antiballistic missile system.

Fourth, it is desirable that an agreement should contain provisions dealing specifically with compliance. To this end, delegates should draft provisions that seek a balance between the desirable restraints and the optimum acceptable verification methods. Agreement on a "common currency" or "unit of account" such as naval tonnage or missile throw-weight is very useful, though not absolutely vital, to conferees so that the terminology used in accounting procedures is mutually understood. It also greatly facilitates bargaining if the units of weaponry—battleships, tanks, troop formations, and so on—are similar since disparities among these elements can pose challenges in balancing the ledgers. Negotiators have found various ways to balance the accounting of units that do not match. Thus, asymmetries should not be allowed to prevent an agreement.

Fifth, the delegates ought to include in the treaty text a mechanism for the quiet, orderly resolution of future differences as they arise. And most assuredly they will. The 1972 ABM Treaty created the Standing Consultative Commission (SCC) to deal quietly with compliance issues in private sessions (see Chapter 8). Throughout the 1970s, the SCC met twice yearly in Geneva (and occasionally in special sessions) where delegates contemplated and resolved a multitude of issues ranging from implementation to compliance. The SCC was, according to Krass, "one of the more important and successful innovations of the Cold War era and it has provided a model for consultative groups in virtually all subsequent agreements." Presidents Nixon, Ford, and Carter found the SCC's performance adequate.

The critics of arms control, however, created such a hostile political environment during President Reagan's first term that their actions led to the demise of the SCC. A new consultative agency, the Special Verification Committee, was created for the 1987 Intermediate Nuclear Forces (INF) Treaty. It met only at the request of one of the parties and functioned otherwise much the same as the discredited SCC. A new consultative body, the Joint Compliance and Implementation Commission (JCIC), was formed for the START I Treaty. The JCIC was to meet in sessions and special sessions, for most urgent matters related to compliance, but subsequently found itself in an almost continuous session during the treaty's implementation during the next several years. The JCIC's tasks, which were handled rather well, were nevertheless complicated by a complex text and the break-up of the Soviet Union.[8]

Finally, verification provisions need to meet certain "standards" and those individuals responsible for interpreting the process for compliance purposes need to understand them. An "adequate" standard according to Bunn and Panofsky requires that as a minimum:

1. no violation that could endanger national security should remain undetected and unidentified;
2. a violation should be identified in sufficient time to allow remedial action to protect national security; and
3. no violation that interferes in a basic way with the essential purpose of the treaty should remain undetected and unidentified.

Yet no matter how verification *terms* are stated, they also, as a practical matter, will raise questions regarding compliance.

Consequently, since no provision can ever identify all possible violations, there must be a balance of values. Is the evasion or violation of such significance as to jeopardize the existence of other positive values stemming from the treaty? How precise need be the observation, especially if quantitative measurements are involved? Any accounting of stipulated numbers, estimate of physical quantities, or evaluation of qualitative measures, may also involve a certain imprecision. Therefore, negative findings or evasions must be weighed against intent on the one hand and their general significance relative to the overall accomplishments of the treaty on the other hand.

As Abram and Antonia Chayes have concluded: "Almost all nations observe almost all principles of international law and almost all of their obligations almost all of the time."[9]

Compliance and Politics. Charges of arms control violations or evasions, with or without adequate evidence, have been employed for political objectives. The issue of compliance during the twentieth century frequently has been manipulated to fit preconceived assumptions. The U.S. Arms Control and Disarmament Agency, for example, for years issued two versions of an annual report dealing essentially with compliance—one for public consumption and one classified for official use. "Both versions [were] the result of an intensely competitive interagency process," according to Allan Krass. "It can be compared to a war, in which bureaucratic armies fight for small parcels of ideological or political turf, intelligence evidence and estimates are the ammunition, and interagency meeting rooms are the battlefields." Since there was usually uncertainty about and different interpretations of the evidence, the final report could "be muted or amplified to serve different politically agendas. If violations are politically inconvenient, even the smallest residual ambiguity can be exploited to preserve the presumption of compliance."[10] Because it was politically inconvenient for the Clinton administration to come down harshly on China for its missile shipments to Pakistan, this evasion of the understandings of the informal Missile Technology Control Regime was ignored.

Conversely, there were occasions when evasions—even those based on the most meager "scraps of evidence"—could be seen as politically convenient. Ardent American anticommunists propagated the belief during the late 1970s and 1980s that the Soviets had ignored or failed to honor their arms control commitments. Staunch Cold Warriors from both political parties, especially Republicans, found strident allegations of Soviet treaty violations played well at home. The 1980 Republican Party platform—without offering any evidence—claimed that Moscow had not complied with its arms control commitments and condemned the Carter administration for failing to challenge the Soviets for their violations.

Early in the Reagan administration, the U.S. Arms Control and Disarmament Agency and its General Advisory Committee were instructed to concentrate on identifying Soviet arms control violations. Congressional hard liners picked up the issue and, as part of Public Law 99–145 passed in the summer of 1985, charged the White House with reporting annually on Soviet noncompliance. The number of listed Soviet violations increased yearly from 7 in 1984, to 13 in 1985, to 18 in 1986. When these charges were examined by less ideologically motivated analysts, however, the evidence frequently proved ambiguous or no longer relevant. While this diplomatically crippling process ignored evidence of U.S. noncompliance, it created a domestically satisfying indictment, but a largely erroneous image of the Soviet's overall arms control behavior. Moscow of course responded in tit-for-tat fashion with what they saw as U.S. violations of various arms control provisions. Most American analysts not infected by a "faith-based" assessment agreed with House Armed Services Committee chairman Les Aspin that the military significance of the charges did not "amount to a hill of beans." In the end, little was accomplished by this bashing of the "evil empire," because during his second term President Reagan sought positive outcomes from the arms control process.[11]

The different conclusions regarding the Reagan administration's pursuit of Soviet noncompliance depended, in Michael Krepon's view, as much "on basic assumptions as on the evidence at hand. For those who suspected the worst from the Kremlin ... the evidence is convincing because the Soviets can be expected to cheat. Those who suspect the worst from the Reagan administration—and who see little or no military value from cheating—will be inclined to dismiss the allegations." Others with less subjective opinions may find themselves with more questions than answers.[12]

President George W. Bush engaged in another round of "faith-based" analyses and, sometimes, simply deceit. Following the UN coalition's defeat of Iraq in the first Gulf War, the Security Council banned Iraq from the possession of nuclear, chemical, or biological weapons, and levied severe limitations on weaponry. In March 1991, a Security Council review of its supervised disarmament of Iraq concluded that "the bulk of Iraq's proscribed weapons programmes have been eliminated." Since this report, in large measure confirmed by the U.S. intelligence agencies, could not say with absolute certainty that Iraq was *completely* disarmed, suspicions remained. A decade later, President Bush ignored information from new inspections that essentially confirmed Iraq's compliance and, instead, argued that Iraq possessed weapons of mass destruction that posed a threat to U.S. security. After American forces occupied Iraq, no weapons of mass destruction were found. It became evident that the Bush administration, in a concentrated barrage of propaganda, used scraps of erroneous "gossip" regarding noncompliance to justify the president's decision to invade that nation.[13]

Evaluating the Data. As already noted, achieving an objective evaluation of arms control compliance, whether by contemporary analysts or historians, has always been challenging. This appears to be the case from ancient times, where merchants and spies supplied intelligence, and in the era of nation-states, where military attachés and radio intercepts provided additional data. Since the 1950s, increasingly sophisticated verification capabilities have had a considerable impact on the issues of compliance and noncompliance. This enhanced detection has resulted in much more data gathered, yet interpreting the data, including identifying what comprised a minor evasion or significant violation, continued to be much more difficult than the actual monitoring or collecting of information. This is because there has always been the tendency over the centuries for the analysts to see what they expected to see, to find the "evidence" of compliance or noncompliance that they expected to find.

As analysts find themselves confronting questions regarding compliance, they need to determine whether the treaty, despite possible evasions, remains in their nation's best interests. They must assess the political and military impact of the arms control regime, and compare the sturdiness of the nation's security with and without the treaty. If the arms control treaty is found to improve national security, then if minor or even substantial disputes relating to compliance are found, it should not be discarded out-of-hand since these questions are inherent in such agreements.

However if an arms control regime is to retain its legitimacy and respect, Krass emphasizes that two general imperatives must be met. First, "violations or disputes over implementation must be taken seriously and dealt with promptly and fairly, and second, motivations, extenuating circumstances, and changing conditions must be recognized and allowed for." Unfortunately, rarely can both of these conditions be dealt with simultaneously, and rarely will all parties to an arms control regime agree upon what incentives or trade-offs should be offered to alter the situation. Nevertheless, past experiences offer some suggestions that encourage compliance. Positive incentives, despite the risk of enticing states to do only what they already had promised, is a better policy than the use of threats and sanctions that may only further antagonize the offender without gaining any satisfactory resolution. A private approach to resolving an arms control dispute is more likely to reap positive results than public charges and political posturing. Employing unilateral declarations, vindictiveness or insensitivity as a compliance policy may satisfy domestic constituents, but it is unlikely to resolve the differences between antagonistic states satisfactorily.[14]

Treaty Status. The legal status of arms control treaties varies considerably. The determination of compliance consequently becomes complicated when neglect or political circumstances lead to the frequent failure of states to ratify previously signed agreements. Since most arms control measures are initially anticipated to fall under international law, agreements not ratified may find their provisions being "less than full legal commitments." This problem grew in seriousness during the twentieth century—especially the last decades of the Cold War—when more legislative bodies became involved in the ratification process. The status of arms control agreements, according to the experienced observer Gloria Duffy, may be placed into various categories:

(1) agreements are force, that are signed and ratified; (2) agreements that are signed, but not ratified, with ratification pending; (3) agreements that are signed, but not ratified, with the ratification process discontinued; (4) agreements that are "declaratory," that is, based on declarations of intent (executive agreements) by national leaders; and (5) agreements, such as moratoriums or declaratory acts that are announced as being in force for fixed terms.

Treaties, negotiated or imposed, that have been signed and ratified have the full force of domestic and international law and can be held to the strictest obligations for compliance. Too many arms control agreements belong to this category to list them all; however, the early-twentieth-century ones included the Versailles Treaty, the major interwar naval treaties, and the Geneva Convention on the law of war. The list grew substantially during the Cold War to include the ABM Treaty, Antarctic Treaty, the Limited Test Ban Treaty, the Outer Space Treaty, the Latin American Nuclear Weapons-Free Zone pact, the Non-Proliferation Treaty, the Biological and Chemical Warfare conventions, INF Treaty, and the START Treaties.

Arms control agreements that have been signed and are waiting intended ratification are subject to the customary norms of international law. While compliance with every provision of such an agreement may not be necessary, all parties should refrain from any steps inconsistent with, or damaging to, implementation once the treaty is ratified. A significant example of this situation was the SALT II pact from 1979 to 1981, when the Reagan administration withdrew it from Senate consideration. During the intervening period, the Soviet Union remained in compliance with SALT II, even though its strategic missile launchers totaled 2,504—the total at the signing of the treaty—rather than lower limits of 2,400, then to 2,250 by January 1981, as required by the agreement.

Where the ratification process has been discontinued, the obligation of signed parties becomes a political, rather than legal, commitment based on their own interpretations. Consequently, obligations regarding compliance are considerably weaker than in the other two categories discussed above. This situation is not unique as any examination of the multilateral arms control regimes can attest—there is often a disparity, sometimes considerable, between those nations that sign and those that manage to complete ratification. The Geneva Protocol of 1925 is one example; the United States and Japan initially signed the agreement, but did not ratify it until the mid-1970s. The Reagan administration stalled the ratification of the Threshold Test Ban Treaty and the Peaceful Nuclear Explosions Treaty. Several international law authorities, consequently, dismissed the administration's subsequent charge that the Soviet Union had violated these pacts.

Executive agreements, usually bilateral ones, may also be considered to have the full force of domestic and international law. These agreements may take several forms including simply an exchange of diplomatic notes, such as the Rush-Bagot pact demilitarizing the Great Lakes. More formal arms control measures not requiring formal ratification have been used even prior to the nation-state. Of the many examples are those including various arms trade restrictions from the Third Lateran Council in 1179, to European monarchs' pacts in the seventeenth century to the Franco-Prussian imposition of arms limits of 1808. Executive agreements also were much in vogue during the Cold War where they included, for example, such bilateral arrangements as the 1963 Hotline pact and its subsequent updates, the "Accidents Measures" agreement, the Incidents at Sea accord, the Prevention of Nuclear War pact, and the Ballistic Missile Launch agreement.

Declarations of intent by national leaders have related to the arms control process and possess a reasonable compliance record. These declarations have involved temporary suspended actions (moratoriums on nuclear testing), renouncing the "first use" of specific weapons (no-first-use pledges), or withdrawn or renounced possession of specific weapons. In 1969, President Richard Nixon unilaterally renounced the United States' use of bacteriological or biological weapons, closed all facilities producing these offensive weapons, and ordered existing stockpiles of biological weapons and agents destroyed. In the 1990s, the United States, Russia, and France employed unilateral Presidential Nuclear Initiatives to declare restrictions and withdrawal of stipulated weapons systems. For example, in 1991, President George H. W. Bush ordered the removal of all U.S. nuclear weapons from South Korea and the following year, the unilateral withdrawal of all U.S. tactical nuclear weapons from Europe. In one of his many unilateral moves, Mikhail Gorbachev in 1988 ordered the reduction of Soviet forces in the USSR and Eastern Europe by 10,000 tanks, 8,500 artillery pieces, 800 combat aircraft, and 500,000 personnel.

While compliance is normally presumed in all treaties, including arms control agreements, there are several opportunities for assessments to determine that noncompliance has taken place.

ASSESSING NONCOMPLIANCE

Noncompliance of an arms control treaty, as Duffy defined it, is a "limited category of behavior that involves the abrogation, violation, or evasion of a signed international agreement to which the violator is a party." It takes place for several reasons, among which are ambiguity, incapacity, unintentional time lag, and rational choice. Intentionally or unintentionally, ambiguity is often built into provisions of arms control agreements. Thus, given the different focus of these agreements and the varying compliance expectations, individual treaty members should exercise a substantial degree of flexibility in evaluating each other's compliance. Seeking out the motivation and extenuating circumstances for an issue of noncompliance may be more significant than the actual violation. Does the evasion have military significance and, if so, to what degree? Reprisal, if taken, then could be proportional. Officials in the Reagan administration, who took the opposite view, made searching out examples of Soviet noncompliance a cottage industry by taking a strictly legal approach that critics caricaturized as "a violation is a violation is a violation." Nor were they even slightly interested in why an evasion might have taken place: "no violation, regardless of military significance is acceptable."

Incapacity and unintentional circumstances may be defined as accident, inadvertence, or unauthorized activities. "All are indications," according to Krass, of the inability of "the state to control its own affairs, whether technically and administratively in the case of accidents and inadvertence, or politically in the case of unauthorized behavior by subordinate officials or citizens." Noncompliance may, of course, occur as the result of "unintentional consequences." Despite intending to comply with an arms control agreement, it is possible for a state to violate its provisions unintentionally.[15] It would be unusual, for example, not to find some unintended violations of the law of war in almost any hostilities. The incidents involved noncombatants and prisoners of war (POWs), with the noncombatants inevitably bearing the brunt of brutal individual acts, and falling victim to modern weapons technology. Even when noncombatants are not targeted, they often become "collateral damage." If twentieth-century treatment of POWs has occasionally matched the brutality of earlier times, optimists believe that overall respect for the law of war regarding their treatment has steadily improved.

Another example of unintentional violations was the Limited Test Ban Treaty (1963) that restricted nuclear tests to underground caverns, and prohibited the venting or release of radioactive debris that might be carried beyond national borders. Poor planning resulted in both the United States and the Soviet Union unintentionally venting radioactivity into the atmosphere detectable beyond their borders. After tests in 1964–1965 and especially in 1970, had vented significant amounts of radiation, the United States revisited its operations and allocated substantial funds to minimize future venting. The Soviets, however, were apparently unwilling either to bury their explosives sufficiently deep or to spend the funds necessary to correct their venting problems. In recognition of the venting problems, the Threshold Test Ban Treaty (1974) accepted that an occasional explosion might result in venting that exceeded treaty limits—"one or two slight unintended breaches per year would not be considered a violation of the treaty."[16] Such acknowledgment did not prevent the Reagan administration from ignoring America's past transgressions and, in 1985, revisiting the Soviets' past venting of underground tests and charging them with violating the limited test ban treaty.

There is frequently a "time lag" between the signing of an arms control treaty and its implementation. There have been several examples of states asking for more time to implement terms of an agreement fully because they were unable for financial, technical, or other reasons to complete the task on schedule. The Soviets announced in 1976 that they could not meet the schedule for dismantling submarine-launched missiles called for in SALT I. At the same time, they repeatedly complained that the United States had covered their Minuteman ICBM silos so that the missile could not be counted by national technical means. This issue was finally resolved when the United States completed the conversion to Minuteman III and removed the tenting.[17] The United States, Russia, and other states, for example, also have experienced difficulties in destroying the scheduled amount of chemical weapons. Also, states undertaking "demining" efforts occasionally have had difficulty meeting scheduled goals.

Occasionally a state may deliberately decide—a "rational choice"—not to comply with provisions of an arms control agreement. Such a choice may stem from one of several reasons. A state may believe that the benefit of their action outweighs that of compliance, or it may be based on convenience. In the case of imposed pacts, such as the Versailles Treaty, officials justified their ignoring of arms restrictions on the grounds of self-defense or unjust treatment. There are other curious circumstances involving the status of arms control agreements. The 1925 Geneva Protocol, in one example, prohibits nations at war from using chemical or bacteriological agents, but made no mention regarding the employment of chemical agents in domestic policing actions. Many local law enforcement agencies have used tear gas, but its wartime use is often called a violation.

A classic case of evasion for convenience was the Soviet military's construction of a large phased-array radar at Krasnoyarsk, Siberia. Despite their rationale for secretly moving from the initial site of Pechora to Krasnoyarsk, the forbidding geographical features of the Arctic region, the harsh climate, the difficulties of transportation, and the lack of electrical power—their decision did violate its ABM treaty obligations to site early warning radars on the periphery of the country. Analysts disagreed, however, regarding its strategic importance. According to the Stanford study, "At the extremes, there are two general assessments of the Abalakovo [Krasnoyarsk] radar: (1) it is highly significant and could contribute to a Soviet territorial or site defense; and (2) it is not strategically significant because it is vulnerable and therefore could not be relied upon in an ABM defense." Discovered in July 1983 by U.S. satellite photos, the Soviets later acknowledged the evasion and the facility was subsequently abandoned.[18]

Occasionally, the three nations that subsequently developed nuclear weapons—India, Pakistan, and Israel—have been accused of violating the 1968 Non-Proliferation Treaty (NPT). However, since they were not signatories to the NPT, they are not guilty of any violation. "If no agreement specifically restricts a certain type of weapon or behavior, if an agreement is not in force, or if a country is not a party to an existing agreement, then that country cannot be deemed to have committed a violation," Duffy has noted.[19] North Korea and Iran pose somewhat different cases. North Korea signed the NPT, but later claimed to have withdrawn before undertaking the development of nuclear devices; consequently, there are differing opinions regarding its relationship to the treaty. Iran has been accused of attempting to develop nuclear weapons and of not providing adequate access to the IAEA inspectors. If Iran should prove to have built nuclear weapons, it might be considered to be in violation of the NPT because it did sign the agreement. (Also see below, Deliberate Violations.)

Difficulties of Interpretation. Where quantitative and particularly qualitative assessments were necessary to determine compliance, problems may arise from the lack of precise measurements, adequate evidence, or verifiable motive. When evidence is unavailable, some charges on noncompliance are "faith-based"—grounded on the conviction that party in question is simply aggressive, perhaps immoral, and "proven" to be untrustworthy. The verification process and determination of compliance is considerably eased, when an arms control measure establishes a total ban on specific weapons or specific weaponry in a geographical area. While quantitative restrictions raise the issue of the accuracy of counting methods, the more difficult problem that analysts confront, is that of evaluating qualitative compliance. Below are a few examples of these types of problems.

First, there is the matter of measurements or counting. Tallying the number of permitted trained German soldiers was a verification dilemma under the Franco-Prussian pact of 1808 and the Versailles Treaty. Counting the "regulars" was not difficult, but uncertainty arose when assessing whether their "reserve elements" were combat ready. Where the INF Treaty banning intermediate-ballistic missiles in Europe has been found in compliance, the Geneva Protocol of 1925 that banned the use of toxic chemical agents in combat, however, has been verified as being deliberately violated by several signatory nations. Additionally, of course, there are disputed claims of bacteriological and chemical warfare. The Chinese and the Soviets charged the United States with employing these agents during the Korean War, which American officials vigorously denied, and Cuba later accused the United States of spreading crop and animal diseases, which was also denied by Washington. Vietnam's invasion of Kampuchea in 1978, and the Soviets' incursion into Afghanistan during the 1980s, brought more reports of toxic agents emanating from aircraft, artillery, and hand-held devices. A UN investigating team, which was denied access to the sites of alleged incidents, could find no evidence of chemical or toxin weapons, but held that it was possible that "some sort of toxic chemical substances" might occasionally have been employed. In 1981, Washington alleged that the Soviets produced, transferred, and used a toxic agent referred to as "yellow rain" in Southeast Asia. Reports of the toxic substance being sprayed on the mountain tribesmen of Laos appeared in the 1970s. Later a review of the charges, evidence, and studies concluded that there were "errors and inconsistencies in the Reagan administration's case" of Soviet-sponsored toxin warfare. Some U.S. Defense Department studies concluded the charges were unfounded, but no definitive answer has been provided for these incidents.[20]

Evaluation of geographic prohibitions—the Antarctic Treaty's prohibiting all weapons, the Seabed Treaty's ban of the fixed placement of nuclear weapons, the Outer Space Treaty's prohibiting the stationing of weapons of mass destruction, and the Latin American Nuclear Weapons-Free Zone—found that states had complied with the provisions. Problems have arisen, however, with evaluating geographical demilitarization measures. Such was the case with Japan's Pacific mandated islands during the 1920s-1930s, when it was suspected that Tokyo had secretly violated its pledge not to fortify its League-mandated Pacific islands—the Marianas, Carolines, and Marshalls. These charges have persisted even though evidence to support it is virtually non-existent.

After Japanese occupation forces left in 1922, a newly installed civilian authority undertook to encourage immigration, stimulate commercial agriculture, and develop fisheries. The number of Japanese immigrants increased from 5,338 in 1924 to 62,305 by 1937. The "organization and planning, capital and equipment, leadership and qualified personnel, and above all the driving, pioneer spirit of the colonists for economic betterment," created impressive achievements. To support the growing Japanese economic activity, the construction of harbors, airfields, communication systems, and fuel facilities was undertaken between 1934 and 1939. Since many of these facilities, of course, could be enhanced to support military activities, writers have made critical assumptions regarding Japan's main purpose in the island mandates.

A thorough examination of available captured Japanese documents, however, led Thomas Wild to conclude that Japan largely complied with its pledge not to construct fortification on the mandates. The substantial expenditure for the buildup of naval bases and fortifications began after 1939, and long after Tokyo's withdrawal from the League of Nations. "Actually," Wild wrote, Japan began construction of "the Mandate bases in earnest only two years before the war, and never finished them." This finding has not prevented political scientist Robert Kaufman from declaring as recently as 1990 that, since Tokyo "clandestinely violated the terms of the naval treaties," then Japan's role in the mandates should be seen as "one possible example in a pattern of systematic violation." As he presents no new evidence, his assertions must be considered suspect.[21]

Charges of evading qualitative restrictions also have been frequently levied. Two examples, dealing with the naval treaties of the 1920s and 1930s and the ABM Treaty during the late 1980s, are reviewed here. During the interwar years, the various admiralties shared mutual suspicions regarding compliance with the Washington and London naval treaties. Tokyo and London were wary of United States battleship modernization programs; London and Washington were suspicious "of each other's interpretations of parity and the legality of battleship modernization;" and London did not believe published Italian warship displacements.

Reciting frequent post-1945 opinions, Kaufman again insisted that "the Japanese broke the rules seriously, systematically, and often clandestinely." Without question, the Japanese admiralty tried to build the greatest possible combat strength into their vessels, but this often resulted in unstable warships requiring additional weight below the water line. This caused these warships to exceed the stipulated displacement limits. The Japanese sought, for example, to build the capabilities of a 1,000-ton destroyer into the *Tomotsuru,* a 600-ton torpedo boat. With four torpedo tubes and three 5-inch guns, however, the new *Tomotsuru* was top-heavy and in March 1934 the beefed-up vessel capsized in a storm. The 1920s *Takao*-class heavy cruisers exceeded treaty tonnage, but this excess contributed little, for the added displacement reduced the ship's general seaworthiness.[22]

Norman Friedman, in *Battleship Design and Development, 1905–1945,* claimed that the Italian admiralty employed a displacement figure "that referred to an empty ship." Even after 1945, the Italian figures were listed "as the *standard* displacement, so that the *Vittorio Venetos* came out at about 38,000 rather than 41,000 tons." Italy's heavy cruisers thus violated treaty displacement limits by 15 percent. The United States also evaded the Five Power treaty limits when it converted battle cruisers, scheduled for the scrap heap, into aircraft carriers that displaced up to 33,000 tons, and then added 3,000 tons when modernizing deck armor and installing blisters. Thus, the *Lexington* and *Saratoga* were "officially listed as displacing 33,000 tons, although in fact they displaced 35,689 and 35,544 tons."

It was not clear then or now, Professor Goldman has noted in a perceptive study, whether the "abuses mean that treaty provisions were being exploited for purposes outside and contradictory to the agreement, or whether they simply represent attempts to maximize military effectiveness within the constraints created by arms control." Often a 5 percent deviation between projected and actual displacement was not intentional, but the result of design modifications during construction. Thus, she concluded, in spite of various evasions, "throughout the 1920s at least, the behavior of the treaty powers, overall, remained within tolerable limits," while "rampant violations" did not begin until late in the next decade. Meanwhile, according to Goldman, "the treaties kept the naval powers close to specific limits until 1936." By the late 1930s, all nations were evading the treaty restrictions on capital ship displacement.[23]

In 1987, the Reagan administration leveled several charges of Soviet ABM violations: "the aggregate of the Soviet Union's ABM and ABM-related actions (e.g., radar construction, concurrent testing, SA-5 upgrade, ABM rapid reload and ABM mobility) suggests that the USSR may be preparing an ABM defense of its national territory." In turn, Moscow questioned the United States' positioning of the Shemya radar, located in Alaska, and charged that the U.S. Homing Overlay Experiment violated the ABM Treaty prohibiting the development, testing, or deployment of ABM interceptors carrying multiple warheads.

Questions about the design and location of radars played a major role in the allegations of ABM Treaty evasions during the 1980s. During the initial treaty negotiations, both sides had a second generation of much larger and more efficient phased-array radars under development. In the fall of 1984, the Soviets claimed that the American program for modernization and updating of its radars at Thule, Greenland, and Fylingdales Moors, England, violated the ABM pact. They argued that these two radars were not on the United States' periphery and could point inward, thus providing an ABM potential; moreover, the treaty forbade transfer of ABM systems to other countries or their deployment outside either nation's borders. The authors of the Stanford study, *Compliance and the Future of Arms Control,* concluded that "the United States [was] pushing close to the limits of reasonable interpretation of the ABM treaty by deploying the new [radars] at Thule and Fylingdales."

If agreements were eventually reached on several of these issues, the seriousness of the Reagan administration's argument was called into question when the Joint Chiefs of Staff's assessment of the status of Soviet technology was considered. The JCS's 1987 report—assessing U.S. and Soviet standings in the

20 basic technologies relevant to ABMs—found the Americans ahead in 14, the Soviets ahead in none, and the two nations equal in 6.[24]

Deliberate Violations. There is little doubt but that most imposed arms limitation pacts were deliberately evaded. Indeed, the imposed terms faced the possibility of deliberate evasion by agents of the state. This was true of Carthage's actions and certainly the case of the German military's violation of the Versailles Treaty.

Some negotiated arms control agreements also were found to have been deliberately violated, the most prevalent of which involved prohibitions against the sale or transfer of arms, and the use of toxic chemical agents. There are many examples of where the sale or transfer of weaponry violated an embargo, national restrictions, or other agreements. These would include merchants evading the Roman Church's prohibition of selling arms to the Saracens, and the China Arms Traffic Convention. Also, nations chose to ignore or to overlook violations of such pacts as the Spanish Civil War Nonintervention Convention, and various League of Nations and United Nations embargoes.

The deliberate use of toxic chemical agents in violation of signed pledges has occurred. It began with Germany's use of "poison gas" during World War I, in violation of its signature on The Hague Conventions (1899/1907). Later several signatories of the Geneva Protocol (1925) continued the illegal use of such agents: Italy used it against Ethiopia in 1936, Egypt against Yemen in 1967, Iraq against Iran in the 1980s and, of course, Iran responded in kind.

No doubt the most serious such violation was the Soviet Union's secret BW program. The Soviets were guilty of the most egregious treaty violation when, a year after signing the convention, they launched an extensive biological weapons program. Over the next decade, this secret project employed some 30,000 individuals at more than a hundred facilities that were engaged in stockpiling plague, smallpox, anthrax, and other agents for ICBMs and bombers. At the same time, the Soviets' improved immunization techniques included aerosol, jet-injector, and oral vaccines. The 1979 accidental release of anthrax spores at Sverdlovsk, leading to many deaths, had suggested the possible existence of an illicit facility; additionally, the CIA located several possible BW sites but could not verify their activities. A defector revealed the existence of the program in 1989, but Russian President Boris Yeltsin did not confirm it until April 1992, claiming that it had been terminated. The vast dimension of the program was organizationally and technologically astounding; however, it is difficult to comprehend the logic of this costly undertaking. What military or political advantage was expected from it that was not available from the Soviet nuclear arsenal?[25]

SUMMING UP

Noncompliance of specific arms control regimes depended in considerable measure upon the manner in which they were conceived. On the one hand, if a victor imposed it upon his vanquished foe, then the historical record indicates that the vanquished will in all likelihood cautiously, but deliberately, violate the provisions in order to regain its lost status. The examples are numerous—in ancient times it was Athens and Carthage, after World War I it was the Germans and their former allies, and after the World War II it was the Finns.

On the whole, however, negotiated agreements in which elements of common interests were established usually have fared well until those elements evaporated. This is not to discount that negotiated arms control measures were likely to be plagued with ambiguity and controversy, and states party to them were likely to bend and stretch their terms. With any arms control pact, where stipulated activity is banned or restricted by mutual agreement or imposed terms, the risk of noncompliance carries a substantial price. However, any head of state considering deliberately violating these terms would have to consider: (1) the other treaty parties' reaction if and when the activities are uncovered; and (2) the political and possibly security costs, both immediate and long-range, that may accompany discovery of cheating. Premeditated violations may not only cause the loss of benefits from the arms control regime, but the loss of the international community's trust that was needed for future negotiations of any kind. Consequently, few states did demonstrate outright disregard for their pledges.[26]

Reflections—On Nuclear Weaponry: The Cold War and After

The extraordinary increase in destructive potential brought about by thermonuclear weaponry vastly altered the nature and significance of arms control. Before the advent of nuclear weapons, the failure of a conventional weapons arms control agreement might have jeopardized a nation's independence and, in the industrial age, lead to extensive death and destruction—as for example, the decimation of the South during the U.S. Civil War or the devastation of European Russia in World War II. But after those wars, the affected societies recovered, rebuilt, and resumed a sense of normality.

An exchange of thermonuclear weaponry, however, would probably eliminate all involved states as viable societies. Most likely, a number of innocent neighboring states also would face destruction and disarray that ranged from a variety of significant issues arising from spreading radiation and a possible "nuclear winter" that could greatly reduce of availability of food. This stark reality has given modern arms control agreements greater significance and, apparently, even more sturdiness because of the devastating potential consequences of a nuclear conflict.

In retrospect, three distinct features of this new era stand out. First, nuclear weaponry rapidly lost its military utility and gradually assumed a virtually independent, political role in international affairs. Superpower arms control negotiations soon took on a new dimension. Second, as realization of the consequences of a nuclear conflict took hold, political leaders realized that the use of this weaponry was much too destructive and must be avoided. Thus, a modern arms control "custom" was born—the nuclear weapons taboo. And third, in the twenty-first century the specter of "nuclear terrorism" surfaced. This situation presents a challenge that requires imaginative, innovative forms of arms control to assist in preventing its occurrence.

Nuclear Arms Negotiations. In the pre-nuclear era, political, trade, or territorial disputes among nations often sparked threatening military buildups in preparation of using force to resolve the fundamental differences. Up to World War II, states could attempt to head off a mounting arms race or the prospect of hostilities by negotiations that might combine arms control measures with resolution of the initial contemporary economic, political, or territorial issues that prompted the military buildup. During the Cold War, there were few superpower negotiations of the traditional nature that focused on basic economic, political, or territorial disputes. Instead, major diplomatic activities came to emphasize attempts to control and limit strategic weaponry (nuclear warheads and delivery systems) and formal consideration of other traditional issues were only occasionally directly involved. Because it was much too dangerous for the superpowers to ignore each other in this new era, control of nuclear weaponry became *the* fundamental issue that Moscow and Washington were willing to discuss jointly.

From the outset, American and Soviet diplomats took opposing stances regarding the Truman administration's ill-fated 1946 proposal (the Baruch Plan) for international control of atomic weapons. While some writers blamed Washington for the failure of the negotiations, historian Barton Bernstein suggests a more realistic perspective: "Neither the United States nor the Soviet Union was prepared in 1945 or 1946 to take the risks that the other power required for agreement. In this sense, the stalemate on atomic energy was a symbol of the mutual distrust in Soviet-American relations." Former Soviet President Mikhail Gorbachev has emphasized, "The arms race ... was both *a result* of the Cold War and *a cause,* as it constantly provided new stimuli for continued rivalry" [italics added].[1]

In an early essay, Australian scholar Hedley Bull argued that the ever-changing, contentious nature of the nuclear arms race required continuous superpower negotiations. "It is for this reason that there is great value in recent suggestions that an aim of the strategic arms talks might be to establish institutions or procedures that would be charged with the business of continuous negotiation."[2] Indeed, this is essentially what took place. A participant in various presidential administrations, Paul H. Nitze acknowledged that arms control endeavors had played a major role in negotiations between Moscow and Washington. "Of course," he wrote, "Soviet-American arms control was not the sole cause of the relaxation of superpower tensions and the end of the Cold War. However, in the political vacuum of much of the era, arms control became the principle conduit for Soviet-American relations." Acknowledging the significance that arms control negotiations played as a political conduit during the Cold War, Nitze goes on to say, "Even in times of [political] tension, arms control trudged ever on in some form."[3]

The arms control pacts that gradually emerged from various multilateral and bilateral negotiations helped neutralize the Cold War political insecurities brought on by the constant arrival of new configurations of nuclear weapons and their delivery systems. Following the disquieting Cuban Missile crisis, President John F. Kennedy and Premier Nikita Khrushchev agreed in 1963 to a "hotline" connecting Moscow and Washington, and a limited ban on tests primarily to restore stability to American-Soviet relations. From then on there were almost continuous negotiations dealing with nuclear proliferation and outer space, and finally a decades-long meeting over strategic weaponry. Secretary of State Dean Rusk labeled the SALT arms control negotiations "history's longest permanent floating craps game." Nonetheless, even if the deliberations went badly, "they provided a forum in which Soviet and American officials sat across from each other at long tables, sipped mineral water and discussed military matters that used to be the stuff spies were paid and shot for. So in that sense, even ... [the] disagreements were often salutary. The process was the product."[4]

Nuclear weapons, it seemed, had created a new situation. Instead of being a traditional instrument of foreign policy to help resolve international disputes, during the Cold War and after, nuclear weaponry itself became the fundamental objective of statecraft, separate and largely apart from the usually ignored fundamental economic, political, and territorial differences. To alter one of Churchill's admonitions: the superpowers armed to negotiate—about the arms.

Nuclear Weapons "Taboo." "It has already been more than five decades since the first, and the last, use of nuclear weapons in warfare," an active Cold War strategic analyst Thomas C. Schelling wrote in 2000. "Who could have believed it 50 years ago." He viewed these five decades of nonuse as "a stunning achievement" and, also perhaps, "some stunning good luck." What had happened was that without formal negotiations or a treaty, a convention took root that nuclear weapons were different and their use was *taboo*. Indeed, an abhorrence of nuclear weapons *use* had become encased in political/military doctrine by American and Soviet—after Stalin—leaders without anyone entirely understanding or appreciating the fact until the later 1980s.[5]

By signing NSC-30 in September 1948, the United States' first formal position on atomic policy, President Harry Truman agreed that the Soviets should "never be given the slightest reason to believe that the United States would even consider not to use atomic weapons ... if necessary." He initially saw nuclear bombs as weapons of last resort. This position was taken by the chief executives of succeeding administrations. In his January 1953 farewell address, however, Truman revealed he recognized the devastating consequences of a nuclear conflict: "starting an atomic war is totally unthinkable for rational men." In December that same year, Konrad Adenauer accepted the view that "the development of nuclear weapons" meant that their use by one state "might destroy life in any other country, then war destroys itself." War between nuclear powers "is possible, but it is also improbable."

In the 1950s, Secretary of State John Foster Dulles objected to the notion of moral inhibitions interfering with the possible use of the atomic bomb. Somehow, he argued, the emerging taboo on the use of these weapons must be countered. During the Quemoy crisis in March 1955, President Dwight Eisenhower responding to a reporter's question regarding the use of tactical nuclear weapons declared, "I see no reason why they shouldn't be used just exactly as you would use a bullet or anything else." However, in a 1956 letter to an old friend and Army general, Eisenhower clearly revealed that he understood the destructive results of a thermonuclear war. "The true security problem is not merely man against man or nation against nation. It is man against war." We must understand that "the era of armaments has ended and the human race must conform its actions to this truth or die." Despite attempts by the military to gain control of the decision to employ nuclear weapons, both Truman and Eisenhower insisted that only the chief executive could issue such orders, a policy that would continue.[6]

President John F. Kennedy's administration pondered the utility of nuclear weapons during the 1961 crisis over Berlin. Earlier, in February 1959, Adenauer was quite insistent that nuclear weapons not be used in during the impending Berlin crisis. When Lord Mountbatten, the head of Britain's Defense Staff, was asked by Secretary of Defense Robert McNamara about the possibility of employing nuclear weapons, he exploded: "My God, anybody who thinks of that is mad!" McNamara apparently responded that he agreed that using nuclear weapons during the crisis would be "irresponsible." While academics at RAND and planners at the Pentagon discussed various strategies, including a hypothetical all-out nuclear assault on the Soviet Union, Kennedy obviously concurred with McNamara. Even though the Air Force tried to assure him that American casualties would be small if the United States struck first, the president told the *New York Post* that "only fools" could entertain the notion of victory in a nuclear conflict. While Henry Kissinger and other strategists were touting the idea of conducting a limited nuclear war, the missile crisis had convinced McNamara this was another futile, even extraordinarily dangerous, effort to find a use for nuclear weaponry.[7]

Although much staff work was expended considering ways to gain a military or political advantage from the growing, expensive nuclear arsenals, the reality of nuclear war's consequences gradually forced itself upon chief executives. Nuclear weapons were unique, and a good measure of this uniqueness stemmed from their being perceived as unique. In September 1964, President Lyndon Johnson confirmed this uniqueness: "Make no mistake. There is no such thing as a conventional nuclear weapon. For 19 peril-filled years, no nation has loosened the atom against another. To do so now is a political decision of the highest order." By the end of the 1960s, France's Charles de Gaulle also had concluded that nuclear weapons "held the destiny of every people and every individual in suspense" because any war with these awful devices would be "a disaster for everyone, because ... after the conflict, there might be neither powers, nor laws, nor cities, nor cultures, nor cradles, nor tombs."[8] The nuclear weapons taboo was becoming institutionalized.

Much earlier, in January 1955, Soviet leader Georgii Malenkov had stated publicly that "a policy of preparing for a new world war, which given today's weapons, would mean the destruction of world civilization." When this pronouncement was derided as a renunciation of Marxist-Leninist doctrine of the inevitability of war between the capitalist and communist camps, Malenkov reversed himself under pressure. He now agreed that a nuclear war would most likely result in the "collapse of the whole capitalist system;" while Foreign Minister Vyacheslav Molotov joined in with his opinion that such a war would bring a "final victory" over the imperialist powers. If Nikita Khrushchev condemned Malenkov's statement as a sign of weakness, when he assumed power and learned of the consequences of a nuclear war, he "could not sleep for several days." The Cuban missile crisis had a sobering effect on Khrushchev, prompting him to emphasize a policy of peaceful coexistence. Afterwards, he wrote President Kennedy emphasizing that the superpowers should resolve their differences "not by military means" but "on the basis of peaceful competition". Crude, boastful, and blustering, Khrushchev nevertheless understood during his frequent saber-rattling episodes that a nuclear war would be suicide.[9]

Nevertheless, military professionals and civilian officials continued to search for various ways of nuclear war fighting and, as they did so, their plans became more and more exotic. Strategists in the Nixon administration looked for limited nuclear war options; however, as James E. Goodby has concluded, this thinking suggested that "a nuclear war might not be won, but maybe it could be managed." Irritated at critics of the SALT I who argued that it gave the Soviets a strategic advantage, Kissinger asked: "What in the name of God is strategic superiority? What is the significance of it, politically, militarily, operationally, at these levels of numbers? What do you do with it?" Soviet Premier Leonid Brezhnev, too, questioned how a superiority of strategic weaponry, if attainable, would be advantageous. At their first meeting, Brezhnev personally urged Nixon to agree to a Soviet-American détente and to an agreement that neither side would employ nuclear weapons against the other—a move that Washington viewed as trying to drive a wedge between the United States and NATO.[10]

President Ronald Reagan often insisted, "A nuclear war can never be won, and must never be fought," and personally hoped to find a way to eliminate nuclear weapons. Members of his administration, however, continued to augment preparations to fight a nuclear war. Secretary of Defense Caspar Weinberger seemed to agree that nuclear wars could not be won, but he vowed, "We are planning to prevail if we are attacked." White House advisor Thomas C. Reed added, "Prevailing with pride is the principle new ingredient of American foreign policy."[11]

Despite this nonsense, the nuclear taboo was fully recognized by the mid-1980s. Thomas Powers argued in the *Atlantic Monthly* that: "war planners are now faced with an extraordinary dilemma: either we ... plan to run the risk of plunging the Northern Hemisphere into a nuclear winter triggered by the smoke of burning cities, or we ... finally admit we simply cannot fight a war with nuclear weapons." Arms control diplomat Gerald C. Smith added: "Myth, misconception and plain ignorance have often influenced U.S. policy on nuclear technology and weapons" during the Cold War. "We have avoided nuclear cataclysm as much through Providence as through wise or well-informed policy."[12]

Looking back over the Cold War years, political science professor Nina Tannenwald concluded in *The Nuclear Taboo: The United States and the Non-Use of Nuclear Weapons Since 1945* (2008) that the "moral opprobrium" which gradually arose in Washington created a "*de facto* prohibition against the first use of nuclear weapons." This prohibition, however, did not prevent the Bush administration in 2006 from requesting that the Pentagon include nuclear weapons as a possible option should the decision be reached to attack Iran's nuclear facilities. However, according to Seymour Hersh's report in the *New Yorker*, the Joint Chiefs of Staff strongly opposed the idea of employing nuclear weapons against Iran.

Perhaps Alfred Nobel's wish had become partially true. For as the inventor of dynamite wrote a friend: "I wish I could produce a substance or invent a machine of such frightful efficiency for wholesale destruction that wars should thereby become altogether impossible."[13] Since 1945, many serious individuals, especially those controlling the use of nuclear weapons, have thought that these devices were so destructive that they could not be used. Most world leaders, consequently, gradually nourished, much like their primitive ancestors, a *new taboo* or *custom* that constituted a form of arms control.

The Post–Cold War Era. The Cold War was over, but the nuclear age was not. In the years following the end of the Cold War, arms control no longer seemed to attract the media or governmental attention, especially in Washington, that it had earlier. Other issues, such as global warming, trade balances, regional conflicts, and international terrorism, challenged it for recognition and resources. This decline in attention, coupled with an aggressive unilateralism, as exemplified by George W. Bush's administration, does not mean that arms control is unimportant in the twenty-first century. There are many areas where renewed involvement in arms control by the major powers would be beneficial. Among these areas are enhancing the nuclear nonproliferation regime, preventing the placement of weaponry in space, and the elimination of chemical/bacteriological weapons.

Emphasizing a concern with the nuclear programs of North Korea and Iran, George P. Shultz, William J. Perry, Henry A. Kissinger, and Sam Nunn, in January 2007, worried that "the world is now on the precipice of a new and dangerous era." In a *Wall Street Journal* article titled "A World Free of Nuclear Weapons," they argued that without positive steps to enhance the Non-Proliferation Treaty, America "will be compelled to enter a new nuclear era that will be more precarious, psychologically disorienting, and economically even more costly than was Cold War deterrence." The four former officials called for "reversing reliance on nuclear weapons globally as a vital contribution to preventing their proliferation into potentially dangerous hands, and ultimately ending them as a threat to the world." In addition to urging the "continuing to reduce substantially the size of nuclear forces in all states that possess them," they called for, among other things, the U.S. Senate to ratify the Comprehensive Test Ban Treaty.

The prospect of terrorists obtaining nuclear weapons was not lost on Shultz, Perry, Kissinger, and Nunn. "Most alarmingly," they believed, "the likelihood that non-state terrorists will get their hands on nuclear weaponry is increasing. In today's war waged on world order by terrorists, nuclear weapons are the ultimate means of mass devastation. And non-state terrorist groups with nuclear weapons are conceptually outside the bounds of a deterrent strategy and present difficult new security challenges."[14]

Expressing less concern with nuclear proliferation, International Atomic Energy Agency chief Mohamed El Baradei believed that nuclear terrorism loomed larger in the twenty-first century than the possible addition of new states possessing nuclear weapons. The world was in disarray, he warned national leaders at a security conference in February 2008, and the greatest danger was that of extremist groups, nurtured on "anger, humiliation and desperation," obtaining nuclear materials. "This, to me, is the most danger we are facing today. Because any country, even if they have nuclear weapons, would continue to have a rational approach. They know if they use a nuclear weapon, they will be pulverized. For an extremist group, there is no concept of deterrence. If they have it, they will use it."[15]

How long, then, can the nuclear weapons taboo or inhibition be extended? We do not know—but we can hope that all cultures, leaders, and national interests will strive to maintain it, and that the result will be the same for any other new technology that has been or will be developed which could wreak havoc upon a human's life, mind, or rights.

Appendix

Presented here is a representative, chronological listing of the treaties and agreements that demonstrated the lineage of a particular technique or category, many of which, but not all, are developed in the six chapters that make up Part I. These lists do not purport to be all-inclusive. For additional information, see Stockholm International Peace Research Institute's *SIPRI Yearbook: World Armaments and Disarmament* and Jozet Goldblat, *Arms Control Agreements: The New Guide to Negotiations and Agreements* (London: Sage, 2002).

CHAPTER 1
ARMS LIMITATIONS AND/OR REDUCTIONS

From Antiquity to World War I

Sparta-Athens Pact (404 BCE)

Rome-Carthage Treaty (202 BCE)

Peace of Apamea (188 BCE)

Austrian Proposal for Arms Reductions (1766)

Anglo-French Naval Limitation Pact (1787)

Poland Disarmed & Dismembered (1794)

Franco-Prussian Agreement (1808)

Franco-Austrian Agreement (1809)

Limitation of Egyptian Arms (1841)

Black Sea Naval Limitation (1856); *see also* Ch. 2

The Hague Conferences (1899/1907)

Argentine-Chilean Naval Limitation (1902)

Interwar Years—I

Germany, the League, and Other Treaties

League of Nations Covenant, Article 8 (1919)

Treaty of Versailles—Germany (1919)

Treaty of St. Germain—Austria (1919)

Treaty of Neuilly—Bulgaria (1919)

Treaty of Trianon—Hungary (1920)

Treaty of Sevres—Turkey (1920)

Central American Treaty (1923)

Soviet Union's Draft Convention for General and Complete Disarmament (1928)

Turko-Greek Naval Protocol (1930)

Turko-Soviet Naval Protocol (1931)

Preparatory Commission's Draft (1935)

League's One-Year Armament Truce (1931)

Interwar Years—II

Washington Naval Limitation System

Washington Naval Treaty (1922)

London Naval Treaty (1930)

Anglo-German Naval Pact (1935)

London Naval Treaty (1936)

World War II—Aftermath

The Berlin (Potsdam) Protocol (1945)

Rumania, Bulgaria, and Hungary Peace Treaties (1946)

Italian Peace Treaty (1947)

Finland Peace Treaty (1947)

Japanese Constitution, Article 9 (1947)

Austria State Treaty (1955)

Cold War—I

Nuclear Weapons and Systems

U.S. Baruch Plan (1946)

Soviet Proposals for International Control of Atomic Energy (1947)

Soviet Proposal for General and Complete Disarmament (1955–1962)

U.S. Proposal for General and Complete Disarmament (1962)

Strategic Arms Limitation Talks [SALT I] Interim Agreement (1972)

Anti-Ballistic Missile Treaty (1972)

Strategic Arms Limitation Treaty [SALT II] (1979)

Intermediate-Range Nuclear Forces [INF] Treaty (1987)

South African Unilateral Nuclear Disarmament (1990)

Reduction and Limitation of Strategic Offensive Arms [START I] (1991)

UN Security Council Resolution 687 [Iraq] (1991)

Unilateral Presidential Nuclear Initiatives [U.S.-Soviet/Russia] (1991–1992)

Reduction and Limitation of Strategic Offensive Arms [START II] (1993)

Unilateral Nuclear Initiative [France] (1996)

Strategic Offensive Reductions Treaty [SORT] (2002)

Cold War—II

Conventional Arms Limitation
Mutual and Balanced Force Reductions talks (1973)

Conventional Forces in Europe [CFE] Treaty (1990)

CHAPTER 2
DEMILITARIZATION, DENUCLEARIZATION, AND NEUTRALIZATION

Defortification

Sparta-Athens Pact (404 BCE)

Azov Fortifications [Russia-Turkey] (1605)

Defortification of Dunkirk (1713–1783)

Treaty of Versailles [Heligoland] (1919)

Demilitarization

Athens-Persia Accord [Aegean Sea] (448 BCE)

Rush-Bagot agreement [Great Lakes] (1817)

Clayton-Bulwer Treaty [Panama Canal Zone] (1850)

Neutralization of Luxembourg (1867)

The Straits of Magellan pact (1881)

Convention of Karlstadt [Norway-Sweden border] (1905)

Treaty of Versailles [Baltic Channel, Rhineland, Saar] (1919)

Pacific Mandated Islands (1920, 1922)

Spitzbergen Treaty (1920)

Aland Islands Convention (1856, 1921)

Washington Naval Treaty (1922)

Demilitarizing the Moon (1979)

Turkish Straits, Black Sea, and Suez Canal
Straits Conventions (1833, 1841)

Black Sea Convention (1856–1871)

Pontus Treaty (1871)

Convention of Constantinople [Suez Canal] (1888)

Treaty of Sevres [Turkish Straits] (1919)

Treaty of Lausanne [Turkish Straits] (1923)

Neutrality

Declaration of Swiss Neutrality (1815)

Neutralization of Belgium (1831)

Neutralization of Luxembourg (1867)

Austrian State Treaty (1955)

Denuclearization

Nuclear Weapons-Free Zones
Antarctic Treaty (1959)

Rapacki Proposals [Europe] (1957, 1962)

Outer Space Treaty (1967)

Treaty of Tlatelolco [Latin America] (1967)

Seabed Treaty (1971)

Treaty of Rarotonga [South Pacific] (1985)

Treaty of Bangkok [Southeast Asia] (1995)

Treaty of Pelindaba [Africa] (1996)

Central Asian Nuclear Weapons-Free Zone (2006)

CHAPTER 3
REGULATING USE/OUTLAWING WEAPONS AND WAR

Prohibitions on Specific Weaponry

Treaty of Zama prohibiting war elephants (202 BC)

Peace of Apamea prohibiting war elephants (188 BC)

Koran's prohibition on use of fire/poison (632)

Lateran Council's Declaration banning crossbows (1139)

King Henry VII/VIII's ban of wheel locks (1485)

Japanese restrict firearms (1597)

St. Petersburg Declaration (1868)

The Hague prohibition on "bombing" (1899)

Protocols on Submarine Warfare (1922–1936)

Efforts to Ban Aerial Bombing (1922–1932)

Convention on "Inhumane Weapons" (1981)

Ottawa Land Mines Convention (1997)

Convention On Cluster Munitions (2008)

Poison and Chemical/Bacteriological Weapons

Treaty of Strassburg on poisoned weapons (1675)

The "Lieber Code" (1863) on poison

The Declaration of Brussels (1874) on poison

The Hague Treaties (1899/1907)

Versailles Treaty "Poison Gas" Ban (1919)

Washington Treaty on Use of Gases (1922)

Geneva Protocol on Poison Gas (1925)

U.S.'s unilateral "no-first-use" gas policy (1943)

U.S. reaffirmation of the "no-first-use" gas policy (1969)

U.S. renunciation of bacteriological/biological weapons (1969)

Biological and Toxin Weapons Convention (1972)

Convention on Chemical Weapons (1993)

Outlawing War

Gondra Treaty (1923)

Kellogg-Briand Pact (1928)

Argentine Anti-war Pact (1934)

Japan's Constitution (1947)

CHAPTER 4
REGULATING ARMS MANUFACTURE, TRADE, AND TRAFFIC

Ancient-Medieval World

Israelite-Philistine prohibition of arms (1100 BC)

Charlemagne's prohibited export of armor (768–814)

Doge of Venice prohibited sale of arms (971)

Third Lateran Council prohibited sale of war material (1179)

Fourth Lateran Council prohibited arms sales (1215)

General Council of Lyon prohibited arms sales (1245)

Early Nation-States

British-Danish Restrictions (1315–1487)

Edward III of England-Low Countries pact (1370)

French, Spanish and Portuguese Regulations (1454–1572)

Anti-Russian Arms Embargo (1558–1583)

Colonial American arms sale prohibitions (1619)

The Nineteenth Century

British-Spain Arms Transfer Pact (1814)

Russian-American Convention (1824)

Brussels Act (1890)

U.S. embargo on arms to Dominican Republic (1905)

U.S. embargo on arms to Mexico (1912)

Interwar Years, 1919–1939

Allied Peace Treaties with Central Powers (1919–1920)

China Arms Traffic Convention (1919)

Chaco War embargo (1934)

Italo-Ethiopian embargo (1935)

Spanish Civil War Nonintervention Convention (1936–1939)

The League of Nation's major initiatives:

St. Germain Convention for the Control of the Trade in Arms and Ammunition (1919)

Geneva Convention on the International Trade in Arms, Munitions, and Implements of War (1925)

Draft Convention for the Supervision of the Private Manufacture and Publicity of the Manufacture of Arms, Ammunition, and Implements of War (1929)

Conference for the Reduction and Limitation of Armaments (1932–1934)

Statistics and information gathering (1924–1938)

Post–World War II

Tripartite Declaration (1950)

UN Arms Embargoes

UN Arms Transfer Register (1991)

Agreed Framework [U.S.-North Korea] (1994)

Inter-American Convention Against the Illicit Manufacture of and Trafficking in Firearms, Ammunition …. (1997)

Inter-American Convention on Transparency in Conventional Weapons Acquisitions (1999)

UN Small Arms Program (2001)

ECOWAS Convention on Small Arms, Light Weapons, Their Ammunition and Other Related Material (2006)

Nuclear Non-Proliferation Regime

International Atomic Energy Agency (1957)

Non-Proliferation Treaty (1968)

Convention on the Physical Protection of Nuclear Material and Nuclear Facilities (1980)

Cooperative Nuclear Threat Reduction Act (1992); *see* Ch. 6

Agreed Framework [U.S.,–North Korea] (1994)

Multilateral Informal Export Control Regimes

Coordinating Committee for Multilateral Export Controls (1949–1994)

The Nuclear Suppliers Group (1974)

The Australia Group (1985)

Missile Technology Control Regime (1987)

Wassenaar Arrangement (1996)

Proliferation Security Initiative (2003)

CHAPTER 5
CUSTOMS AND THE LAW OF WAR

"Warrior" Culture and Customs

Asylum

Ritualized Warfare

Dueling

Noncombatancy

Prisoners of War

Formalizing the Laws of War

Peace of God (989)

Truce of God (1027)

Peace of the Realm (1103)

Hugo Grotious and The Law of War (1625–1631)

U.S.-Prussian Treaty (1785)

U.S. Army's Rules of War (1863)

Geneva Convention (1864)

St. Petersburg Declaration (1868)

Brussels Declaration (1874)

The Hague Conventions (1899/1907)

Modernizing of the Law of War

The Hague Commission of Jurists: Rules of Air War (1923)

Red Cross Conventions (1929)

Roerich Pact (1935)

League of Nation's Resolutions on Aerial Bombing (1938)

Geneva Convention of 1949 (I)—land-based sick and wounded troops

Geneva Convention of 1949 (II)—sea-based sick, wounded, and shipwrecked

Geneva Convention of 1949 (III)—prisoners of war, including guerrillas

Geneva Convention of 1949 (IV)—civilians in enemy territory

The Hague Convention for the Protection of Cultural Property (1954)

United Nations General Assembly Resolution 24 (1968)

Convention Against Torture and Other Cruel, Inhumane or Degrading Treatment or Punishment (1984)

CHAPTER 6
STABILIZING THE INTERNATIONAL ENVIRONMENT

Protecting the Environment

Limited Test Ban Treaty (1963)

Threshold Test Ban Treaty (1974)

Peaceful Nuclear Explosions Treaty (1976)

Environmental Modification Convention (1977)

Cooperative Threat Reduction program (1992)

Comprehensive Test Ban Treaty (1996)

Preventing Unintended Conflicts

"Hot Line" accords (1963)

China's "No-first-use" of nuclear weapons (1964)

U.S.-USSR Accidents Measures Agreement (1971)

U.S.-USSR Prevention of Incidents On and Over the High Sea (1972)

Prevention of Nuclear War (1973)

France-USSR Accidents Measures Agreement (1976)

Great Britain-USSR Accidents Measures Agreement (1977)

Conference on Disarmament in Europe (CDE) (1986)

USSR's "No-first use" of nuclear weapons (1982–1993)

Nuclear Risk Reduction Centers (1987)

Ballistic Missile Launch Notification Agreement (1988)

Reciprocal Advance Notice of Major Strategic Exercises (1989)

Prevention of Dangerous Military Activities (1989)

Treaty on Open Skies (1992)
China-Russia Nuclear "No-first-use" Pact (1994)
Joint Data Exchange Center (1998, 2000)

South Asia Agreements

Nuclear Facilities Agreement (1988, 2005)
Advance Notification Pact (1991)
India-Pakistan "Hot Lines" (1997)
Missile Notification Pact (2005)
Reducing Risk of Nuclear Accidents (2007)

Confidence-Building Measures

Conference on Security and Cooperation in Europe (CSCE) (1972–1983)
Helsinki Final Act (1975)
Stockholm Confidence- and Security-Building Measure Conference (1984–1986)
Stockholm Document (1985)
Vienna Confidence- and Security-Building Measure Negotiations (1986–1992)
Vienna Document (1990)
Vienna Document (1992)

Notes

INTRODUCTION

1. Wayland and Elizabeth Young, "Disarmament vs. Arms Control," *Commentary* 32:1 (1961): 124–34.

2. Philip J. Noel-Baker, *Disarmament* (New York: Harcourt, Brace, 1926): 2.

3. Henry W. Forbes, *The Strategy of Disarmament* (Washington, DC: Public Affairs Press, 1962); William Epstein, *Disarmament: Twenty-Five Years of Effort* (Toronto: Canadian Institute of International Relations, 1971): 3–4.

4. Henry A. Kissinger, *The Necessity for Choice* (New York: Harper, 1960): 213.

5. Thomas C. Schelling and Morton H. Halperin, *Strategy and Arms Control* (New York: Twentieth Century Fund, 1961): 1.

6. Allen R. Ferguson, "Mechanics of Some Limited Disarmament Measures," *American Economic Review* 51 (May 1961): 479.

7. George W. Ball, *Diplomacy for a Crowded World: An American Foreign Policy* (Boston, 1976): 114.

8. Wayland Young, "The Problem of Verification," in John Garnett, ed., *Theories of Peace and Security: A Reader in Contemporary Strategic Thought* (New York, 1970): 199.

9. Charles A. Barker, *Problems of World Disarmament* (Boston: Houghton Mifflin, 1963): 2.

10. Herman S. Wolk, "The Uses of History in the Nuclear Age," *Air University Review* 23 (Nov.–Dec. 1971): 73.

11. J. F. C. Fuller, *Armament and History: A Study of the Influence of Armament on History from the Dawn of Classical Warfare to the Second World War* (New York: Scribner's, 1945): 185.

12. Wolk, "The Uses of History," p. 73, contains Lippman quote.

PART I

1. James E. Dougherty, *How to Think about Arms Control and Disarmament* (New York: Crane, Russak, 1973), 22.

2. R. Ernest Dupuy and Trevor Dupuy, *The Encyclopedia of Military History*, rev. ed. (New York: Harper & Row, 1970), 336–50; also see, Miriam Greenblatt, *Genghis Khan and the Mongol Empire* (New York: Benchmark Books, 2002); Harold Lamb, *Genghis Khan and the Mongol Horde* (Hamden, CT: Linnet Books, 1990); and George S. Goodspeed, *A History of the Babylonians and Assyrians* (New York: Scribner's, 1902), 197.

3. B. H. Warmington, *Carthage* (Baltimore: Penguin, 1964): 235, 244–55; Guglielmo Ferrero and Corrado Barbagallo, *A Short History of Rome* (New York: Capricorn Books, 1964), 190–91, 230–35.

4. Lynn Montross, *War Through the Ages* (New York: Harper & Row, 1960), 145; Morley Roberts, *The Behaviour of Nations* (London: J.M. Dent, 1941), 161.

5. Philip Towle, *Enforced Disarmament* (Oxford: Clarendon Press, 1997), 6.

6. Ibid., pp. 8–9.

7. Ibid., passim.

8. Christopher J. Lamb, *How to Think about Arms Control, Disarmament, and Defense* (Englewood Cliffs, NJ: Prentice Hall, 1988), p. 31n6.

9. U.S. Senate, Committee on Foreign Relations, *Hearings*; *Strategic Arms Limitation Agreement, June 19-July 20, 1972*, 92nd Cong., 2nd Sess. (Washington, DC: G.P.O., 1972), 37.

10. J. F. C. Fuller, *Armaments and History* (New York: Scribner's, 1945), 43–4.

11. Sir Charles Oman, *A History of the Art of War*, vol. II (London: Methuen, 1924), 227.

12. Lance C. Buhl, "Maintaining an American Navy, 1865–1889," in Kenneth J. Hagan, ed., *In Peace and War: Interpretations of American Naval History, 1775–1978* (Westport, CT: Greenwood Press, 1978), 145–47.

13. See Richard Dean Burns, ed., *Encyclopedia of Arms Control and Disarmament*, 3 vols. (New York: Scribner's, 1992), I: 129–30, III: 1367, 1489–93. (Cited hereafter as Burns, *Encyclopedia*.)

14. "Use of Poison Gas," *U.S. Department of State Bulletin* (June 12, 1943), 507; for Nixon's declaration, Burns, *Encyclopedia*, III: 1393–94; for discussion of Japan's constitution, the Austrian State Treaty, and the West German declaration, see Fred Tanner, ed., *From Versailles to Baghdad: Post-War Armament Control of Defeated States* (New York: United Nations, 1992), passim.

15. Stuart Croft, *Strategies of Arms Control: A History and Typology* (Manchester, UK: Manchester University Press, 1996), 76–77.

16. Jeffrey A. Larsen and James M. Smith, *Historical Dictionary of Arms Control and Disarmament* (Lanham, MD: Scarecrow Press, 2005), 176; Jack Mendelsohn, ed. *Arms Control Chronology* (Washington, DC: Center for Defense Information, 2002), 35, 39.

17. These agreements and treaties are all discussed below.

18. Lamb, *How to Think about Arms Control, Disarmament, and Defense*, xvi, 38ff; and Croft, *Strategies of Arms Control*, vii, xi, 40ff.

CHAPTER 1

1. Philip Towle, *Enforced Disarmament: From the Napoleonic Campaigns to the Gulf War* (Oxford: Clarendon Press, 1997), 1–2.

2. Anatoly Dobrynin, *In Confidence: Moscow's Ambassador to America's Six Cold War Presidents* (New York: Times Books/Random House, 1995), 526.

3. Stanley M. Burstein, "Arms Control in Antiquity," in Richard Dean Burns, ed. *Encyclopedia of Arms Control and Disarmament,* 3 vols. (New York: Scribner's, 1993), II: 551–61. Hereafter these volumes are referred to as Burns, *Encyclopedia.*

4. Christopher J. Lamb, *How To Think About Arms Control, Disarmament and Defense* (Englewood Cliffs, NJ: Prentice-Hall, 1988), 31, fn2.

5. Burns, *Encyclopedia,* III: 1138–40.

6. W. R. Morfill, *Poland* (London: T. Fisher Unwin, 1893), 248.

7. William O. Shanahan, *Prussian Military Reforms, 1786–1813* (New York: Columbia University Press, 1945), 129, 178fn.; Towle, *Enforced Disarmament,* 19, 20, 30–5.

8. Sir Thomas E. Holland, *The European Concert in the Eastern Question: a Collection of Treaties and Other Public Act....* (Oxford: Clarendon Press, 1885), chap. 4; John Marlowe, *Anglo-Egyptian Relations, 1800–1956* (London: Cresset Press, 1954); Burns, *Encyclopedia,* III: 1141–42.

9. Calvin DeArmond Davis, *The United States and the First Hague Conference* (Ithaca, NY: Cornell University Press, 1962), 84–5; World Peace Foundation, "Instructions to the American Delegates to the Hague Conference, 1899 (April 18, 1999)," *Pamphlet Series* 3:4 (Apr. 1913): 4; See Tate, *The Disarmament Illusion,* passim.

10. Andrew D. Farrand, "Chile and Argentina: Entente and Naval Limitation," in Burns, *Encyclopedia,* II: 595–604.

11. James Barros, "The League of Nations and Disarmament," in Burns, *Encyclopedia,* II: 605–20; see Ben A. Arneson, "Denmark Votes to Disarm," *Christian Century* 46 (Oct. 9, 1929): 1244–45; Gunnar Leistikow, "Denmark's Precarious Neutrality," *Foreign Affairs* 17 (Apr. 1939): 611 and David Moore Clarkson, "An Analysis of the Defense Policy of the Danish Socialist Democratic Party Until 1949," Senior thesis in History (Lewiston, ME: Bates College, 1960) for Danish sources.

12. Neal H. Petersen, "The Versailles Treaty," in Burns, *Encyclopedia* II: 621–38; Towle, *Enforced Disarmament,* 91–2.

13. Towle, *Enforced Disarmament,* 93–112; Gordon A. Craig and Peter Paret, "The Control of International Violence: Some Historical Notes," *Stanford Journal of International Studies* 7 (Spring 1972): 15.

14. Thomas M. Leonard, *Central America & United States Policies, 1820s–1980s* (Claremont: Regina Books, 1985), 50–2.

15. Richard Dean Burns and Donald Uquidi, *Disarmament in Perspective: An Analysis of Selected Arms Control and Disarmament Agreements Between the World Wars, 1919–1939,* 4 vols. (Washington, DC: U.S. Arms Control & Disarmament Agency, 1968), III: 164–84, hereafter Burns & Uquidi, *Disarmament in Perspective.*

16. Barros, "The League of Nations and Disarmament," in Burns, *Encyclopedia,* II: 605–20.

17. Emily O. Goldman, *Sunken Treaties: Naval Arms Control Between the Wars* (University Park: The Pennsylvania State University Press, 1994), Robert Gordon

Kaufman, *Arms Control During the Pre-Nuclear Era: The United States and Naval Limitation Between the Two World Wars* (New York: Columbia University Press, 1990). (Most readers will find Goldman's analysis superior.)

18. Great Britain, *Documents on British Foreign Policy, 1919–1935* (London: HMSO, 1973): Ser. 3, III, 422, 429; U.S., *Trials of the Major War Criminals before the International Military Tribunal* (Germany: Nuremberg, 1947–1949), XIV: 12–15, 28–33, 144–70, 230–35; Winston S. Churchill, *The Gathering Storm* (Boston: Houghton Mifflin, 1948), 138; D. C. Watt, "Anglo-German Naval Agreement," *Journal of Modern History* 25 (June 1956): 160; Stephen W. Roskill, *The War at Sea, 1939–1945*, 3 vols. (London: HMSO, 1954–1961), I: 57–8.

19. Burns and Uquidi, *Disarmament in Perspective*, III: 225–42.

20. U.S. Department of State Press Release No. 238, March 24, 1947.

21. Mihàly Fülöp, "The Military Clauses of the Paris Peace Treaties with Rumania, Bulgaria and Hungary," in Fred Tanner, ed., *From Versailles to Baghdad: Post-War Armament Control of Defeated States* (New York: United Nations, 1992), 39–54.

22. Illaria Poggiolini and Leopoldo, "The Italian Peace Treaty of 1947: The Enemy/Allied Dilemma and Military Limitations," ibid., 27–38.

23. Pauli Järvenpää, "Finland: Peace Treaty of 1947," in ibid., 55–70.

24. Barton Bernstein, "The Quest for Security: American Foreign Policy and International Control of Atomic Energy, 1942–1946," *Journal of American History* 60 (March 1974), p. 1044.

25. Matthew Evangelista, "Disarmament Negotiations in the 1950s," *World Politics* 42 (July 1990): 502–18; Alessandro Corradini, "General and Complete Disarmament Proposals," in Burns, *Encyclopedia*, II: 1041–52; Dobrynin, *In Confidence*, 147.

26. Dan Caldwell, "From SALT to START: Limiting Strategic Nuclear Weapons," in Burns, *Encyclopedia*, II: 895–99; James A Schear, quoted in Albert Carnesale and Richard N. Haass, eds., *Superpower Arms Control: Setting the Record Straight* (Cambridge, MA: Ballinger, 1987), 91–2; Thomas Graham, Jr., *Disarmament Sketches: Three Decades of Arms Control and International Law* (Seattle: University of Washington Press, 2002), 45–7.

27. Richard Dean Burns and Lester Brune, *The Quest for Missile Defenses, 1944–2003* (Claremont, CA: Regina Books, 2004), 53–76; Duffy, *Compliance and the Future of Arms Control* 33, 39–41, 95–103; Aleksandr' G. Savel'yev and Nikolay N. Detinov, *The Big Five: Arms Control Decision-Making in the Soviet Union* (Westport, CT: Praeger, 1995): 97–9, 102–8.

28. Caldwell, "From SALT to START," 901–907; Graham, *Disarmament Sketches*, 102–3; Christopher Simpson, ed., *National Security Directives of the Reagan and Bush Administrations: The Declassified History of U.S. Political and Military Policy, 1981–1991* (Boulder, CO: Westview, 1995), 645–6.

29. Janne E. Nolan, "The INF Treaty: Eliminating Intermediate-Range Nuclear Missiles," in Burns, *Encyclopedia*, II: 955–66; Rose Gottemoeller, "The Intermediate-Range Nuclear Forces Treaty," *Arms Control Today* (June 2007): 41–8.

30. April Carter, *Success and Failure in Arms Control Negotiations* (Oxford: Oxford University Press/SIPRI, 1989), pp. 172–229; Jack Mendelson and David Grahame, *Arms Control Chronology* (Washington, DC: Center for Defense Information, 2002): 36ff, 44.

31. Stuart Croft, *Strategies of Arms Control: a History and Typology* (Manchester, UK: Manchester University Press, 1996), 144–46.

32. Johan Molander, "The United Nations and the Elimination of Iraq's Weapons of Mass Destruction: The Implementation of a Cease-Fire Condition," in Tanner, ed., *From Versailles to Baghdad*, 137–58; Lester H. Brune, *United States and Two Gulf Wars* (Claremont, CA: Regina Books, 2007), 47–70; David Cortright and George A. Lopez, "Disarming Iraq: Nonmilitary Strategies and Options," *Arms Control Today* (Sept. 2002): 3; "A Chronology of UN Inspections in Iraq," *Arms Control Today* (Oct. 2002): 14–23.

33. Croft, *Strategies of Arms Control*, 76–8.

34. Stephen J. Hadley, "Arms Control and the Bush Administration," in Kenneth W. Thompson, ed., *Presidents and Arms Control: Process, Procedures, and Problems*. 5 vols. (Lanham, MD: University Press of America, 1991–1997), IV: 66–7; for START II, see SIPRI Annual *Yearbooks* sections on "Nuclear Arms Control" for 1998.

35. Wade Boese and J. Peter Scoblic, "The Jury Is Still Out," *Arms Control Today* (June 2002): 4–6. Text and additional commentary appears in same issue.

36. P. Terrence Hoffman, "From MBFR to CFE: Negotiating Conventional Arms Control in Europe," in Burns, *Encyclopedia*, II: 967–90; see also, P. Edward Haley, ed. *Arms Control and the End of the Cold War: An Oral History of the Negotiations on Conventional Armed Forces in Europe* (Claremont, CA: Keck Center for International and Strategic Studies, No. 14, 2002); *Arms Control Today* (May 2009): 29.

CHAPTER 2

1. Allan S. Nanes, "Demilitarization and Neutralization Through World War II," in Burns, *Encyclopedia*, II: 675–93; Stanley I. Kutler, *Encyclopedia of the Vietnam War* (New York: Scribner's, 1996), 156; James I. Matray, *Historical Dictionary of the Korean War* (New York: Greenwood, 1991), 297–298, 327–8.

2. Philip Towle, *Enforced Disarmament: From the Napoleonic Campaigns to the Gulf War* (Oxford: Clarendon Press, 1997), 8–9.

3. Stanley Burstein, "Arms Control in Antiquity," in Burns, *Encyclopedia*, II: 556.

4. James Morton Callahan, "Agreement of 1817: Reduction of Naval Forces Upon the American Lakes," *Annual Report of the American Historical Association for the Year 1895* (1896): 374.

5. William R. Manning, *Diplomatic Correspondence of the United States: Canadian Relations, 1784–1860*, 4 vols. (Washington, DC, 1940–1945): I, 235ff; Ron Purver, "The Rush-Bagot Agreement: Demilitarizing the Great Lakes, 1817 to the Present," in Burns, *Encyclopedia* II: 581–593; James Eayrs, "Arms Control on the Great Lakes," *Disarmament and Arms Control* 2:4 (1964): 372–404.

6. Allan Nanes, "Demilitarization and Neutralization Through World War II," in Burns, *Encyclopedia*, II: 675–93 for additional information.

7. Richard Dean Burns and Donald Uquidi, *Disarmament in Perspective: An Analysis of Selected Arms Control and Disarmament Agreements Between the World Wars, 1919–1939*, 4 vols. (Washington, DC: U.S. Arms Control & Disarmament Agency, 1968), II: 1–63; John J. Teal, Jr., "Europe's Northernmost Frontier," *Foreign Affairs* 29 (1951–52): 263.

8. Richard Dean Burns, "Inspection of the Mandates, 1919–1941," *Pacific Historical Review* 37 (Nov. 1968): 445–562.

9. Nanes, "Demilitarization and Neutralization," in Burns, *Encyclopedia*, II: 675–93.

10. Nanes, "Demilitarization," 675–93.

11. Towle, *Enforced Disarmament*, Ch. 3.

12. Nanes, "Demilitarization," 675–93; Burns and Uquidi, *Disarmament in Perspective,* II:64–139.

13. Burstein, "Arms Control in Antiquity," in Burns, *Encyclopedia*, II: 560.

14. Nanes, "Demilitarization," 675–93.

15. Stephen W. Young, "The Austrian State Treaty: 1955 to the Present," in Burns, *Encyclopedia*, II: 809–16.

16. John R. Redick, "Nuclear Weapons-Free Zones," in Burns, *Encyclopedia*, II: 1079–92.

17. Christopher Joyner, "The Antarctic Treaty: 1959 to Present," in Burns, *Encyclopedia*, II: 817–26.

18. Jozef Goldblat, *Arms Control Agreements: A Handbook* (New York: Praeger, 1983): 231–236; Raymond L. Garthoff, "The Outer Space Treaty: 1967 to Present," in Burns, *Encyclopedia*, II: 877–86; United Nations, *The United Nations and Disarmament: 1945–1985* (New York: UN, 1985), 119–22; also see Garthoff, "Banning the Bomb in Outer Space," *International Security* 5 (Winter 1980/1981): 25–40.

19. Bennett Ramsberg, "The Seabed Treaty: 1971 to Present," in Burns, *Encyclopedia*, II: 887–94.

20. Redick, "Nuclear Weapon-Free Zones," 1081–5; Jose Goldemberg, "Lessons from the Denuclearization of Brazil and Argentina," *Arms Control Today* (Apr. 2006): 41–3.

21. Redick, "Nuclear Weapon-Free Zones," 1083–5.

22. "Appendix 10B: The Nuclear Weapon-Free Zones in South-East Asia and Africa," *SIPRI Yearbook 1998: Armaments, Disarmament and International Security* (Oxford: Oxford University Press, 1998), 443–55, 590.

23. Scott Parrish and William Potter, "Central Asian Nuclear Weapons-Free Zone (2006)," James Martin Center for Nonproliferation Studies, Monterey Institute of International Studies (Sept. 5, 2006), http://cns.miss.edu/pubs/.

CHAPTER 3

1. Paris, Archive de l'Academy, Registre, 1790, fols. 238–9; J.L. Kunz, "The Chaotic Status of the Laws of War and the Urgent Necessity for Their Revision," *American Journal of International Law* (Jan. 1931): 44.

2. Udo Heyn, *Peacemaking in Medieval Europe* (Claremont, CA: Regina Books, 1997), 71–2.

3. Leopold Pospisil, *The Kapauku Papuans of West New Guinea* (New York: Holt, Rinehart & Winston, 1963), 59.

4. Leon Friedman, *The Law of War: A Documentary History* (New York: Random House, 1972), 9; Udo Heyn, "Medieval Arms Control Movements," in Burns, *Encyclopedia*, II: 567.

5. For text of treaties, see Burns, *Encyclopedia*, III: 1137–8.

6. Adrienne Mayor, *Greek Fire, Poison Arrows & Scorpion Bombs* (New York: Overlook Duckworth, 2003), 35; also see the Koran 2.11–12; 2.190–4; 3.172; 22.19–22; 22.39–40 for various bans.

7. Heyn, "Medieval Arms Control Movements," 568; also see Charles H. Ashdown, *British and Foreign Arms and Armour* (New York: Dover, 1970).

8. Michael A. Bellesiles, *Arming America: The Origins of a National Gun Culture* (New York: Knopf, 2000), 21–2.

9. Noel Perrin, *Giving Up the Gun: Japan's Reversion to the Sword, 1543–1879* (Boston: G. K. Hall, 1979), 45ff.

10. Donald Cameron Watt, "Restraints on War in the Air Before 1945," in Michael Howard, ed., *Restraints on War: Studies in the Limitation of Armed Conflict* (Oxford: Oxford University Press, 1979): 59–61.

11. Cynthia Owen Philip, *Robert Fulton, A Biography*, (New York: Franklin Watts, 1985), 95; Archibald M. Low, *The Submarine at War* (New York: Sheridan House, 1942), 51; Richard Dean Burns, "Regulating Submarine Warfare, 1921–41: A Case Study in Arms Control and Limited War," *Military Affairs* 35:2 (Apr. 1971): 56–63; see also W. T. Mallison, Jr., *Studies in the Law of Naval Warfare: Submarines in General and Limited War,* Naval War College, International Law Studies (Washington, DC: GPO, 1968), esp. 79–91.

12. Lester H. Brune, "Regulating Aerial Bombing, 1919–1945," in Burns, *Encyclopedia,* II: 730ff.; also see James M. Spaight, *Air Power and War Rights,* 3rd ed. (London: Longmans, Green, [1924] 1947); Jozef Goldblat, *Arms Control Agreements: A Handbook* (New York: Praeger, 1983), 132; Annette Messemer, "Konrad Adenauer: Defence Diplomat on the Backstage," in John Lewis Gaddis et al., eds., *Cold War Statesmen Confront the Bomb: Nuclear Diplomacy Since 1945* (New York: Oxford University Press, 1999), 236–59.

13. "Banning Anti-Personnel Land Mines: The Ottawa Process and Beyond," *United Nations Forum: The Future of Disarmament* (1998), 105ff; Michael J. Matheson, "Filling the Gaps in the Conventional Weapons Convention," *Arms Control Today* (Nov. 2001): 12–16; UN, Mine Action Service, Department of Peacekeeping Operations, *Portfolio of Mine Action Projects, 2008,* (www.mineaction.org); Miles A. Pomper, "Cluster Munitions Treaty Announced," *Arms Control Today* (June 2008): 42.

14. Of considerable value are the SIPRI studies, *The Problem of Chemical and Biological Warfare: A Study of the Historical, Technical, Military, Legal and Political Aspects of CBW and Possible Disarmament Measures,* 6 vols. (New York: Humanities Press, 1971–1975) and a more recent series: *Chemical and Biological Warfare Studies ("Scorpion" Series),* vols. 1–13 (Oxford: Oxford University Press, 1985–1991). Also Jacques G. Richardson, "The Bane of 'Inhumane' Weapons and Overkill: An Overview of Increasingly Lethal Arms and the Inadequacy of Regulatory Controls," *Science and Engineering Ethics* 10:4 (2004): 670.

15. Mayor, *Greek Fire, Poison Arrows & Scorpion Bombs,* 33; Maurice R. Davie, *Evolution of War: A Study of Its Role in Early Societies* (New Haven: Yale University Press, 1929), 182.

16. *Odyssey* 1, lines 260–263; see also F. Keller, *Homeric Society* (New York, 1915), 298; Mayor, *Greek Fire, Poison Arrows & Scorpion Bombs,* 35.

17. John Ellis van Courtland Moon, "Controlling Chemical and Biological Weapons Through World War II," in Burns, *Encyclopedia,* II: 657–74; also see W. Hays Parks, "The Law of War," in Burns, *Encyclopedia,* II: 1053–68.

18. Moon, "Controlling Chemical and Biological Weapons Through World War II," in Burns, *Encyclopedia,* II: 659; Richardson, "The Bane of 'Inhumane' Weapons and Overkill," 672–3.

19. Frederic J. Brown, *Chemical Warfare: A Study in Restraints* (Princeton, NJ: Princeton University Press, 1968), 233; Thomas H. Buckley, *The United States and the Washington Conference, 1921–1922* (Knoxville: University of Tennessee Press, 1970), 124–5.

20. Moon, "Controlling Chemical and Biological Weapons Through World War II," in Burns, *Encyclopedia*, II: 664; Frederic J. Brown, *Chemical Warfare: A Study in Restraints* (Princeton, NJ: Princeton University Press, 1968), 3–49; Judith Miller, Stephen Engelbert, and William Broad, *Germs: Biological Weapons and America's Secret War* (New York: Simon & Schuster, 2001), 40–1, 166–7, 180; Sheldon H. Harris, *Factories of Death: Japanese Biological Warfare, 1932–1945, and the American Cover-up* (New York: Routledge, 1994).

21. Brown, *Chemical Warfare*, 237.

22. Brown, *Chemical Warfare*, 200–1, 230–38, 263–6.

23. Charles C. Flowerree, "Chemical and Biological Weapons and Arms Control," in Burns, *Encyclopedia*, II: 1005, also see Thomas Graham, Jr., *Disarmament Sketches: Three Decades of Arms Control and International Law* (Seattle: University of Washington Press, 2002), Ch. 2.

24. U.S. Arms Control & Disarmament Agency, *Arms Control and Disarmament Agreements* (Washington, DC: GPO, 1982), 131.

25. Flowerree, "Chemical and Biological Weapons and Arms Control," 1004–6; Miller, Richardson, "The Bane of 'Inhumane' Weapons and Overkill," 677; Engelbert and Broad, *Germs: Biological Weapons and America's Secret War*, 73, 83–4, 150.

26. Allan S. Krass, *The United States and Arms Control: The Challenge of Leadership* (Westport, CT: Praeger, 1997), 57; Miller, Engelberg, and Broad, *Germs*, 63; Jonathan B. Tucker, "The Chemical Weapons Convention: Has It Enhanced U.S. Security?" *Arms Control Today* (April 2001): 8–12; Joby Warrick, "Albania's Farewell to Arms," *Washington Post National Weekly* (Jan. 17–23, 2005), 6–7; "Abandoned Chemical Weapons in China," *SIPRI Yearbook, 2000*, 520; "Old Chemical Weapons," *SIPRI Yearbook, 1999*, 575.

27. Edmund Jan Osmanczyk, *Encyclopedia of United Nations and International Agreements* (New York: Routledge, 2002), 828.

28. Joseph Preston Baratta, "The Kellogg-Briand Pact and the Outlawry of War," in Burns, *Encyclopedia*, II: 695–706; see also Quincy Wright, "The Law of the Nuremberg Trial," *American Journal of International Law* 42 (Jan. 1947): 38–72, "Legal Positivism and the Nuremberg Judgment," *AJIL* 43 (July 1948): 405–14, "The Outlawry of War and the Law of War," *AJIL* 47 (Apr. 1948): 813–16.

29. Philip C. Jessup, "The Saavedra Lamas Anti-War Draft Treaty," *AJIL* 27 (1933): 109–14; Jessup, "The Argentine Anti-War Pact," *AJIL* 28 (1934): 538–41.

30. Mike M. Mochizuki, "The Disarming and Rearming of Japan," in Burns, *Encyclopedia*, II: 801–2.

CHAPTER 4

1. Keith Krause and Mary K. MacDonald, "Regulating Arms Sales Through World War II, in Burns, *Encyclopedia*, II: 707.

2. Robert E. Harkavy, *The Arms Trade and International Systems* (Cambridge, MA: Ballinger, 1975), 212; Keith Krause, "Controlling the Arms Trade Since 1945," in

Burns, *Encyclopedia*, II: 1021–2; Stockholm International Peace Research Institute (SIPRI), *The Arms Trade with the Third World* (Stockholm: SIPRI, 1971), 112.

3. Krause and MacDonald, "Regulating Arms Sales," in Burns, *Encyclopedia*, II:707–24; SIPRI, *The Arms Trade* is also a useful source.

4. Stuart Croft, *Strategies of Arms Control: A History and Typology* (Manchester, UK: Manchester University Press, 1996), 51.

5. Krause and MacDonald, "Regulating Arms Sales," in Burns, *Encyclopedia*, II:707–24; quote in John R. Hale, *War and Society in Renaissance Europe, 1450–1620* (Leicester, UK: Leicester University Press, 1985), 226.

6. Krause and MacDonald, "Regulating Arms Sales," in Burns, *Encyclopedia*, II: 711; quote in Charles Foulkes, *The Gun-Founders of England* (Cambridge, UK: The University Press, 1937), 74.

7. Krause and MacDonald, "Regulating Arms Sales," in Burns, *Encyclopedia*, II: 710; quote in Romain Yakemtchouk, *Les Transferts internationaux d'armes de guerre* (Paris: A. Pedone, 1980), 27–28.

8. Richard Dean Burns and Jeffrey Kimball, "The United States," in Burns, *Encyclopedia*, I: 256.

9. J. Frederick Frausz, "Fighting Fire with Firearms: The Anglo-Powhatan Arms Race in Early Virginia," *American Indian Culture and Research Journal* 3:4 (1979): 43; H. R. McIlwaine and J. P. Kennedy, eds., *Journals of the House of Burgesses of Virginia, 1619–1776*, 13 vols. (Baltimore, MD, 1961) 5: 13, 91; Carl P. Russell, *Guns on the Early Frontiers* (Berkeley: University of California Press, 1957), 10–14; William M. Mallory et al., "Convention as to the Pacific Ocean and Northwest Coast of America," *Treaties, Conventions ... between the United States and Other Powers, 1776–1938*, 4 vols. (Washington, DC: GPO, 1909–1938), II: 1513.

10. Croft, *Strategies of Arms Control*, 51–2.

11. John E. Wiltz, *In Search of Peace: the Senate Munitions Inquiry, 1934–36* (Baton Rouge: Louisiana State University Press, 1963), 4; Krause and MacDonald, "Regulating Arms Sales," 712–13.

12. Krause and MacDonald, "Regulating Arms Sales," 714–719; R. E. Harkavy, *The Arms Trade and International Systems* (Cambridge, MA: Ballinger, 1975): 213.

13. Noel H. Pugach, "The China Arms Embargo and the Policy of Cooperation, 1919–1922," *Diplomatic History* 2 (Fall 1978): 351–371; Harkavy, *The Arms Trade and International Systems*, 217, 219; for a different assessment of the China embargo, see Ch'en, Ts'un-kung, "Lieh Ch'iang Tui Chung Kuo Chin Yün Chun Huo Ti Fa Tuan [The First Prohibition of Arms Sales to China]," *Bulletin of Institute of Modern History, Academy Sinica* [Taiwan] 4:1 (1974): 315–46.

14. Krause and MacDonald, "Regulating Arms Sales," 720–4; Harkavy, *The Arms Trade and International Systems*, 219.

15. Gerald Howson, *Arms for Spain: The Untold Story of the Spanish Civil War* (New York: St. Martin's Press, 1998), 114–9; Barry M. Blechman, *The Control of Naval Armaments: Prospects and Possibilities* (Washington, DC: Brookings Institution, 1975), 34.

16. Krause, "Controlling the Arms Trade Since 1945," in Burns, *Encyclopedia*, II: 1021–2.

17. Ibid., II: 1026–1032; Mark J. Valencia, "The Proliferation Security Initiative: A Glass Half-Full," *Arms Control Today* (June 2007): 19.

18. "Arms Chief Claims that French Officials Aided South African Sales," *Times* (London), Nov. 24, 1970, 5; "VII. International Arms Embargoes," *SIPRI Yearbook, 2000*, List on p. 364

19. *UN Arms Transfer Register, 1991* (New York: United Nations, 1991).

20. Arms Control Association, *Fact Sheet*, online www.armscontrol.org/factsheets; http://www.oas.org/juridico/English/treaties/a-63.html; Holger Anders, "The UN Process on Small Arms: All Is Not Lost," *Arms Control Today* (Mar. 2007): 17–21; http://www.iansa.org/regions/wafrica/documents/CONVENTION-CEDEAO-ENGLISH.PDF

21. William J. Broad and David E. Sanger, "North Korea Feeds Fears of Renewed Global Nuclear Age," *Denver Post* (Oct. 15, 2006), 12A; Walto Stumpt, "South Africa's Nuclear Weapons Program: From Deterrence to Dismantlement," *Arms Control Today* (Dec. 1995/Jan. 1996): 3–8; for Brazil, Argentina, see Jose Goldemberg, "Lessons from the Denuclearization of Brazil and Argentina," *Arms Control Today* (Apr. 2006): 41–3; Paul Kerr, "Libya Vows to Dismantle WMD Program," *Arms Control Today* (Jan./Feb. 2004): 29–30; "Taiwan's Nuclear Past," *Arms Control Today* (May 2008): 47; for India, Pakistan, see Institute for Defense & Disarmament Studies (2005) at www.idds.org/issNucProlifSAsia.html; see *Arms Control Today* for additional information.

22. William Epstein, "The Non-Proliferation Treaty and the Review Conferences, 1965" in Burns, *Encyclopedia*, II: 855ff; Broad and Sanger, "North Korea Feeds Fears," 12A; Stumpt, "South Africa's Nuclear Weapons Program," 3–8; for Brazil, Argentina, see Goldemberg, "Lessons from the Denuclearization of Brazil and Argentina," 41–43; Kerr, "Libya Vows to Dismantle WMD Program," 29–30; "Taiwan's Nuclear Past," 47; for India, Pakistan, see Institute for Defense & Disarmament Studies (2005) at www. idds.org/issNucProlifSAsia.html; see *Arms Control Today* for additional information.

23. SIPRI, *Yearbook of World Armament and Disarmament, 2000* (Oxford: Oxford University Press, 2000), see "Appendix 8B: Nuclear Verification: The IAEA Strengthened Safeguards System," 496–508; International Atomic Energy Agency, "Non-Proliferation of Nuclear Weapons & Nuclear Security: IAEA Safeguards Agreements and Additional Protocols," (Vienna?, May 2005); IAEA, "Measures to improve the security of nuclear materials and other radioactive materials," IAEA document GC(45)14, Sept. 14, 2001 and GOV/INF/2005/10-GC(49)INF/6, Vienna, Sept. 6, 2005.

24. Robert Gallucci, "Ramifications of the North Korean Nuclear Test," *Arms Control Today* (Nov. 2006): 6–8; Michael J. Green, "Making the Best of Bad Options," *Arms Control Today*, 9–13; Richard L. Garwin and Frank N. von Hippel, "Deconstructing North Korea's October 9 Nuclear Test," *Arms Control Today*, 14–16; Peter Crail, "Verification Dispute Stalls NK Nuclear Talks," *Arms Control Today* (Sept. 2008): 29–31.

25. Allan Krass, *The United States and Arms Control: The Challenge of Leadership* (Westport, CT: Praeger, 1997), 168–72.

26. James A. Lewis, "Multilateral Arms Transfer Restraint: The Limits of Cooperation," *Arms Control Today* (Nov. 2005): 45.

27. Jack Mendelson, ed., *Arms Control Chronology* (Washington, DC: Center for Defense Information, 2002): 63–64; James B. Goodby, *At the Borderline of Armageddon: How American Presidents Managed the Atom Bomb* (Lanham, MD: Rowman & Littlefield, 2006), 126.

28. Mendelson, ed., *Arms Control Chronology*, 102, 106, 107; SIPRI, *Yearbook, 2000*, 670.

29. Janne Nolan, *Trappings of Power: Ballistic Missiles in the Third World* (Washington, DC: Brookings Institution, 1991), 82.

30. Waheguru Pal Singh Sidhu, "The Missile Technology Control Regime," *Arms Control Today* (Apr. 2007): 45–8.

31. Lewis, "Multilateral Arms Transfer Restraint," *Arms Control Today* (Nov. 2005): 45–8.

32. Wade Boese, "Interdiction Initiative Results Obscure," *Arms Control Today* (Sept. 2006): 47; Valencia, "The Proliferation Security Initiative," *Arms Control Today* 17–21; Boese, "Interdiction Initiative Successes Assessed," *Arms Control Today* (July/Aug. 2008): 33–4.

CHAPTER 5

1. Michael Howard, ed., "Temperamenta Belli: Can War Be Controlled?" *Restraints on War: Studies in the Limitation of Armed Conflict* (Oxford: Oxford University Press, 1979), 4–5.

2. Geoffrey Best, "Restraints on War by Land Before 1945," in Howard, *Restraints on War,* 23–4, 27–8.

3. Charles G. Fenwick, "Proceedings," *American Society of International Law* 110 (1949): 43.

4. Howard, *Restraints on War*, 4.

5. U.S. Army General Order No. 100: *Instructions for the Government of Armies of the United States in the Field* (1863), Sec. 1, para. 14; U.S. Department of Army Field Manual, *The Law of Land Warfare*, FM 27–10 (Washington, DC: GPO, 1956), 4.

6. W. Hays Parks, "The Law of War," in Burns, *Encyclopedia*, II: 1055; Sir Robert Saundby, "The Ethics of Bombing," *Air Force and Space Digest* (June 1967): 53.

7. Winston S. Churchill, *My Early Life: A Roving Commission* (London: T. Butterworth, 1930), 252–3; Jules Archer, *The Philippines Fight for Freedom* (New York: Macmillan, 1970), 95; W. Hays Parks, "The Law of War," 1060.

8. Camilla H. Wedgwood, "Some Aspects of Warfare in Melanesia," *Oceania* 1 (Apr. 1930): 13, 16.

9. John W. Layard, *Stone Men of Malekula* (London: Chatto Windus, 1942), 597.

10. "*Ancient World of a War-torn Tribe*," *Life* 53 (Sept. 28, 1968): 77–79.

11. Leopold Pospisil, *The Kapauku Papuans of West New Guinea* (New York: Holt, Rinehart & Winston, 1963), 59.

12. K. F. Otterbein, "The Evolution of Zulu Warfare," in Paul Bohannan, ed., *Law and Warfare: Studies in the Anthropology of Conflict* (Garden City, NY: Natural History Press, 1967), 352, 356.

13. Polybius, *The Histories*, Bk XIII, 3: 2–4, trans. by W. R. Paton (London: Heinemann, 1940).

14. Ragnar J. Numelin, *The Beginnings of Diplomacy: A Sociological Study of Intertribal and International Relations* (New York: Philosophical Library, 1950), 78, 81, 94; "Handbook of American Indians," Bureau of American Ethnology, *Bulletin* 30, Pt. II: 145; R. F. Fortune, "Arapesh Warfare," *American Anthropologist* 41 (1939): 331–5.

15. Numelin, *Beginning of Diplomacy*, 72–3; A. H. Keane, "On the Botocudos," *Journal of the Royal Anthropological Institute of Great Britain and Ireland*, XIII, 207; C. B. Humphreys, *The Southern New Hebrides: An Ethnological Record* (Cambridge, UK: Cambridge University Press, 1925), 58–9; A. P Vayda, "Maori Warfare," in Paul Bohannan, ed., *Law and Warfare: Studies in the Anthropology of Conflict* (New York: Natural History Press, 1967), 370.

16. Herodotus, *The Histories*, Bk I, sec. 82, trans. by Aubrey de Selincourt (Baltimore, MD: Penguin, 1954), 45–6; Victor D. Hanson, *The Western Way of War: Infantry Battle in Classical Greece* (New York: Knopf, 1989), 4; II Samuel 2:12–13; 21:18–19; I Chronicles 11:23; Yigael Yadin, *The Art of Warfare in Biblical Lands: In Light of Archeological Discovery* (London: Weidenfeld & Nicolson, 1963), 72–3, 266–7.

17. Pospisil, *The Kapauku Papuans*, 59; Maurice R. Davie, *The Evolution of War: A Study of Role in Early Societies* (New Haven: Yale University Press, 1929), 181, 195; G. Buhler, trans., *The Law of Manu* (Oxford: Clarendon Press, 1886), 231.

18. Stuart Croft, *Strategies of Arms Control: A History and Typology* (Manchester, UK: Manchester University Press, 1996), 49.

19. Udo Heyn, *Peacemaking in Medieval Europe* (Claremont, CA: Regina Books, 1997), x; he shows the evolution and transformation of these campaigns.

20. See texts in Heyn, *Peacemaking*, 91–102, and Burns, *Encyclopedia*, III: 1489–94; Richard Shelly Hartigan, "Noncombatant Immunity: Reflections on Its Origins and Present Status," *Review of Politics* 29 (Apr. 1967): 213.

21. Percy Bordwell, *Law of War Between Belligerents: A History and Commentary* (Chicago, IL: Callaghan, 1908), 12.

22. See texts in Burns, *Encyclopedia*, III: 1497, 1498–500.

23. Best, "Restraints on War by Land Before 1945," 21–3.

24. G. J. Adler, "Targets in War: Legal Considerations," in Richard A. Falk, *The Vietnam War and International Law*, 4 vols. (Princeton, NJ: Princeton University Press, 1968–1976), III: 295; see text in Burns, *Encyclopedia*, III: 1501.

25. James Brown Scott, *Texts of the Peace Conferences at The Hague, 1899 and 1907* (Boston: Ginn, 1908), xv–xvi, ff; Andrew Dickson White, *Autobiography of Andrew D. White* (New York: Century, 1905): II: 265; Calvin DeArmond Davis, *The United States and the Second Hague Peace Conference: American Diplomacy and International Organization, 1899–1914* (Durham, NC: Duke University Press, 1975), 209–210; see *International Commission to Inquire into the Causes and Conduct of the Balkan Wars* (Washington, DC: Carnegie Endowment, 1914); Christopher B. Thomson, *Old Europe's Suicide* (New York: Thomas Seltzer, 1922), 49.

26. Quote in James W. Garner, "The German War Code," *University of Illinois Bulletin* 49:16 (1918): 9; Sheldon Glueck, *War Criminals: Their Prosecution and Punishment* (New York: Knopf, 1944): 193, n.12.

27. Lester H. Brune, "An Effort to Regulate Aerial Bombing: The Hague Commission of Jurists, 1922–1923," *Aerospace Historian* 29:3 (1982): 183–185; also see Morton W. Royse, *Aerial Bombardment and the International Regulation of Warfare* (New York: Harold Vinal, 1928).

28. Texts in Leon Friedman, ed., *The Law of War: A Documentary History* (New York: Random House, 1972), I: 467–477, 493–497; also see W. Hays Parks, "The Law of War," 1058; Herbert P. Bix, *Hirohito and the Making of Modern Japan* (New York: HarperCollins, 2000), 359; Gene Sharp, *The Politics of Nonviolent Action* (Boston: P.

Sargent, 1973), 324; Jonathan Lewis and Ben Steele, *Hell in the Pacific: From Pearl Harbor to Hiroshima and Beyond* (London: Channel 4, 2001), 169; John W. Dower, *War Without Mercy: Race and Power in the Pacific War* (New York: Pantheon Books, 1986), 66.

29. Richard Dean Burns and C. L. Smith, "Nicholas Roerich, Henry A. Wallace and the "Peace Banner": A Study in Idealism, Egocentrism and Anguish," *Peace and Change* (Spring 1973): 40–9.

30. Lester H. Brune, "Regulating Aerial Bombing, 1919–1925," in Burns, *Encyclopedia*, II: 734; *New York Times*, Sept. 28, 1937; Charles Webster and Noble Franklin, *The Strategic Air Offensive against Germany, 1939–1945* (London: HMSO, 1961), I: 134–135. Wesley F. Craven and James Lea Cate's official version, *The Army Air Forces in World War II* (Washington, DC: GPO, 1983), that claimed the United States avoided indiscriminate bombing, has been challenged by Michael Sherry's *The Rise of American Air Power: The Creation of Armageddon* (New Haven: Yale University Press, 1987); Michael Howard, ed., "Temperamenta Belli: Can War be Controlled?" 4. See also Ronald Schaffer, *Wings of Judgment: American Bombing in World War II* (New York: Oxford University Press, 1985); Martin Middlebrook, *The Battle for Hamburg: Allied Air Forces Against a German City in 1943* (New York: Scribner, 1981); and Robert Gullain, *I Saw Tokyo Burning* (Garden City, NY: Doubleday, 1981).

31. For an excellent discussion, see W. Hays Parks, "The Law of War," 1057ff.

32. Dana Priest, "Reinterpreting International Law? A memo allowing the CIA to take detainees out of Iraq is called a breach of Geneva Conventions," *Washington Post National Weekly* (Nov. 1–7, 2004): 16; Dahlia Lithwick, "Getting Away with Torture," *Newsweek* (May 5, 2008): 17.

33. See Jan Hladík, "The 1954 Hague Convention for the Protection of Cultural Property in the Event of Armed Conflict and the Notion of Military Necessity," *International Review of the Red Cross*, No. 835 (Sept. 30, 1999): 621–35; see also Elizabeth Simpson, ed., *The Spoils of War: World War II and Its Aftermath. The Loss, Reappearance, and Recovery of Cultural Property* (New York: Harry N. Abrams, 1997).

34. See http://www.unhchr.ch/html/menu2/6/cat/index.html

CHAPTER 6

1. Benjamin Loeb, "Test Ban Proposals and Agreements: The 1950s to the Present," in Burns, *Encyclopedia*, II: 827ff.; *Science* 222 (Dec. 23, 1983): 1283– 2; *Foreign Affairs* 65 (Fall 1986): 163–168; and Defense Department pamphlet, "The Potential Effect of Nuclear War on Climate," Mar. 1, 1985.

2. UN War Crimes Commission, *History of the U.N. War Crimes Commission and the Development of the Laws of War* [Nuremberg Case No. 7150] (London: HMSO, 1948), 496; SIPRI, *Warfare in a Fragile World: Military Impact on the Human Environment* (London: Taylor & Francis, 1980), 14–19; quote in Leon Friedman, *The Law of War: A Documentary History* (New York: Random House, 1972), 4.

3. SIPRI, *Ecological Consequences of 2nd Vietnam War* (Stockholm: Almqvist & Wiksell, 1976), 86; Jacques G. Richardson, "The Bane of 'Inhumane' Weapons and Overkill: An Overview of Increasingly Lethal Arms and the Inadequacy of Regulatory Controls," *Science and Engineering Ethics* 10 (2004): 680.

4. Loeb, "Test Ban Proposals and Agreements," 830–5; Theodore Sorensen, *Kennedy* (New York: Harper & Row, 1965): 740; Gregg Herken, *Counsels of War* (New York: Knopf, 1985), 186.

5. Loeb, "Test Ban Proposals and Agreements," 836–7; Michael Krepon, "Arms Control: Verification and Compliance," *Headline Series*, No. 270 (Sept./Oct. 1984): 44–5; Gloria Duffy, *Compliance and the Future of Arms Control* (Stanford, CA: Center for International Security and Arms Control, 1988), 203.

6. Loeb, "Test Ban Proposals and Agreements," 837–8.

7. Arthur H. Westing, "The Environmental Modification Convention, 1977 to the Present," in Burns, *Encyclopedia*, II: 947ff; SIPRI, *Ecological Consequences*, 86–7; W. Hays Parks, "Law of War," in Burns, *Encyclopedia*, II:1065; see also Jozef Goldblat, "The Environmental Modification Convention of 1977: An Analysis," in Arthur H. Westing, ed., *Environmental Warfare: A Technical, Legal and Policy Appraisal* (London: Taylor & Francis for SIPRI, 1984), 53–64.

8. Loeb, "Test Ban Proposals and Agreements," 841–3.

9. John M. Shields and William C. Potter, eds., *Dismantling the Cold War: U.S. and NIS Perspectives on the Nunn-Lugar Cooperative Threat Reduction Program* (Cambridge, MA: MIT Press, 1997); James E. Goodby, *At the Borderline of Armageddon* (Lanham, MD: Rowman & Littlefield): 165–7; Senator Richard C. Lugar, "The Next Steps in U.S. Nonproliferation Policy," *Arms Control Today* (Dec. 2002): 3–7, 21; Paul F. Walker, "Nunn-Lugar at 15: No Time to Relax Global Threat Reduction Efforts," *Arms Control Today* (May 2006): 6–11; see also Cristina Hansell Chuen, "Russian Nuclear-Powered Submarine Dismantlement and Related Activities: A Critique," *Center for Nonproliferation Studies* (May 24, 2007); CTR, "Cooperative Threat Reduction Annual Report to Congress, Fiscal Year 2008," 3; Sonia Ben Ouaghram-Gormley, "An Unrealized Nexus: WMD-Related Trafficking, Terrorism, and Organized Crime in the Former Soviet Union," *Arms Control Today* (July/August 2007): 6–13.

10. Webster A. Stone, "The Hot Line: Washington-Moscow Direct Communications Link, 1963 to the Present," in Burns, *Encyclopedia*, II: 847ff; Andrew Bennett, "The Accidents Measures Agreement," in Albert Carnesale and Richard N. Haass, eds., *Superpower Arms Control: Setting the Record Straight* (Cambridge, MA: Ballinger, 1987), 53.

11. Raymond L. Garthoff, "The Accidental Measures Agreement," in John Borawski, ed., *Avoiding War in the Nuclear Age: Confidence Building Measures* (Boulder, CO: Westview, 1986), 56–71; Laura S. Hayes Holgate, "Preventing Accidental War," in Burns, *Encyclopedia*, II: 1094–5ff.

12. These observations are based upon Andrew Bennett, "The Accidents Measures Agreement," 41–61; Raymond L. Garthoff, *The Great Transition: American-Soviet Relations and the End of the Cold War* (Washington, DC: Brookings Institution, 1994), 138–9.

13. For Prevention of Incidents on the High Seas, see David F. Winkler, *Cold War at Sea: High-Seas Confrontation between the United States and the Soviet Union* (Annapolis, MD: Naval Institute Press, 2000), 106–7ff.

14. Bennett, "The Accidents Measures Agreement," 41–51.

15. Bennett, "The Accidents Measures Agreement," 41–51.

16. Holgate, "Preventing Accidental War," in Burns, *Encyclopedia*, II: 1098–9.

17. W. W. Rostow, *Open Skies: Eisenhower's Proposal of July 21, 1955* (Austin: University of Texas Press, 1982); Ann M. Florini, "The Open Skies Negotiations," in Burns, *Encyclopedia*, II: 1113ff.

18. John Steinbruner, *The Significance of Joint Missile Surveillance*, Occasional Paper of the Committee on International Security Studies, American Academy of Arts and Sciences (July 2001), 3; Susan Ellis, "U.S.-Russian Missile Accords to Strengthen Strategic Stability," *Washington File* (June 6, 2000); Wade Boese and Miles A. Pomper, "Strategic Decisions: An Interview with STRATCOM Commander General James E. Cartwright," *Arms Control Today* (June 2006): 9.

19. Wade Boese, "Russia Halts Missile Launch Notices," *Arms Control Today* (Mar. 2008): 46.

20. United Nations, *The United Nations and Disarmament, 1945–1985* (New York: UN, 1985), 102–3.

21. See www.idds.org/issNucProlifSAsia.html; Stuart Croft, *Strategies of Arms Control: A History and Typology* (Manchester, UK: University of Manchester Press, 1996), 92–3; "India, Pakistan Sign Missile Notification Pact," *Arms Control Today* (Nov. 2005): 42; "India Test-Launches Submarine Missile," *Arms Control Today* (April 2008): 44.

22. John Fry, *The Helsinki Process: Negotiating Security and Cooperation in Europe* (Washington, DC: National Defense University Press, 1993), 169; John Macintosh, "Confidence-Building Measures in Europe, 1975 to Present," in Burns, *Encyclopedia*, II: 938.

23. James Macintosh, "Confidence Building in Europe, 1975–1991," in Burns, *Encyclopedia*, II: 929ff; Jussi M Hamináki, "'Dr. Kissinger' or 'Mr. Kissinger'? Kissingerology, Thirty Years and Counting," *Diplomatic History* 27:5 (2003): 654; also see John Fry, *The Helsinki Process*.

PART II

1. Allan S. Krass, *The United States and Arms Control: The Challenge of Leadership* (Westport, CT: Praeger, 1997), 3.

2. See George Bunn, "Negotiating Arms Control and Disarmament Agreements" and James A. Schear, "Political Aspects of Arms Control and Disarmament Agreements," in Burns, *Encyclopedia*, II: 393–404, 425–42.

3. Christoph Bertram, "Arms Control and Technological Change: Elements of a New Approach," in Bertram, ed., *Arms Control and Military Force* (Montclair, NJ: Allanheld, Osmun, 1980), 160–1; Christopher J. Lamb, *How To Think About Arms Control, Disarmament and Defense* (Englewood Cliffs, NJ: Prentice Hall, 1988), 11.

4. Krass, *The United States and Arms Control*, 4.

CHAPTER 7

1. Fred Charles Iklé, *How Nations Negotiate* (New York: Praeger, 1964), 2.

2. Strobe Talbott, "Rethinking the Red Menace," *Time* 135 (Jan. 1, 1990): 36–8; Robert D. English, *Russia and the Idea of the West* (New York: Columbia University Press, 2000), 42, 46–7; Mikhail Gorbachev, *Perestroika: New Thinking for Our Country and the World* (New York: Harper & Row, 1987), 211; Gerald C. Smith, *Disarming*

Diplomat: The Memoirs of Gerald C. Smith, Arms Control Negotiator (Lanham, MD: Madison Books, 1996), xiii.

3. April Carter, *Success and Failure in Arms Control Negotiations* (New York: Oxford University Press, 1989), 284.

4. Quoted in George Bunn, *Arms Control By Committee: Managing Negotiations with the Russians* (Stanford, CA: Stanford University Press, 1992), 8; also see Coit Blacker and Gloria Duffy, eds., *International Arms Control Issues and Agreements* (Stanford, CA: Stanford University Press, 1984), 40.

5. Bunn, *Arms Control By Committee*, 13.

6. Larry G. Gerber, "The Baruch Plan and the Origins of the Cold War," *Diplomatic History* 6 (Winter 1982): 75.

7. Bunn, *Arms Control By Committee*, 144ff; English, *Russia and the Idea of the West*, 206.

8. Stanley Hoffmann, *Gulliver's Troubles: Or the Setting of American Foreign Policy* (New York: McGraw-Hill, 1968), 149.

9. Sadao Asada, "Japanese Admirals and the Politics of Naval Limitation: Kato Tomosaburo vs. Kato Kanji," in Gerald Jordan, ed., *Naval Warfare in the Twentieth Century, 1900–1945: Essays in Honor of Arthur Marder* (New York: Crane Russak, 1977), 158; Dudley W. Knox, *The Eclipse of American Sea Power* (New York: American Army and Navy Journal, 1922), 133–4.

10. Gerald E. Wheeler, *Prelude to Pearl Harbor: The United States Navy and the Far East, 1921–1931* (Columbia: University of Missouri Press, 1963), 178, 184; Stephen Roskill, *Naval Policy Between the Wars: The Period of Reluctant Rearmament, 1930–1939* (Annapolis, MD: Naval Institute Press, 1976), 323.

11. James E. Goodby, *At the Borderline of Armageddon: How American Presidents Managed the Atom Bomb* (Lanham, MD: Rowman and Littlefield, 2006), 30; Raymond L. Garthoff, *A Journey Through the Cold War: A Memoir of Containment and Coexistence* (Washington, DC: Brookings Institution Press, 2001), 46.

12. Thomas Graham, Jr., *Disarmament Sketches: Three Decades of Arms Control and International Law* (Seattle: University of Washington Press, 2002), 102–3; Frances Fitzgerald, *Way Out There in the Blue: Reagan, Star Wars and the End of the Cold War* (New York: Simon & Schuster, 2000), 334–6.

13. Aleksandr' G. Savel'yev and Nikolay N. Detinov, *The Big Five: Arms Control Decision-Making in the Soviet Union* (Westport, CT: Praeger, 1995), 92–3.

14. Smith, *Disarming Diplomat*, 168–169; John Newhouse, *Cold Dawn: The Story of SALT [I]* (New York: Holt, Rinehart, Winston, 1973), 13.

15. Savel'yev and Detinov, *The Big Five,* xii, 20, 28, 184.

16. Quoted in Fitzgerald, *Way Out There in the Blue*, 445.

17. Fitzgerald, *Way Out There in The Blue*, 153–154; Savel'yev and Detinov, *The Big Five,* 124, 136; Robert M. Gates, *From the Shadows* (New York: Simon & Schuster, 1996), 423.

18. Arthur H. Dean, *Test Ban and Disarmament: The Path of Negotiation* (New York: Harper & Row, 1966), 23.

19. See Strobe Talbott, *Endgame: The Inside Story of SALT II* (New York: Harper & Row, 1979), 19–20 and Chapter 10.

20. Christoph Bertram, "Arms Control and Technological Change: Elements of a New Approach," in Bertram, ed., *Arms Control and Military Force* (Montclair, NJ:

Allanheld, Osmun, 1980), 160–1; Christopher J. Lamb, *How To Think About Arms Control, Disarmament and Defense* (Englewood Cliffs, NJ: Prentice Hall, 1988), 11.

21. Liddell Hart, *Deterrent or Defense,* quoted in A. Schlesinger, Jr., *Robert Kennedy and His Times* (Boston: Houghton Mifflin, 1978), 437.

22. Ambassador Ralph Earle, "Arms Control: Myths, Presidents, Transitions and Costs," in Kenneth W. Thompson, ed., *Presidents and Arms Control: Process, Procedures and Problems* (Lanham, MD: University Press of America, 1994), II: 114–5.

23. Quote by Thomas Buckley, "President Warren G. Harding and the Congress," in Thompson, *Presidents and Arms Control,* II: 137–8.

24. Lawrence H. Douglas, "Submarine Disarmament, 1919–1936," Ph.D. diss. (Syracuse University, 1970) 160.

25. Freeman Dyson, *Weapons and Hope* (New York: Harper Colophon Books, 1985), 172; Glenn T. Seaborg with Benjamin S. Loeb, *Kennedy, Khrushchev and the Test Ban* (Berkeley: University of California Press, 1981): 235.

26. Thomas Graham, Jr., *Disarmament Sketches: Three Decades of Arms Control and International Law* (Seattle: University of Washington Press, 2002), 55–6.

27. Earle, "Arms Control: Myths, Presidents, Transitions and Costs," in Thompson, *Presidents and Arms Control,* II: 116; Dyson, *Weapons and Hope,* 173.

28. *Fortune Magazine* (Mar. 1934): 120.

29. Merze Tate, *The United States and Armaments* (Cambridge, MA: Harvard University Press, 1948), 36.

30. Michael Krepon and Dan Caldwell, eds., *Politics of Arms Control Treaty Ratification* (New York: St. Martin's, 1991), 456.

31. Smith, *Disarming Diplomat,* 14; quoted in Sean M. Lynn-Jones, "Lulling and Stimulating Effects of Arms Control," in Albert Carnesale and Richard N. Haass, eds., *Superpower Arms Control: Setting the Record Straight* (Cambridge, MA: Ballinger, 1987), 223; U.S. Senate Committee on Foreign Relations, *Hearings on the Nuclear Test Ban Treaty,* 88th Cong., 1st Sess. (Washington, DC: GPO, 1963): 564.

32. See Arthur Krock, *Memoirs* (London: Casell, 1968), 229.

33. Herbert F. York, *Arms & the Physicist* (Woodbury, NY: AIP Press, 1995), 13.

34. Anatoly Dobrynin, *In Confidence: Moscow's Ambassador to America's Six Cold War Presidents* (Seattle: University of Washington Press, 2001), 472; Mikhail Gorbachev, *On My Country & the World* (New York: Columbia University Press, 2000), 65–6.

35. Michael Krepon, "Arms Limitation Treaties and Their Ratification," in Thompson, *Presidents and Arms Control,* II: 129–46.

CHAPTER 8

1. Mark F. Imber, "Arms Control Verification: The Special Case of IAEA-NPT 'Special Inspections,'" *Arms Control* 3:3 (Dec. 1982): 57.

2. George Bunn and Wolfgang K. H. Panofsky, "Arms Control, Compliance, and the Law," A Working Paper of the Center for International Security and Arms Control (Stanford, CA: Stanford University, May 1988), 6.

3. Bunn and Panofsky, "Arms Control, Compliance, and the Law," 8.

4. U.S., Department of State, *Documents on Disarmament, 1945–1959* (Washington, DC: GPO, 1960): I: 510; Spurgeon M. Keeny, Jr., "The On-Site Inspection Legacy," *Arms Control Today* 18 (Nov. 1988): 2.

5. Thomas G. Mahnken, *Uncovering Ways of War: U.S. Intelligence and Foreign Military Innovation, 1918–1941* (Ithaca, NY: Cornell University Press, 2002), 32; presents an excellent discussion of the role of U.S. attachés.

6. David F. Winkler, *Cold War at Sea: High-Seas Confrontation between the United States and the Soviet Union* (Annapolis, MD: Naval Institute Press, 2000), 20; W. W. Rostow, *Open Skies: Eisenhower's Proposal of July 21, 1955* (Austin: University of Texas Press, 1982), 10.

7. Allan S. Krass, *The United States and Arms Control: The Challenge of Leadership* (Westport, CT: Praeger, 1997), 14–15.

8. Mahnken, *Uncovering Ways of War*, 37, 44, 62ff.; compare with Robert G. Kaufman, *Arms Control During the Pre-Nuclear Era: The United States and Naval Limitation Between the Two World Wars* (New York: Columbia University Press, 1990), 100.

9. Gerald E. Wheeler, *Prelude to Pearl Harbor: The United States Navy and the Far East, 1921–1931* (Columbia: University of Missouri Press, 1963), 88–9; U.S. Dept. of State, *Foreign Relations of the United States, 1929*, III: 256–61.

10. Krass, *The United States and Arms Control*, 15.

11. John Newhouse, *Cold Dawn: The Story of SALT [I]* (New York: Holt, Rinehart & Winston, 1973), 70–1.

12. Krass, *United States and Arms Control*, 16, 419–20; Gloria Duffy, *Compliance and the Future of Arms Control* (Cambridge, MA: Ballinger, 1988), 165–7.

13. Vicount Templewood (Samuel Hoare), *Nine Troubled Years* (London: Collins, 1954), 147; Keith Middlemas and John Barnes, *Baldwin* (London: Collins, 1954), 140.

14. Nicholas G. Papp, "The Anglo-German Naval Agreement of 1935" (PhD dissertation, University of Connecticut, 1969), 292.

15. *Documents on British Foreign Policy*, Ser. 3, IV:628–637, Ser. D, IV:349–350; Templewood, *Nine Troubled Years*, 147; Richard Dean Burns and Donald Uquidi, *Disarmament in Perspective: An Analysis of Selected Arms Control and Disarmament Agreements Between the World Wars, 1919–1939*, 4 vols. (Washington, DC: U.S. Arms Control & Disarmament Agency, 1968), III: 240–2.

16. Krass, *The United States and Arms Control*, 42–5.

17. Krass, *The United States and Arms Control*, 37, 39ff.

18. Krass, *The United States and Arms Control*, 61–2; see Amy E. Smithson, *Resuscitating the Bioweapons Ban: U.S. Industry Expert's Plans for Treaty Monitoring* (Washington, DC: Center for Strategic and International Studies, Nov. 2004).

19. Krass, *The United States and Arms Control*, 47–49; Hendrik Wagenmakers, "The UN Register of Conventional Arms: A New Instrument for Cooperative Security," *Arms Control Today* (Oct. 1994): 8–13.

20. Burns and Uquidi, *Disarmament in Perspective*, II: 35–57; Richard Dean Burns, "Inspection of the Mandates, 1919–1941," *Pacific Historical Review* 37 (Nov. 1968): 445–6.

21. Krass, *United States and Arms Control*, 16, 419–20; Gloria Duffy, *Compliance and the Future of Arms Control* (Cambridge, MA: Ballinger, 1988), 165–7; quote in Michael Krepon, *Arms Control: Verification and Compliance* (New York: Foreign Policy Assoc. [Headline Series #270], Sept./Oct. 1984), 38.

22. Philip Trowle, "The Soviet Union and the Biological Weapons Convention," *Arms Control* 3:3 (Dec. 1982): 37.

23. *Arms Control Today* (July/Aug. 2002): 30; *ACT* (Sept. 2007): 29–30; *ACT* (Oct. 2007): 40.

24. Strobe Talbott, *The Master of the Game: Paul Nitze and the Nuclear Peace* (New York: Knopf, 1988), 381; Spurgeon M. Keeny, Jr., "The On-Site Inspection Legacy," *Arms Control Today* 18 (Nov. 1988): 2; Frances Fitzgerald, *Way Out There in the Blue: Reagan, Star Wars and the End of the Cold War* (New York: Simon & Schuster, 2000), 444–5.

25. Neal Petersen, "The Versailles Treaty, 1919–1936," in Burns, *Encyclopedia*, II: 621–38.

26. Fred Tanner, *From Versailles to Baghdad: Post-War Armament Control of Defeated States* (New York: United Nations, 1992), 86–91; Lawrence Scheinman, "The International Atomic Energy Agency and Arms Control," in Burns, *Encyclopedia* I: 363–369; Imber, "Arms Control Verification," 61–5; International Atomic Energy Agency, *Non-Proliferation of Nuclear Weapons & Nuclear Security: IAEA Safeguards Agreements and Additional Protocols* (Vienna?, May 2005).

27. Christopher C. Joyner, "The Antarctic State Treaty," in Burns, *Encyclopedia*, II: 820.

28. See Shannon Kile, "Nuclear Arms Control" in *SIPRI Yearbook 1998: Armaments, Disarmament and International Security* (Oxford: Oxford University Press, 1998), 403–19.

29. P. Terrence Hopmann, "From MBFR to CFE: Negotiating Conventional Arms Control in Europe," Burns, *Encyclopedia* II: 967–990; see also Joseph P. Harahan and John C. Kuhn III, *On-Site Inspections Under the CFE Treaty: A History of the On-Site Inspection Agency and CFE Treaty Implementation, 1990–1996* (Washington, DC: The On-Site Inspection Agency, Department of Defense, 1996).

30. *Arms Control Today* (Sept. 2002), 23.

31. Krass, *The United States and Arms Control,* 56–8.

32. "A Chronology of UN Inspections in Iraq," *Arms Control Today* (Oct. 2002), 14–23; see Chapter 3 in Lester Brune, *United States and Two Gulf Wars: Prelude and Aftermath* (Claremont, CA: Regina Books, 2007).

33. Richard Dean Burns, "International Arms Inspection Policies Between World Wars, 1919–1934," *Historian* 31 (Aug. 1969): 583–603; Burns, "Supervision, Control and Inspection of Armament: 1919–1941," *Orbis* 15 (Fall 1971); 943–52; and various issues of *Arms Control Today.*

CHAPTER 9

1. Allan Krass, *The United States and Arms Control: The Challenge of Leadership* (Westport, CT: Praeger, 1997), 163.

2. Gloria Duffy, "Arms Control Treaty Compliance," in Burns, *Encyclopedia* II: 279–80.

3. George Bunn and Wolfgang K. H. Panofsky, "Arms Control, Compliance, and the Law," Center for International Security and Arms Control, (Stanford, CA: Stanford University, May 1988), 2.

4. Bunn and Panofsky, "Arms Control, Compliance, and the Law," 3–5.

5. Wade Boese, "Russia Casts Doubt on Conventional Arms Pact," *ACT* (June 2007): 36.

6. Bunn and Panofsky, "Arms Control, Compliance, and the Law," 3–4.

7. Strobe Talbott, *The Master of the Game: Paul Nitze and the Nuclear Peace* (New York: Knopf, 1988), 130–4; Raymond Garthoff, *Policy versus the Law: The Reinterpretation of the ABM Treaty* (Washington, DC: Brookings Institution, 1987).

8. Krass, *The United States and Arms Control,* 19–20, 41–2.

9. Bunn and Panofsky, "Arms Control, Compliance, and the Law," 8–10; Abram Chayes and Antonia Handler Chayes, "On Compliance," *International Organization* (Spring 1993): 177.

10. Krass, *The United States and Arms Control,* 173.

11. Gloria Duffy, *Compliance and the Future of Arms Control* (Stanford, CA: The Center for International Studies and Arms Control, 1988), 12; Aspin quoted in Krass, *The United States and Arms Control,* 20.

12. Michael Krepon, "Arms Control: Verification and Compliance," *Headline Series,* No. 270 (Sept./Oct. 1984): 44–5.

13. Lester H. Brune, *The United States and Two Gulf Wars* (Claremont, CA: Regina Books, 2007), chs. 3 and 4.

14. Krass, *The United States and Arms Control,* 186–7.

15. Duffy, *Compliance and the Future of Arms Control,* 279–80; Krass, *The United States and Arms Control,* 166–8.

16. Albert Carnesale and Richard N. Haass, eds., *Superpower Arms Control: Setting the Record Straight* (Cambridge, MA: Ballinger, 1987), 331–2, 308.

17. Duffy, "Arms Control Treaty Compliance," in Burns, *Encyclopedia,* II: 286–7.

18. Aleksandr' G. Savel'yev and Nikolay N. Detinov, *The Big Five: Arms Control Decision-Making in the Soviet Union* (Westport, CT: Praeger, 1995), 97–99, 102–8; Duffy, *Compliance and the Future of Arms Control,* 109.

19. Duffy, "Arms Control Treaty Compliance," in Burns, *Encyclopedia,* II: 279–80.

20. Charles C. Flowerree, "Chemical and Biological Weapons and Arms Control," in Burns, *Encyclopedia,* II: 1002–3.

21. Midori Nishi, "An Evaluation of Japanese Agriculture and Fishery Developments in Micronesia, During the Japanese Mandate, 1914–1941," *Micronesica* 4:1 (June 1968): 1–18; Robert G. Kaufman, *Arms Control During the Pre-Nuclear Era: The United States and Naval Limitation Between the Two World Wars* (New York: Columbia University Press, 1990), 100–1; Thomas Wild, "How Japan Fortified the Mandated Islands," U.S. Naval Institute *Proceedings* (Apr. 1955): 401–8; see also Richard Dean Burns, "Inspection of the Mandates, 1919–1941," *Pacific Historical Review* 38 (1968): 445–562.

22. Kaufman, *Arms Control During the Pre-Nuclear Era,* 32, 99; Stephen E. Pelz, *Race to Pearl Harbor: The Failure of the Second London Naval Conference and the Onset of World War II* (Cambridge, MA: Harvard University Press, 1974), 32; Eric Lacroix, "The Development of the 'A Class' Cruisers in the Imperial Japanese Navy," Part 3, *Warship International* 16:4 (1979): 341.

23. Norman Friedman, *Battleship Design and Development, 1905–1945* (New York: Mayflower Books, 1978), 154–64; Anthony Preston, *Cruisers* (London: Bison Books, 1980), 80, 99–101; Emily O. Goldman, *Sunken Treaties: Naval Arms Control Between the Wars* (State College: Pennsylvania State University, 1994), 156, 173, 178–80.

24. Sidney N. Graybel and Patricia McFate, "Strategic Defensive Arms Control," in Jeffrey Larsen and Gregory J. Rattray, eds., *Arms Control Toward the 21st Century* (Boulder, CO: Lynn Rienner, 1996), 123–5; Duffy, *Compliance and the Future of Arms Control,* 33, 39–41, 95–103.

25. Judith Miller, Stephen Engelbert, and William Broad, *Germs: Biological Weapons and America's Secret War* (New York: Simon & Schuster, 2001), 73, 83–4, 150.

26. See Fred Charles Iklé, "After Detection—What?" *Foreign Affairs* (Jan. 1961): 208–20.

CHAPTER 10

1. Barton Bernstein, "The Quest for Security: American Foreign Policy and International Control of Atomic Energy, 1942–1946," *Journal of American History* 60 (March 1974): 1044; Mikhail Gorbachev, *On My Country & the World* (New York: Columbia University Press, 2000), 196.

2. Hedley Bull, "The Scope of Soviet-American Agreement," *Adelphi Papers* 65 (Feb. 1970): 10.

3. Paul H. Nitze, "Foreword," in Aleksandr' G. Savel'yev and Nikolay N. Detinov, *The Big Five: Arms Control Decision-Making in the Soviet Union* (Westport, CT: Praeger, 1995), xi–xii.

4. Strobe Talbott, *Endgame: The Inside Story of SALT II* (New York: Harper & Row, 1979), 19–20.

5. Thomas C. Shelling, "A Half-Century Without Nuclear War," *The Key Reporter* (Phi Beta Kappa quarterly) 65:3 (Spring 2000): 3–5.

6. Campbell Craig, *Destroying the Village: Eisenhower and Thermonuclear War* (New York: Columbia University Press, 1998), 49, 52; Annette Messemer, "Konrad Adnauer: Defence Diplomat on the Backstage," in John Lewis Gaddis et al., *Cold War Statesmen Confront the Bomb* (New York: Oxford University Press, 1999), 242–3; Robert A. Strong, "Arms Control and the Presidency in the Nuclear Age," in Kenneth W. Thompson, ed., *Presidents and Arms Control* (Lanham, MD: University Press of America [for the Miller Center, University of Virginia], 1994) I: 17; James E. Goodby, "How Presidents Make Decisions on Nuclear Weapons," in Thompson, ed., *Presidents and Arms Control*, I: 37.

7. Messemer, "Konrad Adnauer," 257; Gregg Herken, *Counsels of War* (New York: Knopf, 1985), 159, 161, 167.

8. Johnson quote in McGeorge Bundy, *Danger and Survival: Choices About the Bomb in the First Fifty Years* (New York: Random House, 1988), 537; Philip H. Gordon, "Charles de Gaulle and the Nuclear Revolution," in Gaddis et al., *Cold War Statesmen Confront the Bomb*, 226.

9. Vladislav M. Zubok, *A Failed Empire: The Soviet Union in the Cold War from Stalin to Gorbachev* (Chapel Hill: University of North Carolina Press, 2007), 126–7, 220–1; William Taubman, *Khrushchev: the Man and His Era* (New York: Norton, 2003), 449.

10. James E. Goodby, *At the Borderline of Armageddon: How American Presidents Managed the Atomic Bomb* (Lanham, MD: Rowan & Littlefield, 2006), 98–9; Kissinger quote in Herken, *Counsels of War*, 266; Melvyn P. Leffler, *For the Soul of Mankind: the United States, the Soviet Union, and the Cold War* (New York: Hill & Wang, 2007), 158.

11. Lou Cannon, *President Reagan: The Role of a Lifetime*, 2d ed. (New York: Public Affairs, 2000), 246–50; Christopher Paine, "A False START," *BAS* 38 (Aug./Sept. 82): 14.

12. Thomas Powers, "Nuclear Winter and Nuclear Strategy," *Atlantic Monthly* (Nov. 1984): 63; Gerald C. Smith, *Disarming Diplomat: the Memoirs of Gerald C. Smith, Arms Control Negotiator* (Lanham, MD: Madison Books, 1996), xiii.

13. Nina Tannenwald, *The Nuclear Taboo: The United States and the Non-Use of Nuclear Weapons Since 1945* (New York: Cambridge University Press, 2008), reviewed by William Burr in *Arms Control Today* (Sept. 2008): 54–8; Nobel quoted in Strong, "Arms Control and the Presidency in the Nuclear Age," 5.

14. George P. Shultz, William J. Perry, Henry A. Kissinger, and Sam Nunn, "A World Free of Nuclear Weapons," *The Wall Street Journal* (Jan. 4, 2007), A15.

15. Kim Murphy, "ElBaradei Warns About Extremist Nuclear Threat," *Los Angeles Times* (Feb. 10, 2008), A4.

Glossary

A-bomb	Atomic bomb
ABM	Anti-Ballistic Missile
ACA	Agency for the Control of Armaments
ACDA	Arms Control and Disarmament Agency, U.S.
AEC	Atomic Energy Commission
ASEAN	Association of Southeast Asian Nations
BMD	Ballistic Missile Defense
BMLN	Ballistic Missile Launch Notification Agreement
BWC	Biological Weapons Convention
C/B	Chemical and Biological
CBW	Chemical and Biological Weapons
CFE	Conventional armed Forces in Europe
CIA	Central Intelligence Agency
CPSU	Communist Party Soviet Union
CSBMs	Confidence and Security Building Measures
CSCE	Conference on Security and Cooperation in Europe
CTB	Comprehensive Test Ban
CTR	The United States' Cooperative Threat Reduction program
DMZ	Demilitarized Zone
ENDC	Eighteen Nations Disarmament Conference
EnMod	Environmental Modification Convention
FRG	Federal Republic of Germany

H-bomb	Hydrogen bomb
HCOC	Hague Code of Conduct
IAAC	Inter-Allied Control Commission
IAACC	Inter-Allied Aeronautical Commission of Control
IAEA	International Atomic Energy Agency
IAMCC	Inter-Allied Military Commission of Control
ICBM	Intercontinental Ballistic Missile
INF	Intermediate-range Nuclear Forces
IRBM	Intermediate Range Ballistic Missile
JCIC	Joint Compliance and Implementation Commission
LNTB	Limited Nuclear Test Ban
MAD	Mutual Assured Destruction
MBFR	Mutual and Balanced Force Reduction
MIRV	Multiple Independently targeted Reentry Vehicle
MRBM	Medium Range Ballistic Missile
NATO	North Atlantic Treaty Organization
NIE	National Intelligence Estimate
NNWS	Non-Nuclear Weapon State
NPT	Non Proliferation Treaty
NRRC	Nuclear Risk Reduction Centers
NSC	National Security Council
NWFZ	Nuclear Weapons-Free Zone
OAS	Organization of American States
OAU	Organization of African Unity
OPANAL	Agency for the Prohibition of Nuclear Weapons in Latin America and the Caribbean
PIN	Presidential Nuclear Initiative
PNEs	Peaceful Explosions of Nuclear Devices
SAC	Strategic Air Command
SALT I	Strategic Arms Limitation Treaty (Talks)
SALT II	Strategic Arms Limitation Treaty (Talks)
SAM	Surface-to-Air Missile (Soviet)
SCC	Standing Consultative Commission
SDI	Strategic Defense Initiative ("Star Wars")
SDIO	Strategic Defense Initiative Organization
SLBM	Submarine Launched Ballistic Missiles
SORT	Strategic Offensive Reductions Treaty—the "Moscow Treaty"

SRAM II	Short Range Attack Missile
START	Strategic Arms Reduction Talks
START I	Strategic Arms Reduction Treaty
START II	Strategic Arms Reduction Treaty
UNSCOM	United Nations Special Committee on Iraq
VPK	The Soviet Union's Military Industrial Commission
WEU	Western European Union
WMD	Weapons of Mass Destruction

Essential Resources

The notes listed in these chapters provide many references to specific arms control activities; however, for those desiring materials for more extensive investigations, the following suggestions may be of assistance. Christopher Lamb, *How to Think About Arms Control, Disarmament, and Defense* (New York: Prentice Hall, 1988) and Gunji Hosono, *International Disarmament* (Societe D'Imprimerie D'Ambilly-Annemasse, 1926) provide brief surveys of historical endeavors. For the modern era, see B.J.C. McKercher, ed., *Arms Limitations and Disarmament: Restraints on War, 1899–1939* (Westport, CT: Praeger, 1992), Philip Towle, *Enforced Disarmament: From the Napoleonic Campaigns to the Gulf War* (Oxford: Clarendon Press, 1997), Emily O. Goldman, *Sunken Treaty: Naval Arms Control Between the Wars* (University Park: Pennsylvania State University Press, 1994) and the United Nations' *The United Nations and Disarmament: A Short History* (New York: UN, 1988). These accounts also contain useful bibliographies.

Any search for sources and information dealing with pre-1945 arms control agreements and treaties should include Richard Dean Burns, *Arms Control and Disarmament: A Bibliography* (Santa Barbara, CA: ABC-CLIO, 1977) and the review of pertinent chapters in Burns, ed., *Encyclopedia of Arms Control and Disarmament*, 3 vols. (New York: Scribner's, 1993), Vols. I & II. Volume III provides the texts of agreements and treaties from antiquity to the nuclear age. Other useful sources include Trevor N. Dupuy and Gay Hammerman, *A Documentary History of Arms Control and Disarmament* (New York: R.R. Bowker, 1973); Leon Friedman, ed., *The Law of War: A Documentary History*, 2 vols. (New York: Random House, 1972); and Adam Roberts and Richard Guelff, eds.,

Documents on the Laws of War (New York: Oxford University Press, 2000). Although it has little information on pre-twentieth-century arms control activities and focuses on Cold War weaponry, military episodes, and political events, Jeffrey A. Larsen and James M. Smith, *Historical Dictionary of Arms Control and Disarmament* (Lanham, MD: Scarecrow Press, 2005) provides 100-plus bibliography pages.

Several important yearbooks provide substantial information on arms control during the post–World War II era. Excellent resources with worldwide coverage include Stockholm International Peace Research Institute's *SIPRI Yearbook: World Armaments and Disarmament* (Stockholm/Oxford: 1968/1969), the United Nations' *The United Nations and Disarmament, 1945–1985* (New York: UN, 1985), and *The United Nations Disarmament Yearbook, 1976–* (New York: UN, 1977–). Also see Thomas Graham, Jr., and Damien J. LaVera, *Cornerstones of Security: Arms Control Treaties in the Nuclear Era* (Seattle: University of Washington Press, 2003), William C. Greene, *Soviet Nuclear Weapons Policy: A Research Guide* (Boulder, CO: Westview, 1984), and Andres McGlean, *Security, Arms Control and Conflict Resolution in East Asia and the Pacific: A Bibliography, 1980–1991* (Westport, CT: Greenwood, 1993). The International Institute of Strategic Studies' *The Military Balance* (London) provides an annual update of various armed forces.

Of additional assistance are Jack Mendelsohn and David Grahame, *Arms Control Chronology* (Washington, DC: Center for Defense Information, Winter 2002), U.S. Information Agency, *A Chronology of United States Arms Control and Security Initiatives, 1946–1990* (Washington, DC: USIA, May 1990), and Steve Tulliu and Thomas Schmalberger, *Coming to Terms with Security: A Lexicon for Arms Control, Disarmament, and Confidence Building* (New York: UN Institute for Disarmament Research, 2001). For agreements and treaties, see also Jozet Goldblat, *Agreements for Arms Control: A Critical Survey* (Cambridge, MA: Oelgeschlager, Gunn & Hain, 1982)—frequently updated; Goldblat, *Arms Control Agreements: The New Guide to Negotiations and Agreements* (London: Sage, 2002); and U.S. Arms Control & Disarmament Agency, *Arms Control and Disarmament Agreements: Texts and History of Negotiations* (Washington, DC: AC&DA, 1990).

Index